**Don't Just Look—See!**

## Praise for Don't Just Look - See! My Parents' War

"Excellent read. Extremely well researched and written. I could feel the emotions of Marine Corps training and the loneliness of separation from family and loved ones. Highly recommended for a great study of the American people during World War Two." **--Steve "Smitty" Smith, Curator, Flying Leatherneck Aviation Museum**

"Vieregg brings us a fascinating story of love, loss, risk, intrigue, and courage in the time of World War II. I was particularly drawn to Vernice, her work as a Code Girl, and her willingness to rise to the challenges of this difficult period in history. You will be, too!" **--Cindy Crosby, author of** *Chasing Dragonflies: A Natural, Cultural, and Person History* and *The Tallgrass Prairie: An Introduction*

"Don't Just Look--See! My Parents' War is a highly readable and well researched account of one young couple's navigating university life and wartime service in the years leading up to, during, and following World War II. With an engaging writing style, Mary Vieregg pulls you in by interweaving personal and world events and just enough of the occasional "clip" from a later point in the story to underscore the drama in this couple's experience. It is a compelling personal story of coming of age at a time of momentous historical events and social change. The narrative is strengthened by frequent but judicious quotes, facts, and reports of events. Its real power is the sense it gives the reader of how vibrant but worrying life was at the moment when the outcome we know now was quite uncertain. As the University of Illinois archivist, I can say that no matter how many boxes of records I have examined from these years, not one has provided the immediacy and breadth of scope found in Vieregg's engaging and informative story of Vernice Milleville and Steve Lynn." **--William J. Maher, University Archivist, University of Illinois at Urbana-Champaign**

"As the daughter of a Marine who served with Lt. Lynn, **Don't Just Look--See!** rings true. Readers wanting to learn more about two aspects of World War II---the role of the First Marine Division in the Pacific and the vital code breaking work by women at Arlington Hall Station---will find this book of great interest. Based on her extensive research, Vieregg describes and humanizes both the horrific battle scenes and the pressure of decrypting critical enemy messages."**--Barbara Rossow**

-------------------------------------

*Mary Lynn Vieregg earned undergraduate and graduate degrees at the University of Illinois at Urbana-Champaign prior to teaching high school and college science and restoring tallgrass prairie in northern Illinois. Over the years, the backstories of American history have become a compelling personal interest. She lives in the Chicago area.*

# Don't Just Look—See!
# My Parents' War

## Mary Lynn Vieregg

Mary L. Vieregg
Wheaton, Illinois

Copyright © 2021 by Mary Vieregg, Second edition 2022

All rights reserved. Short excerpts of this book may be used without permission by a reviewer when writing a book review. For permission to use or reproduce portions of this book for any other purpose, please contact the author at: maryvieregg@gmail.com.

ISBN: 978-1-7372564-4-1 (hard cover);
ISBN: 978-1-7372564-3-4 (paperback);
ISBN: 978-1-7372564-2-7 (ebook)

Subjects: 1. History/Military/World War II; 2. Biography & Autobiography/Personal Memoirs; 3. History/United States/Cryptography/20th Century; 4. History/United States/20th Century

*This book is a biographical memoir. It reflects the author's careful research of actual events and her subsequent recreation of dialogue and letters.*


Distributed by Ingram Books, www.ingramcontent.com
Printed in the United States of America

*For my family*

# Contents

| | |
|---|---|
| Introduction | 1 |
| *Chapter 1*: Steve, Massac County, IL, 1934–1940 | 3 |
| *Chapter 2*: Vernice, Champaign, IL, 1931–1940 | 11 |
| *Chapter 3*: Steve and Vernice, University of Illinois at Urbana-Champaign, September 1940–March 1943 | 18 |
| *Chapter 4*: Steve, San Diego, CA, and Quantico, VA, March 1943–January 1944 | 28 |
| *Chapter 5*: Vernice, Champaign, IL, March 1943–January 1944 | 44 |
| *Chapter 6*: Steve and Vernice, Champaign, IL, January 1944 | 50 |
| *Chapter 7*: Steve, California, January–March 1944 | 53 |
| *Chapter 8*: Vernice, Champaign, IL, February–March 1944 | 57 |
| *Chapter 9*: Steve, California, At Sea, New Caledonia, and Pavuvu, April–June 1944 | 62 |
| *Chapter 10*: Vernice, Champaign, IL, and Washington, DC, April–June 1944 | 78 |
| *Chapter 11*: Steve, Pavuvu in the Russell Islands, July–August 1944 | 83 |
| *Chapter 12*: Vernice, Arlington, VA, July–August 1944 | 99 |
| *Chapter 13*: Steve, Peleliu in the Palau Island Group, September–October 1944 | 114 |
| *Chapter 14*: Vernice, Arlington, VA, September–October 1944 | 155 |
| *Chapter 15*: Steve, Pavuvu Revisited and En Route to Okinawa, October 1944–March 1945 | 165 |
| *Chapter 16*: Vernice, Arlington, VA, and Washington, DC, November 1944–March 1945 | 193 |
| *Chapter 17*: Steve, Okinawa, April–June 1945 | 204 |
| *Chapter 18*: Vernice, Arlington, VA, and Washington, DC, April–June 1945 | 256 |
| *Chapter 19*: Steve, Oahu, Hawaii, July 1945 | 262 |
| *Chapter 20*: Vernice, Arlington, VA, and Washington, DC, July–August 1945 | 269 |
| *Chapter 21*: Steve, Oahu, Hawaii, August 1945 | 277 |
| *Chapter 22*: Vernice, Arlington, VA, and Washington, DC, September–December 1945 | 281 |

*Chapter 23:* Steve, Tientsin, north China, and Home,
September-December 1945     287
*Chapter 24*: Vernice, Arlington, VA, and Washington, DC,
January-March 1946     301
*Chapter 25*: Steve, Illinois, January–March 1946     304
*Chapter 26*: Steve and Vernice, Champaign, IL,
April–May 1946     310
*Chapter 27*: Steve, Champaign, IL, May–September 1946     313
*Chapter 28*: Vernice, Arlington, VA, and Washington, DC,
May–September 1946     318
*Chapter 29*: Steve and Vernice, Illinois and Into the Future
Together, September 1946–March 1950     323

Acknowledgments     334
Notes     339
Bibliography     351

# Introduction

This narrative is a true story about my parents' contributions to the war effort during World War II. I never really knew much about it until after they died. Perhaps if I had begun this narrative when my father and mother were still living, I could be assured it was more completely accurate than what I've written ... but probably not.

My mother would never talk about her work in Washington, DC, during the war. She had vowed never to do so, and she kept her promise her entire life. Until I began my research, the only piece of hard evidence I had that she was even there was a faded War Department Notification of Personnel Action record indicating my mother had resigned from her position as "Cryptographic Clerk" working for the Army Security Agency at Arlington Hall Station in Arlington, Virginia, on September 9, 1946, "to be married." Attached to it was a certificate acknowledging her "loyalty and devotion to duty ... while serving with the Military Intelligence Division, War Department." Her silence was noble, but it also deprived her of the respect she was entitled to for the services she rendered. During her lifetime, her children and extended family never learned enough about the important contribution she made to the war effort to appreciate it, and she felt she could never share with potential employers the invaluable skills she had acquired working for the War Department. I had to glean her story from her declassified personnel record and other historical documents declassified many years after World War II ended.

My father would never talk much about his war experiences until well into his old age. Even then, he was reluctant, reticent, and sometimes confused. His battle experiences were traumatic, and late in his life, the symptoms of his untreated posttraumatic stress disorder were acute and dramatic. Revisiting his wartime experiences exacted a heavy toll paid in frightening flashbacks, nightmares, and intense sadness. He was proud of his service, and his family was proud of him, but my mother warned us not to bring up the old times. Sometimes, my father was playful, funny, generous, and thoughtful, but knowing what I know now, I better understand his unpredictable impatience, restlessness, insomnia, moodiness, and occasional rage. At times, he could be very difficult to get along with. Now I understand why.

My mother died in 2010. My father died three years later. After his death, I found a battered cardboard box squirreled away in the back of his closet. In it was a collection of brown, tattered "flimsies"—thin sheets of paper which turned out to be his copies of most of the orders he received as an officer in the United States Marine Corps. They reflected the geographic outline of his service during World War II. I was curious enough to spend time deciphering the acronyms and military language in the orders to create a bare-bones timeline of his experiences. Each new discovery led to a score of new questions, and my parents' intertwined stories began to slowly reveal themselves as I doggedly chased down the answers. Here is what I learned.

# 1
## Steve
### Massac County, Illinois
### 1934–1940

Get up, Jack ... Step up, Jack! Gee ... gee ... gee ... Step up, Jack! Easy! Haw! Haw! You lazy old mule!
—"S A" Lynn to his family's mule team in the 1930s

Trust the dreams, for in them is hidden the gate to eternity.
—Kahlil Gibran, *The Prophet*

As soon as he left the warm farmhouse, twelve-year-old Steve lowered his head and curled his shoulders into the wind. It was still dark, and it was bitter cold as he and his younger brother, George, ran to the barn through the new snow to complete their morning chores. Steve's dog, Teddy, faithfully trotted along behind them.

The brothers sleepily mumbled to each other as they completed their morning tasks: shovel out the animal manure, feed the ten mules, feed the horse, feed the cows, fill the water troughs, and then milk the cows. Only after they were done could Steve (or "S A," as his mother called him) and George (also called "Joe" or "Dub") run back into the warm kitchen. Their mother would have a hearty breakfast of eggs, bacon or ham, grits, biscuits, and gravy ready for them.

Breakfast smelled wonderful! After pumping the well handle in the sink to bring water up to wash their hands, the boys started chowing down the hot meal. As they ate, S A and Joe listened to their mother, Elva, humming the harmonies of the gospel tunes she and her brother, Delmar, would sing at the Mount Olive Baptist Church social the next weekend. The boys' jovial older sister, Tillie, teased the boys as she waited patiently for them to finish breakfast and run along the dirt roads with her to the one-room schoolhouse they all attended. Their oldest sister, Frances, attended high school in nearby Brookport.

Elva woke up earlier than the boys to start breakfast and make sure S A and Joe began their chores before their father sat down for breakfast. Stephen Sr. was sitting at the large oak table when the boys rushed into the kitchen. He regarded them sternly, wanting confirmation that they had completed their morning chores. He was a disappointed, angry man who lost a good farm management job in Iowa when the Great Depression hit and the bank foreclosed on the farm owner. Stephen Jr. had been born in 1922 during the happier days the family had spent in Iowa.

**One-year-old Stephen with his sisters Naomi (Tillie, *left*) and Frances in Iowa, 1923**
(Photograph in family collection)

Now, in 1934, the family of six was back on the Lynn family farm about three miles northeast of Brookport at the edge of the Shawnee Hills near the southern tip of Illinois. The rolling landscape had been settled by the Lynns and other extended family members back in the mid-1800s, but the soil is mediocre, and the prospects for getting ahead financially were poor.

The Lynns came from a long line of feisty, stubborn, and independent Scotch-Irish people who arrived in America in the early 1700s and moved over the generations from North Carolina into Tennessee and then into Kentucky and north into southern Illinois. They had always been self-sufficient and hardworking, but the elder Stephen would never fully recover from the financial or psychological blows rendered by the Great Depression.

Sundays were good days. Red-haired, blue-eyed Steve and his family always went to his maternal grandparents' farm farther up in the wooded Shawnee Hills for a big family get-together. His many uncles and male cousins played ball and wrestled. The women chatted and prepared food together in the kitchen. Grandma Rilla doted on S A. She fixed his favorite foods—fried chicken and her famous white cake with sweet coconut frosting.

His grandfather Samuel Phillips, a justice of the peace and an active leader in the nearby Mount Pleasant United Church of Christ, led the prayer after everyone gathered for supper.

**Steve's maternal grandparents, Samuel and Rilla Phillips**
(Photograph in family collection)

After the big meal, everybody in Elva's family pulled out a guitar or a fiddle, and the singing and dancing began. Even Steve's father loosened up a bit and smiled occasionally. Everyone joined in, but Elva and her brothers were the musical stars. Their voices and fiddle playing were so good, they were sometimes booked on radio programs to sing gospel songs together. Burl Ives was a favorite local musician, too, and remained one of Steve's favorites his entire life. Ives had grown up in Jasper County north of Massac County. In the 1930s, he was still in the early days of his career, but Steve and his family knew about him from the singing he'd done on radio station WBOW out of Terre Haute, IN. They'd heard his renditions of popular folk songs like "Wayfaring Stranger" and "On Top of Old Smoky" at local venues, too.

On Sundays, Steve still had the morning chores to do, but he usually got a break from the field work. The other days of the week, he drove a mule team to do the plowing, tilling, cultivating, and harvesting. There was no money for a tractor. Steve's loyal canine companion Teddy stayed by his side as Steve worked the fields barefoot behind the mules. They both watched for the snakes kicked up by the mules' hooves to avoid a painful snakebite. Shoes were a luxury the family couldn't afford to waste on farm work; they had to be saved for church, school, and special occasions.

**Steve and his dog Teddy on the farm in 1938**
(Photograph in family collection)

Steve knew every mule's personality as well as he knew those of his brother and sisters: which mule would kick the other mules, which mule was eager to please him, which mule would bite him if given a chance. Jack was the most annoying mule. Jack would let the other mules in the team do all the work if Steve let him, and the ornery beast seemed to enjoy aggravating Steve by shirking his duties every chance he was given.

There was very little cash in the Lynn family during the Depression years. They managed to survive on what they could raise on the farm and what they could barter for with other people in the area. No one had any cash to buy the farm's output, so it was used instead to trade for goods they couldn't grow, hunt, gather, or make themselves. Steve and Joe became expert shots hunting for deer, wild turkey, rabbits, ducks, geese, and other small game to add to the food supply for the whole family. They headed down to the creek east of the farm fields or searched along the fence lines for the best chance to score a meal-worthy target.

In 1936, Steve and Joe started attending high school in Brookport. Now they had to complete all the morning chores as quickly as they could so they'd have time to eat their breakfast before running the half mile to catch the school bus that stopped at the end of the dirt road that bordered the farmland. The boys had to run especially fast past the run-down hog farm down the road, where the farmer's two sons yelled out their scorn and bullied the brothers if they could. They'd been pulled out of school after the eighth grade to help at home.

As the drought years of the 1930s dragged on, even water became scarce. In the summer of 1937, the stone-lined well in the farmyard ran completely dry. Several times a month the boys and their father had to load large heavy barrels onto a wagon, hook up the mule team, and travel several miles to a relative's farm to get water for their livestock and for themselves. The work was a backbreaking addition to the daily farm chores, and it was all done under the angry supervision of the boys' bitter father. He was a hard man to please, and Steve did what he could to avoid confrontation.

The small, square, redbrick, two-story Brookport High School building was Steve's haven. He'd always stood out academically, and he read every book he could lay his hands on. Sometimes he was harassed for his love of learning anything and everything. At Brookport High School, Mr. Carl Ammon's math classes were a revelation. Mr. Harry Wright's science classes proved to Steve that he had a knack for learning how the physical world works. Both teachers took note of Steve's curiosity and aptitude for learning, and Steve took note of the fact that both Mr. Ammon and Mr. Wright were graduates of the University of Illinois. Mr. Wright was elected to the respected office of Massac County school superintendent during Steve's senior year.

The English teacher at his small high school, Mr. Max Murphy, loved poetry, and Steve memorized boatloads of it—poetry he'd remember and recite to others for the rest of his life. Mr. Murphy also introduced Steve to the poetry and philosophy of Kahlil Gibran, whose books Steve kept near his side until he died. Steve even had a role in a school play during his senior year. The play was entitled *Fireman, Save My Child!* It was an old-fashioned melodrama featuring a romance between the characters Chester Quingle and Daisy Dorriance, respectively played by S. A. Lynn and classmate Imogene Russell.

Mr. C. H. Ammon, Principal, Math   Mr. Harry Wright, Science

Mr. Max Murphy, English
(Photographs courtesy of the Brookport Public Library, Brookport, IL)

When he could get time away from the farmwork, Steve played baseball, basketball, and football on the Brookport High School Bulldog teams, too. The blue-and-white uniformed basketball team was pretty good; it won the district championship in the 1939–1940 school year with a record of 19–5 under the direction of coach Clovis Wallace.

Mr. Ammon, Mr. Wright, Mr. Murphy, and Coach Wallace all recognized Steve's determination, ambition, and academic gifts, but could they help him escape the arduous and mind-numbing rural poverty of the farm and his father's overbearing control?

During those years, every county in Illinois offered a glimmer of hope for young people like Steve. It was called the County Competitive Exam. It was administered every spring, and the high school senior who scored highest on the exam received a four-year scholarship that paid the tuition at the University of Illinois in Champaign-Urbana, the state's flagship university. For a poor kid like Steve, it was only a small light at the end of a long, dark tunnel because he had no money for books, room, or board. Even so, it was still an enticing dim beacon of opportunity.

Stephen Sr. had other ideas for Steve's future. He needed and wanted Steve to stay on the farm as his primary farm laborer. Steve's younger brother, Joe, was too easygoing to get the work done the way Steve did, and the elder Stephen felt entitled to Steve's labor. He wasn't in favor of Steve taking the County Competitive Exam. The idea of Steve's doing well enough on the test to leave the farm was a threat he felt to the core of his being.

Had Stephen Sr. forgotten his own desire to escape the poverty of southern Illinois by taking the more lucrative farm management job in Iowa twenty years earlier? Was controlling his son's life one of the very few parts of his own life he thought he could control? Did he even think about why he opposed his son's desire for a different life? Surely, he must have.

Fortunately, Steve's teachers and the principal of Brookport High School, Mr. Ammon, teamed up with Steve's mother, Elva, to override his father's veto. They persuaded him to allow Steve to take the county exam, and the arrangements were made.

On that all-important early spring Saturday morning in 1940, Mr. Ammon personally drove Steve over the muddy dirt roads of Massac County to the countywide test site at the school superintendent's office in Metropolis, the county seat. With a pat on the back and a few words of encouragement from Mr. Wright, Steve walked into the room where the test was given, and he focused on the task at hand. He did his best, but would it be good enough?

Stephen A. Lynn Jr., Brookport High School graduation photo, 1939

## 2
## Vernice
## Champaign, Illinois
## 1931–1940

*If you're not going to do it right, there's no sense doing it at all.*
—Vernice Lynn to her children

"Necie, there's a letter for you on the kitchen table. It's from the university."

Millie had heard her daughter Vernice come in the door after staying late at Champaign High School. Vernice was midway through the last semester of her senior year in the spring of 1940. She was the business manager for the school's newspaper, the *Chronicle*, and she had stayed late to enter the advertising revenue sums into the accounting ledger before she left for home.

"Okay, Mom. I see it."

When she walked in the door, Necie had been tired from the long walk home and hungry and a bit low about all the schoolwork she had to do that evening. Now she felt both anxiety and excitement growing as she looked at the long envelope from the University of Illinois. It sat there on top of the huge oak table where she helped her mother serve breakfast and dinner to the boarders living in their rooming house at 1109 S. Fourth Street in Champaign, 250 miles north of the Lynn farm.

Vernice set her books down and leaned against the kitchen counter. So much depended on the contents of that letter. She was the youngest of the four daughters born to George Phillip Milleville and Ludaemilia "Millie" Elizabeth Goers. The oldest daughter, Anita, had already graduated from the university and was teaching business courses in a small rural high school nearby. The second oldest, Norma, would graduate in June and then marry Carl Wilfong and move to Flora, Illinois. Dolores was finishing her sophomore year. It was expected that Vernice would follow in their footsteps. More than expected, really—willed, mandated—no choice. Even though George and Millie had only completed the eighth grade, they were determined that all four of their daughters would get a college degree. They were *resolutely* determined to make it happen, and Vernice felt the weight of that fierce determination as she looked at the envelope sitting on the table.

**Vernice's mother, Ludaemilia "Millie" Elizabeth Goers, as a young woman**
(Photograph in family collection)

George and Millie were the grandchildren of devout, well-educated German Lutherans who immigrated to the United States in the mid-1800s after refusing to accept the government-mandated standardization of Lutheran doctrine in Prussia. It had taken two generations to first transition through the German Lutheran settlement near Buffalo, New York, to the rich farmland and small towns of central Illinois and then navigate the years of virulent World War I anti-German sentiment in America. Now it was time to get the train back on the track. George and Millie's girls needed to be well educated. They needed to excel academically. They needed to graduate from university.

Millie walked into the kitchen and glanced at her youngest daughter impatiently.

"Well, are you going to open it? We need to get those *Kartoffeln* peeled so we can start boiling them," she said, her gaze drifting in the direction of the potatoes.

Millie had been washing sheets and cleaning rooms most of the day and was pretty tired herself. She and George had made the decision nearly nine years earlier that she would move north to Champaign with the four girls when it was time for Anita to begin her studies at the university. George would remain in their home in Altamont, ninety miles southwest of Champaign, to manage the grocery store he had acquired from his mother's family shortly after he and Millie had married in 1913. He drove up to visit the family often, and Millie and the girls returned to Altamont whenever possible to go to the Lutheran church potlucks and visit the many Millevilles and Goers living in town and on the nearby farms.

**Vernice, the youngest of Millie and George Milleville's four daughters, 1923**
(Photograph in family collection)

As she watched her youngest daughter reach for a sharp knife to carefully slice open the top of the envelope, Millie remembered the small rented rooms in the Hotel Walker at 315 E. University Avenue where she and the four girls had all lived together when they first arrived in Champaign in the fall of 1931. As the youngest, Vernice had begun fourth grade that fall at Marquette School just a few blocks away on Clark Street.

Back then there was still enough money generated from the George Milleville Store in Altamont and George's other investments to support the move. That changed as the Depression years dragged on.

One of George's investments that took a dive because of the Depression was the one he had in the Altamont Garment Factory building. George and his brother Clarence held shares in the building along with six other men and the owners of the Altamont Manufacturing Company. As the economy constricted, the sale of garments dropped, and the factory closed in 1934. In 1935, George and the other men agreed to forfeit their financial investment in the empty building. With the deed in hand, the owners of the Altamont Manufacturing Company could get a government subsidy to reopen a New Deal garment factory and employ out-of-work Altamont residents. As part of the deal, the company promised not to move the factory from Altamont.[1] It was good for the town but not necessarily for the Millevilles.

**Vernice's father, George Phillip Milleville, 1940**
(Photograph in family collection)

Gregarious and good-hearted, George had always generously extended store credit to his customers, too. As the economic downturn lingered through the decade, fewer and fewer of the debts were paid as the Altamont bankers foreclosed on business owners and farmers who couldn't meet their loan payments. Trying to keep the store afloat, George decided in 1937 to sell a half interest in the store to Herman Stettbacher, who had worked for George for more than twenty years.[2]

Millie and George could see the handwriting on the wall. To accomplish their driving parental goal of graduating all four of their daughters from the University of Illinois, they would have to sell their home in Altamont for pennies on the dollar and find a rooming house to rent and run in Champaign.

By 1940, George and Millie were renting the rooming house on Fourth Street, which provided housing for university students. George was working as a sales clerk at the Jos. A. Kuhn Company, a well-established men's clothing store in downtown Champaign, while Millie managed the boardinghouse with her two youngest daughters' assistance.

Millie paused and watched Vernice slowly and carefully try to open the envelope. Vernice had been trained to do everything in a neat and orderly fashion—even something like this that was seemingly so important to them both. Necie's hands were shaking and her big brown eyes were wide as she tried not to tear the envelope apart. Finally, Millie gently took the envelope from her hands.

"Pour yourself a glass of milk, Necie, and have a piece of the *Apfelkuchen* I baked this afternoon. We'll open it together after you have a bite to eat."

Vernice exhaled. She took a glass out of the cupboard and the milk out of the metal icebox. As she poured the cold, creamy milk into her glass, she caught the delicious smell of the cooling *Apfelkuchen* on the counter. How had she not noticed it earlier? She cut first through the firm apple layer on top and then through the soft crumbly cake layer beneath. As she lifted the first piece out of the pan, the escaping aroma filled the room and made her mouth water. She also cut a small piece for her mother, who had done something she rarely did: she had stopped working. She had actually taken a seat at the large table to share a few quiet moments with her youngest daughter.

**Vernice's mother, Millie Milleville, 1940**
(Photograph in family collection)

"Tell me about school today, Schatzi," she said affectionately.

"There's so much going on, Mom. I can barely keep up. I have an essay due for my history class tomorrow, and I have lines to learn for our spring play. The type is being set for the next issue of the *Chronicle*, and I still have to finish the articles I'm writing on the Girl Reserves and GAA activities. I'm going to have to stay up late every night this week to get everything I promised to do done on time."

"Well, you said you would do it all, Necie, so you'll just have to buckle down and get it done. You will, I'm sure."

Vernice was involved in so much with so many of her fellow high school students. Her 1939–1940 senior yearbook lists her many activities and accomplishments: secretary of the Wig and Paint Club (a theater group); business manager of the school newspaper, the *Chronicle*; cast member in the school play *Dark House*; member of the Girl Reserves, the Girls Athletic Association (GAA), the Book Club, Thespians, Student Council, as well as the honorary societies of Quill and Scroll and the National Honor Society. She rarely had time to just relax with her good friends Marilyn, Carolene, and Georgia.

Looking out of the many activity photos in the yearbooks from her junior and senior year, Vernice expresses so much of herself—her vulnerability and intelligence, her cheerfulness and determination, her warmth and pensiveness, her energy and fatigue, her curiosity and occasional boredom—and accompanying her formal senior portrait in the yearbook is the sentence, "Vernice disapproves of irresponsibility." One doesn't doubt that it was true or have to wonder how and from whom she had learned that point of view, but one also wonders how she felt about it being memorialized in print for all her classmates to read.

Gently interrupting her daughter's thoughts, Millie asked, "Shall we open the letter now, Necie? What has the University of Illinois decided about your application for admission?

**Vernice Marilyn Milleville, Champaign (IL) high school senior picture, 1939**
(Photograph in family collection)

## 3
## Steve and Vernice
## University of Illinois at Urbana-Champaign
## September 1940–March 1943

**A Marine Corps recruiter would tell me that I'd find boot camp easier than living at home.**
J. D. Vance, *Hillbilly Elegy*

"Necie, I'm not sure how long I can keep doing this. It's getting too hard."

Steve and Vernice were walking east under the emerging canopy of elm trees along John Street on their way to the quad at the University of Illinois in Champaign. Steve was headed for the Illini Union building where he had a meal service job. Vernice was walking to her job as a clerical and laboratory assistant in the Home Economics Department in the Woman's Building (later to be renamed the English Building). Spring was in the air that early April day of 1942, but their mood was somber.

So much had happened in the past nineteen months.

After getting the highest score ever attained on the Massac County Competitive Exam, Steve Lynn enthusiastically began his freshman year in the College of Engineering at the university in the fall of 1940. He found a cheap room to live in on East Healey Street in Champaign and hustled for meal service jobs at sororities, fraternities, and independent houses and clubs. Sometimes the sororities and fraternities just gave him a meal instead of cash, but he was still able to scrape up enough money for his rent and books. His required freshman courses in rhetoric and composition, hygiene, general engineering, algebra, trigonometry, geometry, chemistry, physical education, and military training (required of all male students at land grant colleges since 1862) were manageable even with his work schedule, and he did well. He also met some guys from Club Topper, an independent housing men's "club" at 509 E. John Street in Champaign. Most of the students living there were studying engineering and seemed welcoming, so he decided to move in at the beginning of the second semester.

It turned out that the very best part of living at Club Topper was the opportunity it gave him to meet Vernice Milleville, an outgoing, pretty brunette with big brown eyes. Her parents ran the boardinghouse, the Illini Club, across the street at 508 E. John Street. The two of them met informally on the sidewalk one afternoon, and they discovered they had a lot in common even though their backgrounds were so different. They both enjoyed literature and dramatics, and they found it easy to enjoy each other's company. He even found the time to watch her portray the role of Mamie, the cook, in the Illinois Theatre Guild's production of the Clare Booth Luce comedy *Kiss the Boys Goodbye*. Performed with great reviews during March 1941, the title of the play seemed in retrospect to be a premonition of what would happen after Pearl Harbor was attacked nine months later.

Vernice was taking the required courses for liberal arts students—rhetoric and composition, general science courses, an introduction to literature, and physical education—as well as continuing with the French she had begun studying in high school. Even though her help was still needed to run the family's boardinghouse, she also began working in the Home Economics Department in January 1941 as a clerical and laboratory assistant for Dr. Julia Outhouse, a professor of nutrition who was researching information for the first Recommended Dietary Allowances report (which would be issued in 1943). The extra money covered the cost of her books and an occasional luxury item such as a new hat.

The economic condition of the country was slowly improving as the New Deal programs and the material demands of the war in Europe kicked into effect. One sign of the times was the February 8, 1941 opening of the new Illini Union building on the quad, which was built using federal money for the materials and alumni-donated money for the labor costs. The dining hall at the new Illini Union was popular and sorely needed, and Steve was able to get a regular cash-paying job there, which made his financial position a little more secure even though it didn't reduce any of the time pressures on his life.

**University of Illinois Illini Union Building, 2018**
(Photograph by M. Vieregg)

During the summer of 1941, Vernice and Steve parted ways. Vernice stayed in Champaign, working both at home and for the university. Steve returned to the Lynn farm near Brookport to work for his father. Steve's paternal grandmother, Melida Lynn, had died in January at the age of seventy-one, and Steve's father was still grieving. Steve's maternal grandfather, Samuel Phillips, had died during the winter at the age of seventy-two, but Steve would still get to spend those wonderful Sunday afternoons with his beloved maternal grandmother, Rilla Cleomane Phillips, for one more summer. She passed away in May 1942 at the age of seventy-four, very proud of her favorite grandson, the first person in the family to go to college.

Being back on the farm during the summer of 1941 wasn't so bad. At least Steve had three solid meals he could depend on, and he loved his mother's cooking. Only his Grandmother Rilla could fry the fresh chicken from the barnyard like his mother could, and the fresh green beans, tomatoes, and strawberries from the kitchen garden were abundant and delicious. The southern Illinois peaches came into season in July, and his mother and grandmother knew how to make the best peach pie and peach cobbler in the world. Add the homemade ice cream from the fresh cream gathered in the morning, and Steve's stomach was full for a change.

Steve's father was still difficult and overbearing, but the farm economy had improved enough so the farm now had a tractor—one of the 690,000 tractors replacing two million horses and mules between 1940 and 1945.[1] The well was full of water again, too. European agricultural production was so disrupted by the expanding war, demand for American farm products increased dramatically. The Lend-Lease Act—passed on March 11, 1941, promising food for the Allies—ensured that American farm productivity would need to remain high for the duration of the war.

Even small "dirt" farmers like the Lynns were beginning to see their economic prospects improve after twenty years of depressed farm prices. The farmers of America were now feeding not only American civilians but also the exponentially growing number of Americans in the U.S. military and the Allied civilians and military forces overseas. "Keep them eating" became the American farmers' mantra, and they were rapidly mobilizing to efficiently grow, process, store, and transport huge amounts of farm products. To fill just one freighter with dried eggs and milk, evaporated milk, cheese, canned meat and vegetables, sacks of flour, and boxes of lard required the output of 3,824 average farms.[2] All this increase in agricultural production had to occur simultaneously with the migration of farm workers away from marginal farms to war industry jobs in cities and with the enlistment of sons of farm families into the military.

When the first semester of the 1941–1942 school year began, Steve and Necie were both living at the Milleville boardinghouse, the Illini Club, on East John Street! It was a bit less expensive than Club Topper, and the Millevilles were willing to give Steve even more of a break if he would help out with maintenance around the house. The skills he'd gained from working for years on the family farm buildings and machines came in handy, and Necie's mom, Millie, appreciated his help with the kitchen garden and her prized peonies in the backyard of their "new" old boardinghouse. Steve needed all the breaks he could get because he was still receiving no financial help from his family for his expenses. He hadn't even been paid any money for the farmwork he'd done over the summer.

Steve enjoyed being part of the Milleville family. Sometimes Vernice's sister Norma and her gregarious husband, Carl, also called "Pat" (short for Patrick Henry because he spoke so much and so eloquently), would visit with their toddler Marge (Margaret Ann). Sometimes Vernice's oldest sister, Anita, would travel into town from Newton, Illinois, where she taught school. Vernice's other sister, Dolores, had earned her university degree at the end of the 1940–1941 school year and was serious about

Norman McQuown, aka "Mac," who would soon be doing classified work for the U.S. Department of War in New York City.

**Carl, Margaret Ann, and Norma (Milleville) Wilfong, 1941**
(Photograph in family collection)

Steve went back to school in the fall of 1941 refreshed (and poor), and he tackled a heavy course load of calculus, physics, mechanical engineering, theoretical and applied mechanics, physical education, and military training, while at the same time working as many as forty-nine hours a week, mostly at meal service jobs, to make ends meet. He was determined to succeed, and he passed all his courses with a C or better during the first semester of his sophomore year. No doubt it helped being in a supportive living arrangement that included the person who was fast becoming his best friend and favorite study companion, Necie.

At the beginning of her sophomore year, Vernice landed the role of Aunt Valentine in the Theater Guild's Homecoming and Dad's Day production of *Seventh Heaven*, a popular play written by Austin Strong. In the play, the young woman Diane falls in love with the young man Chico in World War I France. Maybe Vernice herself was falling in love with "Stevie," as she was calling the new boarder by then. Stevie no doubt wondered the same thing as he sat in the audience watching Necie's performance.

Even as she found the time to rehearse her role in *Seventh Heaven*, Vernice continued to work both at home and at the university while she dived into more sociology, psychology, French literature, and history classes. Her grades were great as she became more confident in herself and her abilities. Still, she squeezed time out of her busy schedule to spend time with Steve.

During all of this time, an anxious sense of uncertainty hung over not only the University of Illinois campus but also the rest of the country. The news from Europe was dire, and the Japanese were acting aggressively in the Pacific. Would the United States be going to war?

The answer, of course, came on December 7, 1941. In response to the radio broadcasts of the Japanese predawn attack on the U.S. Pacific Fleet at anchor in Pearl Harbor in Hawaii and President Franklin Delano Roosevelt's declaration of war on Japan the next day, future film critic Roger Ebert wrote in the school newspaper, the *Daily Illini*, on December 8 about the crowds of "smiling, laughing, yelling" students packing campus restaurants and drugstores and parading up and down Green and Wright Streets in the campus area:

> Few were serious-faced ... seemingly confident of an easy American victory, and slightly hysterical over the suddenness of the war.[3]

Apparently, the relief of certainty replaced the prior months of uncertainty. Six hundred students marched by torchlight to the university president's house, chanting along the way, "Hi Ho, Hi Ho, we're off to Tokyo! We'll wipe the Jap right off the map, Hi Ho, Hi Ho."[4]

Not all students reacted that way. Many were stunned. Many were shocked. Many looked around at one another wondering what roles they would play in the war. How many would fight? How many would die? How many would lose brothers? Sweethearts? Husbands? Friends? An editorial in the *Daily Illini* on December 9 chastised the revelers, "Think it over before you depravedly shout 'We don't give a damn for Japan' and rattle your silly cowbell."[5]

The mood shifted as most junior and senior men on campus realized they were immediately eligible for the draft because they were age twenty-one or older. And, too, it was learned fairly soon that William Schick, a University of Illinois alumnus and a flight surgeon in the medical corps, had died in the Pearl Harbor raid. He was the first of the university's 738 alumni to be killed in World War II.[6]

Students were encouraged by university officials to stay in school. University President Willard published an open letter to students on December 19, saying in part:

> You will best serve your country and yourselves if you will continue (your) education exactly as you had planned.[7]

Provost Albert J. Harno, longtime dean of the College of Law, told students that by staying in school:

> Your action will be consistent in full measure with the ideals of patriotism and the highest interests of our country ... until your country needs and calls you.[8]

Nevertheless, the ratio of men students to women students on campus went from three-to-one to one-to-four within a year.[9]

The nation had been turned upside down by Pearl Harbor, and even though both Vernice and Steve finished their fall semester courses successfully and their relationship continued to strengthen, they weren't immune to the impact the war would have on everyone.

During the new academic term beginning in January 1942, Vernice's intellectual worldview continued to expand as she studied European history, more sociology and psychology, speech, and writing. A black-and-white photo of her and her friend Carolene in riding chaps commemorates the horseback riding class she took for a physical education requirement. Vernice became proficient in dressage. She was able to find time to listen to Carl Sandburg recite his poetry on campus as well as to First Lady Eleanor Roosevelt's remarks at the first anniversary celebration of the Illini Union building on February 2, 1942.

**Vernice (*right*) and her best friend, Carolene, in riding chaps, April 1942**
(Photograph in family collection)

Steve, on the other hand, struggled with the burdens of both working nearly fifty hours a week to make ends meet and a difficult course load of German, two physics classes, a second calculus class, a mechanical engineering class, a theoretical and applied mechanics course, physical education, and military training. His grades were sliding downward as he was ground between working, studying, and the social pressure of current events. He was not eligible for the draft because he was still only nineteen years old, but all men in his age group were grappling with the tough dilemmas posed by their country being at war.

His discouragement as he and Necie walked east along John Street under the elm trees on that beautiful April day in 1942 was understandable.

"It's just getting to be too much of a grind."

"But Stevie, you've got to get as much of your education behind you as you can before you reach draft eligibility. Can you ease your course load somehow? Can you find a better-paying job so you don't have to work so many hours?"

"I've tried, Necie. I just don't see a way. I'm tired. I'm running out of steam…"

Silence as Steve shrugged his shoulders dejectedly.

"Well, Stevie, can you give up the idea of going back to the farm this summer and stay here in Champaign to make a little money? Maybe take a few courses during the expanded summer session? Then maybe you'll know for sure what you want to do."

"I'll think about it… See you later, Necie."

And that's what Steve decided to do. He stayed in Champaign during the summer of 1942, and he was able to find a regular part-time job at the University Physical Plant. He registered for two theoretical and applied mechanics courses, a physics course, a mechanical engineering course, and a weight lifting class, the latter to satisfy his last physical education requirement. He later withdrew from physics and weight lifting, but he finished the other three courses with decent grades. He had nine more credits toward his degree.

At the same time, he and Vernice experienced the sugar rationing taking effect on campus. It required all campus housing units to register for their quotas. Rationing of meat, processed foods, gasoline, and shoes soon followed. They watched uniformed U.S. Navy and Army students and trainees swarm the campus as the military established a wide range of specialized training courses using the university's facilities and faculty. By the end of the summer, there were more military students and trainees on campus than civilian students like Steve and Vernice.[10]

In late June, Vernice quit her job in the Home Economics Department and started working for the Illinois Bell Telephone Company as a local and long-distance operator with starting pay of forty-five cents per hour. She took the job for the higher pay, not knowing it would later draw the attention of government recruiters.

By the end of the summer term, Steve had had enough. It was time to make some hard decisions. He was ready for a change from the grueling work/school schedule he had been enduring. It was wearing him down both mentally and physically. It didn't help being on the campus teeming with uniformed military trainees as intense social pressure was being put on healthy young students to enlist. It didn't make the decisions any easier when he called home only to hear his parents ask him to come back to help on the farm, which was at last turning a profit.

On November 13, 1942, the U.S. Congress lowered the minimum draft age from twenty-one to eighteen. Steve had turned twenty on June 13 and had registered for the draft on June 29 at the National Guard Armory in Champaign. At about the same time, Steve learned that if he went back to work on the family farm, he would be eligible for II-C draft deferment, "Men necessary to farm labor." The farm labor shortage was dire, and by mid-1943, more than a million farmers and farmworkers were deferred by the Selective Service System; the number would reach nearly three million by the end of the year.[11] Women, both urban and rural (the Women's Land Army), youth volunteers ages eleven to seventeen (Victory Farm Volunteers), workers brought in from Mexico, the Bahamas, Barbados, Jamaica, and Canada, and nearly 270,000 Italian and German prisoners of war would all be needed to address the farm labor shortage during the war. Individually grown "victory gardens" became not only patriotic but often essential for Americans to get fresh vegetables into their diet.

Could Steve really think seriously about going back to the farm to work with his father and his brother Joe? What would Vernice think if he took a farm labor deferment? What would he think of himself both now and later? He was young, healthy, strong, and smart. Didn't he have an obligation to enlist in the military like so many others?

Steve took some more time to think about it. He worked full-time at the University of Illinois Physical Plant in Urbana, and he helped the Millevilles around the Illini Club on John Street in Champaign, where he continued to live. He spent time with Necie even as she continued working at Illinois Bell and began the fall semester of her junior year, signing up for more psychology, sociology, history, and literature classes.

Finally, Steve made up his mind. He enlisted in the United States Marine Corps to serve for the "Duration of the Emergency."

"I'll write when I can, Necie, and they've promised me I'll have leave before I ship out."

"Please take care of yourself, Stevie. I'll miss you. I'll write, too."

Stephen A. Lynn Jr. climbed into the white van sent to pick him up in Champaign on March 10, 1943. He was driven up to Chicago, where he caught an assigned train to San Diego to start Marine recruit training. He made the decision to move forward into the unknown instead of backward to the farm life he knew all too well.

Meanwhile, Vernice continued her studies in sociology, psychology, history, and literature, and by the time Steve left for the Marine Corps, she was well on her way to completing her university degree.

# 4
# Steve
## San Diego, California, and Quantico, Virginia
## March 1943–January 1944

**Marine Corps training taught us to kill efficiently and to try to survive. But it also taught us loyalty to each other—and love. That esprit de corps sustained us.**

E. B. Sledge, With the Old Breed

*March 15, 1943*
*Dear Necie,*
 *I'm on the train headed for San Diego. Our van from Champaign was met at Union Station in Chicago by a Marine recruiter who hustled us onto the right train. The station was a madhouse, and I'm not sure we would have found the right train if he hadn't been there to show us the way.*
 *I guess the trip is going to take several days because there's so much traffic on the train lines---military equipment, tractors, troop trains ... you name it. Sure is a big country, too. I hope you'll want to see more of it with me after the war. The farther west we get the more different it looks than Illinois.*
 *There are only Marine recruits on this train, and we're getting to know each other a little bit on the long ride out there. We keep being called the "Dago people" because we're all headed out to San Diego instead of Parris Island. There are guys from all over---some from farms, some from cities. We're playing a lot of cards and joking around a lot. We've eaten some meals in the dining car, but sometimes when the train gets pulled onto a siding to wait for other trains, we get to eat in a restaurant along the line.*
 *None of us really knows exactly what we're getting into...*
Steve

  By the time Steve Lynn's troop train arrived in San Diego, all the recruits had been issued green wool Marine uniforms and been assigned buses to board at the station. The NCOs (noncommissioned officers, i.e., corporals and sergeants) started yelling at them right away: "Fall out!" "Board your assigned buses!" In his legendary book *With the Old Breed at Peleliu and Okinawa*, E. B. Sledge recounted his initial experiences after the buses arrived at the Marine Corps Recruit Depot in San Diego in 1943, shortly before Steve arrived:

> We scrambled out, lined up with men from other buses, and were counted off into groups of about sixty. Several trucks rolled by carrying work parties of men still in boot camp or who had finished recently. All looked at us with knowing grins and jeered, "You'll be sorreee." This was the standard, unofficial greeting extended to all recruits.[1] Then the recruits met their drill instructor: "Your soul may belong to Jesus, but your ass belongs to the Marines. You people are *recruits*. You're *not* Marines. You may not have what it takes to be Marines."[2]

Herded through the physical exam and haircut, Steve's 70-inch (5-foot, 10-inch) height, 170-pound weight, blue eyes, red hair, and ruddy complexion were all recorded for posterity in his personnel records. Poked, prodded, and immunized for smallpox, typhoid fever, tetanus, cholera, and yellow fever, Steve followed the shouted instructions of the drill instructor as each man in his unit was evaluated. As required by law, each recruit received his first introduction to the Articles of War, or military law, which they were now subject to. They all became quick studies in basic military drill, customs, and courtesy.

During the first week of training, Steve also would have had an interview with a psychiatrist, psychologist, or a specially trained Marine officer or enlisted man. The interview was designed to evaluate his probable likelihood of completing recruit training. It would also have a huge bearing on what his subsequent assignment within the Marine Corps might be. Each recruit was asked about his family background, education, sports and hobbies, previous military training, and business experience. In this interview, the Marines learned about Steve's high school baseball, basketball, football, and dramatics; his tractor- and car-driving abilities; his two-plus years of engineering education; and his two years of military training at the university.

The recruit interview procedure began in early 1943 after President Roosevelt ordered the Marines to begin accepting draftees as well as enlistees after December 1942. Prior to that time, Marine recruiters had handled the screening of volunteers. Only volunteers who were in excellent physical condition, were able to read and write, and showed an aptitude for learning had been accepted into the Corps. Now the Marines had to sort personnel at the recruit training depots. Men with inadequate education, learning disabilities, and physical "defects" were initially placed in "casual" platoons for further observation. Some men were culled out of the Corps entirely. By August 1943, men who only had educational deficiencies were directed into units where elementary schooling was provided for three to six months (up to the sixth-grade level) before they would then join a regular platoon for recruit training.

In addition to his personal screening interview, Steve took several written tests during the week of March 21, 1943. There were tests on algebra, trigonometry, and geometry as well as electrical systems and radios. He also took the GCT, or General Classification Test.[3] The 150-question multiple choice GCT was designed to assess the ability of recruits and officer applicants to learn the duties and responsibilities of a soldier or Marine. It was divided into three sections: vocabulary, arithmetical reasoning problems, and block counting. The first two sections were more dependent on what a recruit had learned; the third section was a test of abstract reasoning ability. Scores on the GCT were highly correlated with success in both recruit training and officer candidate class (OCC). Any score of 130 or higher was considered "very superior"; the cutoff for officer training school was 110. Steve's score was 136. He also performed well on the MA-3, a mechanical aptitude test and the ROA1X1, a reserve officer aptitude test. Depending on how well he managed recruit training, his path forward seemed likely to be that of becoming a U.S. Marine Corps officer in a specialty requiring an aptitude for mechanical and mathematical reasoning.

Marine recruit training itself was a grueling physical and mental ordeal in 1943. Not everyone successfully completed it. A typical day began at 4:00 a.m. and ended around 10:00 p.m. All recruits were relentlessly pushed to perform with a sense of urgency. They were constantly harassed with demanding long runs through soft sand, lengthy physical training sessions, and stressful marching and rifle drills as their drill instructor watched every move and vocally criticized every small mistake. Several times they were ordered to move to different housing units on very short notice, collecting all their gear and marching off at quick time to new huts. Upon arrival, they would get immediate orders to "fall in" to military formation for inspection. In Sledge's words, "the discipline we were learning in responding to orders under stress often would mean the difference later in combat—between success or failure, even living or dying."[4]

The U.S. Marines had left the brutal fighting on Guadalcanal in December 1942, and by the time Steve began boot camp in San Diego in March 1943, several veteran NCOs from the campaign were serving as drill instructors. They brought with them not only the toughness of their experience but also the fighting techniques they had learned the hard way in battle. Specifically, Guadalcanal had taught the Marines that recruits needed to develop competency in the martial arts used by Japanese troops. Consequently, Steve and the other recruits in the Tenth Recruit Battalion were taught hand-to-hand and bayonet fighting techniques derived from judo and karate. Wearing protective gear initially and then later without it, the recruits practiced with each other as the NCOs loudly and constantly critiqued them. The emphasis in physical training had shifted, too, from calisthenics to physical contact exercises like boxing, wrestling, hand-to-hand fighting, and daily half hour swimming periods for recruits who couldn't meet the minimum swimming qualifications.[5]

On the eve of World War II, Marine recruit training had been a rigorous eight weeks, but after President Roosevelt called for a dramatic ramp-up in personnel numbers in 1939, the Marines tried to do the same training in four weeks. Found to be highly unsatisfactory at both the San Diego and Parris Island, South Carolina, training depots, the shortened training period was quickly extended to six weeks and then to seven weeks in 1940. Still the rifle proficiency scores of the recruits were not as good as those of prewar Marines. After Pearl Harbor, an even more dramatic mobilization challenged the Marine Corps' ability to house the increasing number of recruits and find drill instructors to train them. For a while in early 1942, recruit training time was reduced to only five weeks, two of which were spent on the rifle range.[6]

By 1943, however, the Marines had built seven hundred sixteen-man huts for housing recruits at the San Diego depot, and the rifle range at Camp Matthews in La Jolla, California, had been expanded. Steve's boot camp lasted seven weeks but with longer days than in 1940. The first three weeks were spent at the San Diego training camp, the next three weeks were spent on the rifle range at Camp Matthews, and the final week was back in San Diego. In addition to the aforementioned physical training (a minimum of 42 hours), Steve's recruit training consisted of a minimum of 138 hours of weapons training, 62 hours of garrison instruction, and 57 hours of field training.⁷

Weapons training included developing proficiency first and foremost with the Marines' semiautomatic rifle, the Garand M1, which had completely replaced the 03 Springfield by 1943. While dismantling and cleaning their rifles several times a day, the recruits had the mantra "The rifle is a Marine's best friend" embedded into their brains. Steve and the other recruits also trained with M1 carbines, rifle and hand grenades, and bayonets. Sledge describes the first week of rifle training this way:

> We were divided into two-man teams ... for dry firing, or "snapping in." We concentrated on proper sight setting, trigger squeeze, calling of shots, use of the leather sling as a shooting aid, and other fundamentals. ... During this snapping in, each man and his buddy practiced together, one in the proper position (standing, kneeling, sitting, or prone) and squeezing the trigger, and the other pushing back the rifle bolt lever with the heel of his hand, padded by an empty cloth bandolier wrapped around the palm. This procedure cocked the rifle and simulated recoil.⁸

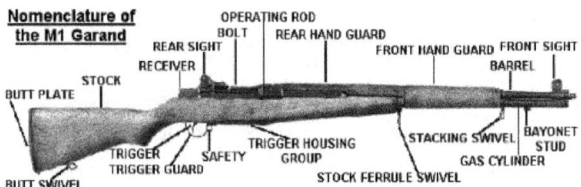

(Wikimedia photograph in public domain)

Live ammunition wasn't used until the second week, which is when recruits learned what it was like to hear the sound of bullets overhead. All the rifle training was done under the strict oversight of the drill instructor and rifle coaches who continually stressed safety and discipline while at the same time teaching effective marksmanship. E. B. Sledge noted, "Punishment for infractions of the rules came swiftly and severely."⁹

Sometimes recruits like Steve who had hunted throughout their childhood and teen years realized they had to relearn everything they thought they already knew to learn the "Marine Corps' way" of firing a rifle, and Steve's hunting certainly had not been done with an M1. Nevertheless, on Qualification Day, April 29, 1943, Steve earned the Maltese Cross–shaped Rifle

Sharpshooter's badge, which he wore proudly. He qualified as a Bayonet Expert by the end of his recruit training as well.

*April 30, 1943*
*Dear Necie,*

*I'm sorry it's taken me so long to write to you. This is the first personal time they've given us. I've really appreciated your letters. They've meant the world to me. Champaign and the university seem like another world to me now, and it's great to hear about what you've been up to.*

*The drill instructor is always yelling at us to do this and that and do it in a hurry and do it perfectly. Some of the guys are struggling but I've done pretty well. It's not that different from growing up with my dad—only in spades.*

*The physical training is okay, too. I guess there's an advantage to having grown up on a farm working from dawn to dark, and God knows I had to learn some serious wrestling and boxing moves back in southern Illinois to avoid getting beaten up. The wrestling class I took at the U of I came in handy, too. Compared to a lot of guys, I guess I'm in pretty good shape.*

*We finished our training on the rifle range yesterday, and they're giving us a few hours today to transition back to main camp. I did fine, but it was sure a lot different than hunting rabbits back on the farm. I think the hardest part of boot camp may be over, but you never know what these guys have up their sleeves so I might be wrong about that.*

*And, by the way, getting three square meals a day without having to pinch pennies is a welcome change. The food's not great, but it's filling...*

*Steve*

Upon graduation from boot camp on May 7, 1943, Stephen A. Lynn Jr., "recruit," became Stephen A. Lynn Jr., "Marine." He was given three bronze globe-and-anchor Marine Corps emblems, one for each lapel of his green wool coat and one for his cap. His initial rank was that of private.

(U.S. Marine Corps image in the public domain via Wikimedia Commons)

Private Lynn's platoon in the Tenth Recruit Battalion was disbanded as, one by one, each Marine reported to a specific truck for transport to his next training location. The majority went to Camp Elliott twelve miles north of San Diego or to the brown hills of Camp Pendleton farther north of San Diego in Oceanside for advanced infantry training. Others were selected to become enlisted specialists in as many as twenty-one different occupational fields each of which contained a number of specialties (e.g., artillery, administration, communications, engineering, food, intelligence, ordnance, supplies) and required specific advanced training.[10]

Steve's courses in college, including his military training, and his test scores from the first week of boot camp pegged him as a potential officer candidate from the get-go, and in mid-1943, the Marines were in dire need of new second lieutenants. Steve was one of a limited number of recruits selected by special screening boards set up at the San Diego and Parris Island recruit training centers to be considered for officer training. He was asked to submit the names of people who could provide character references, and before his seven weeks of recruit training were completed, the Marine Corps had received five letters of recommendation from men back home in Massac County, Illinois.

Harry Wright, who had been Steve's science teacher at Brookport High School, was now the Massac County superintendent of schools. On April 19, he wrote, "I consider [Stephen A. Lynn Jr.] one of the finest young men of my acquaintance." Walter Roberts, Massac County judge, wrote, "[I] have always found him to be one of the outstanding young men of this community ... honest, truthful, sober and dependable in every way." The state's attorney, Robert A. Chase, wrote on April 16, "It is a pleasure to recommend Mr. Lynn to you. I do so with the hope that other applicants may come to you as well qualified." On the same day, the Massac County sheriff, George Krueger, wrote, "Pvt. Lynn is a hard worker, honest, intelligent, of good character, and pleasing personality." Even the farm advisor of the Massac County Farm Bureau, J. R. Strubinger, chimed in with, "He has a pleasing personality, a good cooperator, industrious, and I do not hesitate to recommend him for consideration for Officers Training School."

Not much for the Marine Corps to worry about there.

Except for those officers commissioned in the field or recruited from civilian life as specialists, Marine officers in 1943 were trained as infantrymen first. Then perhaps they trained to become officers in artillery, ordnance, or some other specialty. Consequently, Steve found himself with the majority of Marines graduating from the Tenth Recruit Battalion who headed for six weeks of additional advanced infantry training in California. He was ordered to retain his personal M-1 rifle and personal equipment and board the bus with so many others headed for Camp Elliott.

Sledge wrote that the atmosphere in this part of training was much less tense than during recruit training. There wasn't as much screaming and bullying by NCOs, and there was an enlisted men's club and more time to go to the PX (post exchange—i.e., the base store). It was assumed that since these men were now "Marines" and not just "recruits," they would work hard to learn what they needed to know to defeat the enemy and survive the war.[11]

The emphasis was on learning about additional weapons systems, participating in amphibious landings, practicing combat tactics for rifle squads, and maintaining physical fitness. The infantry training began with lectures and demonstrations of weapons that had not been introduced during recruit training: antitank guns, 81 mm and 60 mm mortars, machine guns of various sizes, and the Browning automatic rifle. Five-man squads competed with other squads to handle the weapons the fastest and most precisely. Repeated weapons drills were followed by live ammunition exercises.

Hand-to-hand combat continued to emphasize the judo and knife-fighting techniques introduced in recruit training. Each Marine was issued a Ka-Bar knife, the "foxhole companion." More important in fighting the Japanese, who more often than the Germans tried to infiltrate American lines during the night, the foot-long knife with "USMC" stamped on its five-inch leather handle and a seven-inch-long by one-and-a-half-inch-wide blade was (is) a light and necessarily effective fighting weapon. It was adopted by the Marine Corps in November 1942. The last phase of the training was a series of swimming tests.

**Marine Corps Ka-Bar combat knife**
(Displayed in Flying Leathernecks Aviation Museum; photograph by M. Vieregg)

Steve's Infantry Training School ended on June 17, 1943, and he immediately headed cross-country by train to Quantico, Virginia, to begin Officer Candidates School (OCS) in Company K of the Thirty-first OCC. He was promoted to "(Temp) Private First Class" on June 21.

Before the run-up to World War II, Marine Corps officers came from a pool of U.S. Naval Academy graduates, enlisted men of special note, honor graduates of college NROTC (Naval Reserve Officer Training Corps) and ROTC (Reserve Officer Training Corps) programs, exceptional officers from the Marine Corps Reserve, and selected graduates of the Marines' Platoon Leader's Class. They experienced rigorous nine-month-long training at the Basic School in the Marine barracks at the Philadelphia Navy Yard. During the entire year ending in June 1939, only sixty-seven second lieutenants were graduated from the Basic School.[12]

Gradually throughout the period leading up to Pearl Harbor, the Marine Corps worked on ways to expand its officer corps. The challenge was to transform civilians into competent combat leaders in a shorter period. The Corps settled on a two-part program requiring officer candidates to successfully complete OCC and then ROC (Reserve Officer Class). The program went through several iterations between Pearl Harbor and V-J Day (commemorating victory over Japan) in 1945, varying in the duration of the classes and specific additional requirements for certain groups of men, but during that period, a total of 16,084 officers completed Marine Corps officer training.[13]

The Marine barracks at the Philadelphia Navy Yard was too small to handle the larger number of trainees, so all officer training was moved to Quantico, Virginia. Initially, the Marines had to use nearby Civil War battlefields for training, but in 1942, the base expanded in size by fifty-one thousand acres. The new area was named the Guadalcanal Area after the Corps' first successful offensive action of the war. It included topography similar to some of the terrain the Marines would encounter in the Pacific. Now all officer training, including artillery officer training, could be done on Marine Corps property.

An officer candidate had to graduate first from OCC to participate in ROC, and not every candidate completed the rigorous program. As Jack H. McCall Jr. wrote in the introduction to Christopher S. Donner's memoir, *Pacific Time on Target*:

> OC was not—and is not—for the weak of mind or infirm of body or character: Its intent is to weed out those unfit to be officer-leaders of the Marine Corps. To assess future officers' strengths and shortcomings rigorously, this training program is even more relentlessly focused than the enlisted Marines "boot camp" in finding each candidate's shortcomings and testing the candidate to (or beyond) his breaking point.[14]

Donner wrote about his experience in OCC/ROC that took place a few months earlier than when Steve went through the program:

> I obtained from it ... the conviction that actual combat could never be much worse. And, in fact, it had proved more of a struggle for me to get through those twenty weeks at Quantico than it was to keep going through any of the fighting I personally met. There were times in OC[C] when I very much wanted to quit, and when my conception of the responsibilities an officer must shoulder seemed mountainous.[15]

Donner did survive OCC and ROC and later wrote a book recounting his harrowing experiences as a forward ground observer for the Eleventh Marines at Okinawa at the same time Steve was there serving as an aerial artillery observer for the same regiment.

Company K's platoon sergeant, platoon commander, and company commander closely and aggressively scrutinized Private First Class Lynn and each of the other officer candidates as they were put through their paces during OCC. Their studies and drills focused on marksmanship, small arms, combat principles, map reading, physical conditioning, troop inspection, amphibious operations, Japanese weapons, Marine Corps customs and traditions, and so on. Each candidate was graded using "a detailed and uniform system" of criteria within two general categories: "General Characteristics" and "Military Proficiency." Candidate classes in this time frame showed an average 20 percent attrition rate.[16]

Private First Class Lynn proved to be tough enough to graduate from the OCC. On August 10, 1943, he was appointed a second lieutenant in the Marine Corps Reserve, accepted the commission, and executed the oath of office at the Marine barracks in Quantico. The very next day he was assigned to active duty at Barracks B in the Thirty-fourth ROC at Quantico for another ten weeks of advanced leadership and infantry training. ROC training included a minimum of 517 hours of instruction, and each class had about 250 officer students. In 1943, a new ROC of officer students began every two weeks to provide a steady stream of graduates.

Along with additional instruction in small arms marksmanship, physical conditioning, map reading, naval law, and administration, emphasis was placed on field fortifications, landing operations, tank tactics, drill and command exercises, and infantry tactics up to and including company level. Instruction and tactical demonstrations were conducted in the field. Officer candidates spent their field training time in tent camps in the Guadalcanal Area scouting and attacking vacated farms and experiencing live fire artillery exercises.

Marine Corps property along the Potomac River was used for amphibious landing exercises. Officer students had to demonstrate competency in following strict tactical principles and directing troop loading in these exercises. In addition, there was a troop-leading exercise:

> It consisted of a series of squad, platoon, and company tactical exercises in which the student, acting as unit commander, was presented with a tactical problem, given an approved solution, and required to perform all the steps necessary for the movement of the unit in carrying out the given solution.[17]

Second Lieutenant Lynn graduated from the Thirty-Fourth ROC on October 20, 1943, as an Infantry Officer (MOS [Military Occupation Specialty code] 1542) in the United States Marine

Corps. His certificate indicates he received satisfactory marks in the following subjects: Combat Intelligence, Interior Guard Duty, Signal Communications, Estimates and Decisions, Field Supply and Evacuation, Hygiene and Field Sanitation, Tanks, Combat Orders, Chemical Warfare, Landing Operations, Aerial Photograph Reading, Organization and Tactics of Marine Corps Aviation, Tactics of the Organic Units of the Infantry Battalion, Naval Law, Administration, Drill and Command, Terrain Appreciation, Rules of Land Warfare, and Artillery in Support of Infantry.

It was quite a bit to master in ten weeks.

United States Marine Corps 2nd Lt. Stephen A. Lynn
upon completion of ROC, October 1943
(Photograph in family collection)

Of the 5,584 ROC graduates designated for ground duty during the calendar year 1943, 2,478, or 44 percent, were ordered directly to formal specialist schools for additional training before taking up their duty assignments.[18] Lieutenant Lynn was one of them. He graduated from ROC at Quantico on October 20, 1943, and the next day began training as a field artillery officer at the same base.

Prior to the buildup for the war, Field Artillery and Base Defense were included in one officer school at Quantico. (Field

Artillery generally supports and reinforces the infantry, while Base Defense defends advance bases from attack.) Base Defense training was moved to Camp Lejeune, North Carolina, in early 1943, while Field Artillery officers continued to be trained at Quantico. By early 1944, training artillery officers was the third largest training function at Quantico, after OCC and ROC.[19]

When Second Lieutenant Lynn began the twelve-week Field Artillery Class (FAC) for Battery Officers, he found himself back in the classroom and out in the Guadalcanal Area of Quantico learning all the Marine Corps could cram into his head about artillery. Organized in November 1942, the Field Artillery Training Battery was equipped with 105 mm howitzers and 75 mm guns mounted on half-tracks, which allowed observed firing by student officers. "Study in the classroom then fire in the field" was the course organization.[20] By late 1943, 155 mm guns were also being successfully used as field artillery in ground support missions in the Pacific. Fortunately, the basic methods for adjusting and conducting fire were essentially the same for these guns as for the smaller weapons.

Artillery officers took courses in all three divisions of Ordnance School: Artillery Mechanics, Fire Control Equipment, and Ammunition. Artillery mathematics, base line surveying, computation of firing data, position finding, spotting and adjustment of fire, field artillery communication, and firing tactics of the weapons and their associated range-finding equipment were some of the areas of study within in the FAC. Second Lieutenant Lynn's artillery "bibles" included a red-covered booklet entitled *Logarithmic, Trigonometric, and Short Base Tables* and two beige booklets of *Firing Tables*, one for the 75 mm pack howitzers and another for the 105 mm howitzers.

The *Firing Tables* booklets describe the gun and carriage characteristics, the projectile weights, and the various fuse types used in certain situations. They also include numerous tables dealing with probability, wind components, air density and temperature, safe elevation for low-angle fire over friendly crests with particular charge types, and other relevant information.

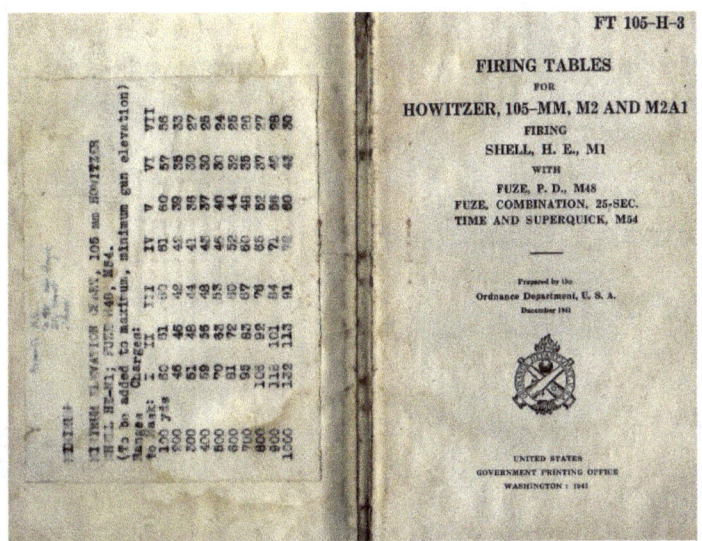

*Firing Tables* booklet for the 105 mm howitzer

**Pouch for artillery handbooks and *Tables* booklet**
(Booklet and pouch property of Lt. Seeley G. Lodwick, Fourth Battalion, Eleventh Marines; photographs by M. Vieregg, with permission from Barbara Lodwick Rossow)

Lieutenant Lynn's mechanical aptitude and training in mathematics and engineering helped him master the large amounts of information presented. They didn't help him protect his ears much from the loud percussive noise during the live firing exercises, and he, like many other artillerymen of the era, would endure lifelong and progressive hearing loss as he grew older.

In late November 1943 while Lieutenant Lynn was still attending FAC at Quantico, the commandant of the Marine Corps directed Marine Corps Schools to organize an Artillery Observers Course:

> From each class graduating from the Artillery course, six officers were to be selected for training as aerial observers. Their instruction was to include tactical instruction in aerial artillery spotting and technical instruction photography.[21]

Even though Lieutenant Lynn would later serve as an aerial observer at both Peleliu and Okinawa, he did not attend the school located in Pearl Harbor, Hawaii, until after both campaigns were over in mid-1945. The Marine Corps had another plan for Lieutenant Lynn in California.

Lieutenant Lynn would personally orchestrate a third plan for the Marine Corps.

Just before Christmas 1943, Lieutenant Lynn received orders to report on January 29, 1944, to Camp Elliott when the FAC ended, specifically to the Commanding General, Fleet Marine Force, San Diego Area. On January 12, 1944, Second Lieutenant Stephen A. Lynn (USMCR) graduated from the Field Artillery Class for Battery Officers and became a Field Artillery Officer (MOS 1193).

Having been away from home and training intensively for ten months, Lieutenant Lynn finally had a few days to catch his breath. He had sixteen days for travel and "delay"—that is, seven days leave. To expedite his trip, the Marine Corps ordered him to travel first class on the Richmond, Fredericksburg, and Potomac Railroad from Quantico to Washington, DC, and then on the Chesapeake and Ohio Railway to Cincinnati; then on the New York Central Railroad to St. Louis; and then on the Missouri Pacific Railroad to Kansas City, where he was to catch an Atchison, Topeka, and Santa Fe Railway train to San Diego.

Somehow, he found a way to interrupt his trip mid-route to visit Necie in Champaign, Illinois.

*December 25, 1943*
*Dear Necie,*

 *Merry Christmas! I wish I could have been in Illinois for the holidays. The Corps fed us well, and all of the guys in my FAC spent time around the makeshift Christmas tree we put together in the barracks, but it's not the same as being home. Guess I shouldn't complain too much, though. Sounds like the 2$^{nd}$ Marine Division had a hell of a time on Tarawa. Still mopping up, I bet, and recovering.*

 *Here's the good news, though! I just got my orders for where I'm going after FAC ends. There's a lot to talk about, but the most important thing is that I'll have some leave time to spend with you in Illinois. It looks like I might be able to get there around January 15$^{th}$ or 16$^{th}$ depending on how the train connections work. Will you keep the time open for me?*

 *It's been a long ten months since we were together. I'm a little nervous about whether I've changed to someone you won't care for as much as you seemed to when I left Champaign. Guess there's no way to find out except to show up on your doorstep. I'll try to call or telegram the exact date as soon as I know it myself...*

                   *Steve*

## 5
## Vernice
## Champaign, Illinois
## March 1943–January 1944

We are every second being born.
—Richard Powers, *The Echo Maker*

*September 15, 1943*
*Dear Steve,*

*Being here in Champaign without you is just not the same. Sure, I'm busy with work and school, but I miss your company studying, walking around campus, meeting at the Union for lunch—everything. I hope your training is going as smoothly as it can go. I keep hearing how rough it is, but I know you can do it.*

*I decided to take a really heavy course load this term so I can graduate early, but all the hours I'm working at the phone company are really making it hard to get everything done. I have to write a lot of papers for three of my classes, and the others move along so fast that I can barely keep up. And you know how it really bothers me to do just so-so in my classes. If I want to take as many courses next term, I think I'll have to find a job on campus where I can work fewer hours closer to home. Just when I've gotten so good at working all of the switchboard equipment, too...*

*The number of soldiers and sailors on campus just gets bigger and bigger. It feels like a military camp. Don't worry, though. I'm only interested in one particular Marine...*

*Necie*

Still living at home in the Illini Club on East John Street in Champaign, Vernice Milleville began her senior year at the University of Illinois in March 1943. Her help at home was needed more than ever since her sister Dolores had graduated the spring before, married "Mac" McQuown, and moved to New York City. Vernice was also working long hours at the telephone company while at the same time earning good grades in her coursework. Her course lineup that spring included more liberal arts courses: Latin American history, two sociology classes (Criminology and Immigration & Assimilation), two psychology classes (Genetic Psychology and Educational Psychology), and another American literature class.

Vernice thought she was interested in pursuing a career in the growing field of social work, and she was part of the first cadre of students to be specifically trained for such a career by the university. She pursued and accepted membership in the international sociology honor society, Alpha Kappa Delta, in early 1943.

During the following summer, Vernice took only one course, Methods of Speech Correction, and worked as many hours as she could at the phone company. Taking that one course would allow her to graduate after the fall semester of the 1943–1944 academic year if she successfully completed the heavy course load she signed up for in her last term: two sociology classes, a speech course, an English literature class, a clinical psychology class, and an education course. Like so many wartime students, she was anxious to finish up. During the "national emergency," the university was running an accelerated term schedule, which allowed her to finish her degree in less than four years if she was willing to do the work in a shorter time.

To accommodate her demanding course load, Vernice started a new job in October 1943 at the University Engineering Library. She earned thirty-five cents an hour until she graduated the next February. She had been making forty-eight cents an hour working at the phone company, but her focus had shifted to finishing her degree. She liked the work, but she learned to be a bit wary about shelving books by herself back in the quieter parts of the huge library. Apparently, she experienced a bit of an "incident" with a male engineering student when she happened upon him back in the stacks.

Campus life had changed dramatically since the war began. Civilian enrollment dropped from 12,624 in 1938–1939 to a low of 5,824 during the 1943–1944 school year.[1] It would drop to 4,451 civilian students during the term following Vernice's graduation in February 1944 before returning veterans began to swell the enrollment numbers again later in the year.

That doesn't mean the campus was "empty," though. The U.S. Navy and Army "told" the University of Illinois (and many other schools) that they would use its facilities for special personnel training. The first two hundred military arrivals were trainees in the Navy signal school established on campus in May 1942. As the training school geared up, the Navy rotated eight hundred to a thousand men through the school every sixteen weeks. Two campus gyms were converted into housing for the Navy trainees, and the new Illini Union ballroom was converted into a mess hall.

The Navy also took over university facilities to train diesel engine operators and officers, cooks, and bakers. During the summer of 1943, the Navy began its V-12 program on campus as well. The V-12 trainees were taught by university faculty under Navy supervision to be medical, dental, and engineering officers. All in all, there were, over the course of the war years, about thirteen thousand U.S. Navy personnel on the Urbana-Champaign campus.[2] The naval trainees were allowed to join fraternities and play on university sports teams while they were on campus. In 1943, the U of I men's basketball team won the Big Ten title.

The Army Specialized Training Program (ASTP) was organized in late 1942 on many campuses across the nation, including the University of Illinois. Its goal was to provide younger students with rigorous instruction in engineering, psychology, foreign languages, medicine, dentistry, or veterinary science. By December 1943, there were nearly thirty-four hundred ASTP students living in several university fraternity houses, but they were not given time to be involved in campus life. Their twelve-week-long terms were closely supervised, and the pressure on the young student-soldiers (some as young as seventeen) was probably excessive. Complaints about the program were fairly widespread.

By the time Vernice graduated in early 1944, the campus had become quite militarized. The *Illinois Alumni News* reported:

> All over campus—from old Illinois field on the north to the stock pavilion on the south—you see lines of soldiers marching to the sound of "Hup, two, three, four-hup, two three, four," and the sailors to a weird chant which sounds something like: "Follow your LEFT, right, left, right, follow your LEFT, right, left, right..." one boy doing most of the chanting and hitting a high pitch on the words we've put into capital letters. We've never heard anything like it; it has a south seas sound about it—which is appropriate.[3]

Vernice, like many civilian students, had mixed feelings about all this military activity. On the one hand, everyone wanted to support the war effort, and Steve was, after all, doing his part in the Marines. If it meant warily avoiding the military trainees' sometimes "inappropriate" behavior (back in the stacks of the engineering library and elsewhere) and tolerating their constantly marching units as you made your way to class across campus, well, that's just what you needed to do to be patriotic. Vernice and others were perturbed, though, when parts of her beloved Illini Union—including the cafeteria—were closed to civilian students during the summer of 1943. Fortunately, she could eat at home nearby on John Street between work and classes. The Illini Union cafeteria reopened in October when the ASTP mess hall was moved to the ice-skating rink near the campus Armory Building, and civilian feathers were smoothed as a result.

Vernice participated in student activities on campus that were designed to support the war effort—USO fund-raisers; collections of playing cards, magazines, and other supplies for wounded soldiers; war stamp sales; bandage rolling and wrapping in the Red Cross work rooms—but mostly she tried to keep up with her coursework so she could graduate early.

Especially as a sociology student, Vernice must have had her worldview challenged during late 1943 and early 1944 by the inevitable roiling of the social status quo on campus. Some Army and Navy trainees were African American and experienced service refusals by local businesses. Such treatment began a deep soul-searching among white university students and administrators, which accelerated as more and more veterans of all stripes began to return to campus in 1944. Imagine the debate that ensued when the U of I Board of Trustees agreed in January 1944 to admit a small number of Japanese American students "for a trial period."[4]

On campus, too, women students moved into unfamiliar roles as male student numbers dwindled. Women took positions editing the student newspaper, the *Daily Illini*, and the yearbook, *Illio*, for the first time. The Illini Union Board was led by women, as was the Theater Guild. Most notably:

> A few women even enrolled in the College of Engineering—a traditional bastion of maleness; the education of many of these engineering students was financed by the Pratt-Whitney aircraft corporation.[5]

During Vernice's senior year, a woman assumed the role of Chief Illiniwek, the university's longtime symbol. For about a year, too, women had the option to receive military training for the first time, in the Women's Auxiliary Training Corps, but there wasn't much interest.

In October 1943, George and Millie Milleville celebrated their own personal achievement. They had finally saved enough money to buy the Illini Club from H. Gladys Reilly, the woman from whom they had been renting the boardinghouse they both lived in and managed.

As the neighborhood elm, oak, and sweet gum leaves changed color and fell, George, Millie, and Vernice were all leading busy lives. Vernice worked at the Engineering Library and studied diligently. Millie maintained and managed the Illini Club. George worked full-time at the Jos. A. Kuhn store in downtown Champaign. The days went by quickly even as the war news worried them all.

Vernice could not have known that Christmas 1943 would be one of the last holidays she would spend with her mother. Millie had carefully reserved the rationed sugar and flour to make their traditional German cookies and cakes for Christmas Eve and Christmas Day dinner. They were even able to spare enough dried fruit, canned pickles, and canned tomatoes to put together a few gift baskets traditionally given to neighbors or friends living alone nearby. Because of rationing, gifts were modest, but the best gift that Vernice was going to be giving her parents was her college graduation in just a few short weeks.

It was an exhilarating time for Vernice Marilyn Milleville. The world was changing before her eyes in more ways than she could have ever imagined. The adult version of Vernice was being born. She shared most of it with Steve through the letters she wrote him. On very rare occasions, they were able to talk on the phone when he had the time to wait in the long lines on base to use a phone for just a few expensive minutes. Maybe it was during one of those brief conversations that she learned she would soon see Steve in Champaign!

*January 2, 1944*
*Dear Stevie,*

*I can't wait to see you here in Champaign! I can hardly believe you were able to arrange the train schedule to make it work to stop here on your way to California! How long will you be able to stay? Mother is already planning what room you'll stay in. I think she's nearly as excited as I am. I'll hardly be able to keep my mind on my studies between now and then. And with final exams just around the corner, too... but I don't care!*

*We all missed you at Christmas, but I was glad to hear that at least the Marine Corps fed you a nice Christmas dinner. Mother planned for the holiday for months scrounging sugar and flour and eggs and everything else she needed to put together a traditional German feast — a beautiful pork roast, potato dumplings, apple and sausage stuffing, and red cabbage. She was even able to bake Berlin bread, almond-filled stolen, and four kinds of German cookies — vanilla crescents, molasses ginger cookies, cinnamon stars, and bars. I put a box of her cookies in the mail to you today. I hope it gets there without the cookies turning into a pile of crumbs...*

*Necie*

# 6
# Steve and Vernice
# Champaign, Illinois
# January 1944

*People will say we're in love…*
Curly and Laurey in Richard Rodgers and Oscar Hammerstein II's
*Oklahoma!* 1943

Without a doubt, the brightest highlight of this period for Steve and Vernice as a couple was their rendezvous in Champaign in January 1944 after Steve completed artillery officer training at Quantico. Even though train seats were hard to come by, Steve found a way to divert from his Marine Corps–dictated rail route to visit Necie. He might have done it by hopping off the New York Central train he'd boarded in Cincinnati when it stopped in Indianapolis. From there he could have taken another New York Central train for the short hop into Champaign.

**Steve and Vernice, January 1944**
(Photograph in family collection)

In one photo taken during Steve's visit, both Steve and Vernice look happy, proud, and relaxed as they face the camera in front of the porch at the Illini Club on John Street. Lieutenant Lynn is wearing his U.S. Marine Corps officer service uniform. His second lieutenant bars sit on his shirt collars, his Marine Corps insignia on his jacket's lapels, and his Rifle Sharpshooter qualification badge and other qualification bars on his chest. He's standing tall and fit beside Necie, who looks delighted to have him at her side; her dark wavy hair and large brown eyes glow. Her beret is fashionably tilted to one side of her head, and a U.S. Marine Corps pin gleams on her own lapel in the winter sunlight. In a second, less formal photo, they gaze into each other's eyes.

**Steve and Vernice, January 1944**
(Photograph in family collection)

One can imagine them walking together along John Street toward the university quad, just as they had walked together during spring 1943. This time they talk about his Marine Corps training and what comes next in California. They talk about her upcoming college graduation and what her postgraduation plans are. They share news about their families and friends. Maybe they talk about the war. And as they walk and talk and laugh, they probe each other's minds and hearts and expectations and dreams, and they try to find out whether the spark is still there. Could they have a future together?

After his brief visit, Necie's dad may have driven Steve down to Mattoon, fifty miles south of Champaign. There Steve could have caught the New York Central's Southwestern Limited at 2:20 p.m. He'd have arrived in St. Louis around 5:00 p.m., in time to catch one of the Missouri Pacific Railroad's Eagles headed for Kansas City. Maybe he snagged a seat instead on the Illinois Central

Railroad's southbound Panama Limited or City of Miami. If he did, he had to wait overnight in Mattoon for the next day's New York Central morning train into St. Louis. Either way, Steve had to hightail it back to St. Louis to catch a train for Kansas City. There he climbed aboard the Atchison, Topeka, and Santa Fe Railroad's San Diegan headed for California.

The visit was a short one, but it was important. It was the last time they would see each other for more than two years.

# 7
# Steve
# California
# January–March 1944

> Though it might be no more than an illusion that he had the power of selection ... in the vast warp of life ... a man might get personal satisfaction in selecting the various strands that worked out the pattern.
> —W. Somerset Maugham, *Of Human Bondage*

*January 21, 1944*
*Dear Necie,*

*It was sure great spending time with you in Champaign. It had been so long since we'd seen each other that I didn't know how we would get along, but it felt just as fine to be with you this time as it did before I left. People say that Marine Corps training changes a person, and I guess it has in some ways, but being with you felt just as comfortable as it always did. I hope you feel the same.*

*I made it back to St. Louis just in time to catch my assigned train. I'm writing this letter on the train to Kansas City. From there, I'll catch another train that will take me into San Diego. The cars are filled with soldiers, sailors, and Marines. Some of the guys want to talk and play cards; others just sit quietly looking out the windows. After our busy time in Champaign together, I've dozed off a few times only to be jostled awake by either stops at train stations and along sidings or by other guys bumping into me.*

*As I explained in Champaign, I've heard the Marine Corps has ideas about me linking up with the Navy for liaison work, but I'm not buying it. I want to be with Marine artillerymen like I was trained to be so I'm going to figure out a way to go in another direction than the Corps has in mind. Wish me luck...*

*Steve*

After spending time with Necie in Champaign, Steve headed west. He reported for duty at the Fleet Marine Force headquarters at Camp Elliott near San Diego on January 29, 1944.

Steve had spent formative time with fellow Marines in his Field Artillery Section of the Thirty-Second Field Artillery Class (FAC). Eleven of them had been through both Officer Candidate Class (OCC) and Reserve Officer Class (ROC) with Steve. Four others had been in the same ROC. Now their Marine Corps paths began to diverge. Twelve officers were ordered to join the Thirteenth Marines, the artillery regiment for the Fifth Marine Division formally activated on January 21, 1944. Eventually, they would go on to play a crucial role in the battle for Iwo Jima during February and March 1945.

Six fellow officers were attending the new Aerial Observers' School in Pearl Harbor (Charles J. Aldrich, Clarence J. Echterling, James L. Frink, Wm. H. Lynch, Gene E. McDonald, and Allen M. Scher). Steve would meet up with them again a few months later out in the Pacific after first taking a circuitous detour in California.

Lieutenant Lynn was one of fourteen Field Artillery officers ordered to report to replacement battalions at Camp Joseph H. Pendleton in Oceanside, California. There he initially joined the Second Field Artillery Battery of the Artillery Training Battalion as a battery officer, but he stayed in that unit for only two weeks. Along with another graduate of his FAC, Lieutenant Lynn was ordered to join the Third Joint Assault Signal Company of the Field Signal Battalion as an artillery officer. He was greatly disappointed and dismayed to learn that he had been selected to attend Naval Gunfire Liaison School at Coronado, California, beginning March 2, 1944.

Since 1933, the U.S. Marine Corps had been working on refining the art of amphibious landing operations. A major element of such operations was naval gunfire support for landing Marines. Naval gunfire support is either *direct*, where the ship has a line of sight with the target, or *indirect*, which to be accurate requires an artillery observer to direct the line of fire. During the early Pacific battles of Guadalcanal and Tarawa, the naval gunfire was not as effective as it could have been and, in fact, too often resulted in "friendly fire" (fire by one's own troops) on American positions. Additionally, the radio channels were sometimes filled with too much garbled and sometimes conflicting firing orders, not only between the shore and ships but also between infantry units and supporting artillery.

The Joint Assault Signal Company concept was created in late 1943 to address the problem. The goal was to improve communications between and among shore units, naval fire control, and air units by creating small mixed units of Navy, Marine, and Army officers who would coordinate all communication related to air, naval, and artillery gunfire. In early 1944, such coordination often entailed having a specially trained Marine artillery officer on board a naval vessel coordinating and directing naval gunfire onto shore. Steve was selected to be trained for the job, but he was clearly not interested in it.

Lieutenant Lynn's first two officer fitness reports covered his time in the FAC at Quantico and his first few weeks at Camp Pendleton in the Second Field Artillery Battery. His ratings in every category from "performance of regular duties" through "physical fitness," "attention to duty," "intelligence," "cooperation," "judgement," and on to "loyalty" ranged from good to very good to excellent in both reports. His next fitness report written by his commanding officer at Naval Gunfire Liaison School reads more like a poor report card from middle school, and it prompted a "fitness report case" with his superiors.

USMC Major John H. Ellis reported that as a student at the Naval Gunfire Liaison School in Coronado, Lieutenant Lynn exhibited notable deficiencies in "performance of duties," "attention to duty," "cooperation," "initiative," "force," and "loyalty." Major Ellis conceded that Lieutenant Lynn had very good "military bearing and neatness" and good "intelligence," but he wrote that the young officer's attitude toward the course was "bad for the morale of the entire group which would be even more undesirable under combat conditions."

Major Ellis reported that Lieutenant Lynn had shown no interest in the course and was almost always tardy to class. On March 16, "while sitting with a group of students working out a Bombardment Plan," the lieutenant fell asleep at the table and had to be awakened and reprimanded by the instructor (a naval officer)! After class that day, Lieutenant Lynn asked to be sent back to an artillery battalion and was told it could happen but only if the transfer was accompanied by the submittal of a bad fitness report. Lieutenant Lynn "promised to do better," but the very next day he was caught reading a novel during the Bombardment Plan class, and on Saturday, March 18, Major Ellis saw him "reading a book during a lecture on rocket launching from landing boats." That was the end of Lieutenant Lynn's days as a student training to join the Third Joint Signal Company as a naval gunfire liaison officer.

By March 20, both the Navy and the Marines jointly decided Lieutenant Lynn was definitely not a good candidate for the job, and Lieutenant C. R. Hammond (USNR) requested a replacement. He wrote that Lieutenant Lynn had shown "no initiative or inclination to benefit from instruction given" and that his "general attitude has been unsatisfactory." His academic marks on ordnance, shore fire control, and communication tests had averaged 1.37 out of 4. For a former engineering student at a competitive university, this poor performance had to be intentional. In response to the unsatisfactory fitness report, Lieutenant Lynn only said, "I do not desire to make a statement." He was detached from the unit and returned to the Headquarters and Services Battery of the Artillery Battalion in the Camp Pendleton Training Center awaiting further assignment.

Later in life, Steve wasn't particularly proud of this stretch with the Third Joint Signal Company, but he was glad it turned out the way it did. Anyone who ever knew Steve Lynn knew that if he made up his mind about something, he would make it happen if it was humanly possible. He'd sweated through long months of Marine Corps training, and as he said later in life, he didn't want to be "stuck on a ship with a bunch of swabbies." He was a Marine Corps artillery officer, and he wanted to serve with other Marines. His behavior at the Naval Gunfire Liaison School was bona fide passive-aggressive, and it worked.

*March 30, 1944*
*Dear Necie,*

*I'm "out of the Navy" and couldn't be happier. I don't know if anything negative will come out of it down the road, but I just had to get back to a Marine artillery unit. I got my new orders today, and I'm catching the bus for Camp Elliott in about an hour. The officers making the decision gave me a good dressing down but I just stood at attention and took it until they let me leave. I think the Marine Corps sergeant in the room knew what the score really was, but he didn't even blink ... until the officers looked away. Then he winked. He took a chance even doing that.*

*I suppose this means I'll be shipped out sooner than later, but I don't have any orders on that yet. I guess I'll find out soon enough.*

*Wish I could have been there for your graduation. Thanks for the photos and the copy of your commencement program. I bet your mother and father were over the moon...*

*More soon...*

*Steve*

# 8
# Vernice
# Champaign, Illinois
# February–March 1944

> When they are young ... at that point in their lives, everything is possible. They are not afraid to dream, and to yearn for everything they would like to see happen to them in their lives.
>
> —Paulo Coelho, *The Alchemist*

*March 29, 1944*

*Dear Stevie,*

*I got your letter today. I hope your transfer back to the artillery battalion works out like you want it to. I have to admit the whole episode makes me a little nervous, but I know you were really unhappy about the possibility of serving on a ship instead of with an artillery regiment.*

*I've been doing a lot of thinking here, too. As I wrote you before, I just haven't been happy with my DCW job. For lots of reasons, I just can't see myself keeping the position much longer. I'm seriously thinking about trying to get a job in Washington, D.C. instead. I just feel like it's a special time in history, and I may never have another chance like this to really test myself. So many people like you have made the choice to really get involved in winning the war. Maybe, I can really help, too...*

*Necie*

On February 6, 1944, Vernice graduated from the University of Illinois with a Bachelor of Arts degree in the College of Liberal Arts and Sciences. She was proud and delighted, and her parents felt gratified. They had accomplished their goal. All four of their daughters had graduated from college. It was quite a feat for two parents, neither of whom had graduated from high school. In 1944, only about 4 percent of American women had earned college degrees.[1]

**Vernice Marilyn Milleville, University of Illinois graduation photo, 1944**
(Photograph in family collection)

Five days after she graduated from the University of Illinois, Vernice began working as a social worker for the Illinois Division of Child Welfare (DCW) at a salary of one hundred dollars a month. She stayed with the job only through May.

It's unclear exactly why Vernice left the social work position only four months after she started it. She was clearly proud to have been part of the first group of students at the university to be trained for social work. There may have been a personality conflict with her supervisor, who later wrote an unflattering letter of reference. Vernice may simply have wanted to earn more money, which is what she stated on her War Department Civilian Questionnaire completed shortly after she left the DCW. Or she may have discovered that she just really didn't have that special worldview effective social workers require. In conversation one time, she said she just couldn't understand how people could live the way some of her clients lived, and it made her very uncomfortable. Maybe it was a combination of all these factors.

Or maybe, and most likely, the lure of working in Washington, D.C., was just too attractive to ignore. In an exciting, dangerous, and uncertain time, Vernice wanted to be part of the war effort. She'd heard the radio programs and seen the recruiting posters encouraging women to do their part in Washington, and the work and the atmosphere in the nation's capital seemed vibrantly alive and connected to momentous world events. Being a social worker in central Illinois and living at home with her parents must have seemed depressingly tame by comparison. She wanted to apply for a government position in Washington, and she probably felt confident she would get one.

Even before the attack on Pearl Harbor in December 1941, the recruitment of educated women to join the work force in Washington, D.C., had been intense because the need for them was anticipated. Now it was dire. The number of government jobs had already been increasing during the 1930s because of Depression-era programs. After the war began, the number of wartime agency jobs skyrocketed as well. In the meantime, the men were being shipped out to the battlefronts. In 1940, almost twelve million American women already worked outside the home. The nation would require over six million more from what Secretary of War Henry Stimson called the "vast reserve of woman power" to aid the war effort---nearly one million in the federal government alone.[2]

The Office of War Information worked with movie producers, newspaper and magazine editors, writers, and artists to develop a strong message that would attract women with "Star Spangled Hearts" to serve their country. It needed to create the ideal of young, single, patriotic women traveling to Washington to help win the war. Part of the messaging was directed at the young women's families, trying to convince them that working in Washington would not corrupt their daughters' character or permanently change them in any negative way. Young women like Vernice were bombarded with magazine articles, radio programs, and even movies (e.g., *The More the Merrier*, *Government Girl*) sending the message they were needed, and their new lives would be important and adventurous.

The characters Rosie the Riveter, Wendy the Welder, and Wonder Woman were created to assist in the effort. Rosie and Wendy were often the somewhat older, often married women who worked in the defense industries near home while still taking care of their children or other family members. Wonder Woman was another story.

Diana Prince was the patriotic single woman who would leave her home to travel to Washington to defend her country in the guise of her powerful secret alter ego, Wonder Woman. She first made an appearance in *All-Star Comics* in 1941 as part of a cadre of superheroes; her solo debut appeared in *Sensation Comics* in 1942.[3]

Diana's clerical job in Washington was with Army Intelligence. Capable and strong, Diana and Wonder Woman would help America win the war.

**Poster featuring Rosie the Riveter**
(U.S. National Archives photograph)

Vernice undoubtedly listened to the radio broadcasts every Monday through Saturday of *Helen Holden–Government Girl*. At the time, nine out of ten people owned at least one radio which they tuned into three to four hours every day.[4] The Helen Holden serial followed the adventures of a young woman who had moved from her home in the Midwest to work in the Washington clerical army. She had "sworn to protect the homeland against enemy infiltration and aggression."[5]

Recruiting women to work in Washington was primarily the responsibility of the Civil Service Commission. Teams of agents traveled the country contacting employment agencies, placing ads in newspapers and magazines and on the radio, holding open recruiting drives in town squares, post offices, and movie theaters, and even helping convince doubtful parents to let their daughters go to Washington.[6] As the labor shortage became even more severe in late 1942 and early 1943, the need was so great that qualifications for a specific position weren't as necessary as the willingness to travel to Washington and be trained there.

There was, however, one branch of government that needed to be more selective. It needed women like Vernice—smart, college-educated women of good character who could "keep their lips zipped."[7] Recruiters for that branch of government found Vernice in the spring of 1944, and in less than two months' time, she would find herself in Washington far from her family home. Soon she would be interacting with many new people from many different parts of the country who had many different lifestyles and different ways of looking at the world. She would begin one of the greatest adventures of her life.

# 9
## Steve
## California, At Sea, New Caledonia, and Pavuvu
## April–June 1944

"I think the Marine Corps has forgotten where Pavuvu is," one man said.
"I think God has forgotten where Pavuvu is," came a reply.
"God couldn't forget because he made everything."
"Then I bet he wishes he could forget he made Pavuvu."
—E. B. Sledge, *With the Old Breed*

*March 15, 1944*
*Dear Necie,*

*I can't say where I am anymore and you can guess why, but I wanted to let you know that right now I'm pretty comfortable and the weather is beautiful. I'll just say there's a lot of deep blue water in the Pacific Ocean, and it's nice to be on land again. On board ship, I spent a lot of time training replacements for the artillery units. We couldn't do any firing, but we were able to go over a lot of the book work on equipment and tactics. It was good review for me, too, and it made the days at sea go faster.*

*I won't be in this particular spot for too long because I received my orders today to report for transport to another location soon. I haven't had any men to supervise here while I've been waiting for orders, so it's been nice to just do a little relaxing and keep in shape. We get radio news from the States so we've all heard about the troops landing in New Guinea. Sounds like they're having a tough go of it. At least we're on the attack and not just defending ourselves everywhere.*

*I reconnected with some of the guys from Quantico in San Diego and onboard ship. They've been good company exploring this place. Some of us will be traveling on together, too.*

*Keep your letters coming.*

*Steve*

After Lieutenant Steve Lynn was transferred out (kicked out) of Naval Gunfire Liaison School, he was reassigned March 30, 1944, and ordered to report April 3 for duty as company officer in Company C of the Fifty-Second Replacement Battalion at Camp Elliott. There were about one thousand Marines in the Fifty-Second Replacement Battalion, and they were all awaiting transport to the

Pacific staging areas. Another Marine assigned to the same battalion on the same day was Second Lieutenant Jack E. Dearmore, who would become a lifelong friend. Steve also reconnected with Lieutenant John Butler, a Field Artillery Class buddy.

When the war began in 1941, the Marine Corps' plan was to only deploy fully equipped units and replace personnel after a combat mission was completed. The policy was based on the sound philosophy that the fighting effectiveness of a unit was greatest when the Marines in it had trained together and established the esprit de corps of a unified group. By September 1942, however, the first replacement battalions had reluctantly been formed.[1] The unexpectedly high number of casualties and losses to disease and combat fatigue in the Pacific theater of operations required the Corps to insert individual Marines into units that had suffered heavy losses of personnel. Ideally, the replacements were absorbed into units when they were regrouping and recovering after a combat operation, but it didn't always happen that way later in the war.

Depending on when replacements joined particular units and what training they brought with them, the replacements' effectiveness in combat was variable. However, as Benis Frank and Henry Shaw wrote in *Victory and Occupation*, volume 5 of the *History of U.S. Marine Corps Operations in World War II*:

> Replacement training was probably as good as it could have been considering the time limitations. ... The inherent shortcomings of the replacement system could be cured only by adopting a different method for replacing combat losses, and none had appeared, even by the end of the war.[2]

Lieutenant Lynn's Fifty-Second Replacement Battalion was one of sixty-seven such battalions raised in San Diego and New River/Camp LeJeune, North Carolina, between September 1942 and June 1944. The function of these administrative and training units was to transfer both officers and men to the war zone to fill in the gaps in deployed units and replace veterans rotating back to the United States. With more than one thousand Marines in the battalion, the Fifty-Second was one of the largest. While awaiting transport, the Marines in replacement battalions (and the later replacement drafts) spent time at their bases working on physical conditioning and small unit training techniques such as cover and concealment, field fortification, and sniper and infiltration tactics.[3]

About two weeks after Lieutenants Lynn, Dearmore, and Butler joined the Fifty-Second Replacement Battalion, they and the rest of the battalion embarked on the transport ship USAT *Robin Doncaster* for the long trip across the Pacific Ocean to Noumea, New Caledonia. The *Robin Doncaster* first sailed in supply convoys in the Atlantic earlier in the war but was converted to a transport ship by the Marines during 1943. It was not luxury cruising. Aboard ship, the replacement Marines had a daily fitness regimen and training lectures. They also had a lot of free time to talk, play cards, write letters, stare out at the ocean and sky, and read the Armed Services Edition books (ASEs) they had grabbed from huge bins on the dock as they embarked.

The small ASE paperbacks were designed to fit into uniform pockets and rucksacks, and they were hugely popular. They would be read and traded not only aboard ship but also after the Marines made their way to their new units. With titles ranging from Mark Twain's *The Adventures of Huckleberry Finn* through C. S. Forester's *The African Queen* to Plato's *Republic*, every conceivable genre was available. They were read by soldiers, sailors, and Marines alike wherever they were stationed.

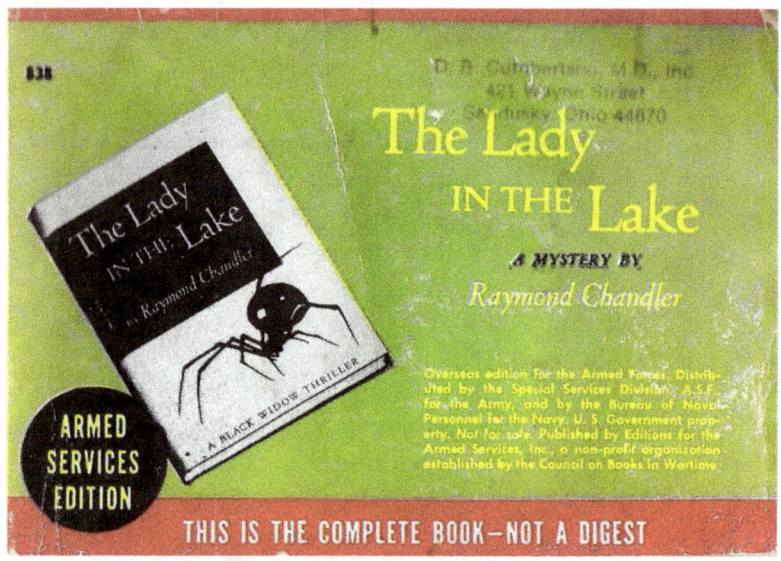

**Example of an Armed Services Edition (ASE) book**
(Photograph of ASE owned by M. Vieregg)

Almost three weeks after leaving San Diego, the *Robin Doncaster* arrived at Noumea on May 6, 1944.

E. B. Sledge recalled his arrival at Noumea:
> The blue water of the Pacific turned to green as we passed into the channel leading into the harbor of Noumea. There was a pretty white lighthouse near the harbor. White houses with tile roofs nestled around it and up the base of slopes of high mountains. The scene reminded me of a photo of some picturesque little Mediterranean seaport.[4]

He also noted that the first Pacific islander he saw there had bleached hair and a bone in his nose, but he was "an admirable tractor driver."[5]

**New Caledonian local in 1944**
(U.S. National Archives photograph)

Located at Noumea in 1944 was the primary Transient Center in the Pacific. At the center, the replacement battalions were gradually disbanded, and individual Marines were assigned to units throughout the Pacific theater. While waiting for transport, enlisted Marines underwent additional training usually conducted by combat veterans who worked hard to create realistic combat scenarios. They often used live fire from Japanese weapons so that the inexperienced replacement Marines could learn the sounds of the weapons. Experienced combat veterans also led bayonet training using Japanese rifles with fixed bayonets against the replacement Marines with M1 rifles, thus honing the replacements' skills and setting new expectations of combat conditions. Long hikes and forced marches ensured that the replacements reached peak physical fitness and endurance levels before shipping out to their new units.

Sledge was at the Noumea Transient Center for about six weeks, and he felt the training he received there probably saved his life on Peleliu and Okinawa. Lieutenant Lynn was there for only three weeks but still had time to undergo additional training and physical conditioning at Camp Magenta, one of the transient officers' camps. Generally, though, Noumea was a bit of a break for officers; Lieutenant Lynn had few duties and no troops to supervise. The weather was beautiful, the food was good and plentiful, and there was a popular bar at the Pacific Club where officers could go when they weren't reading, swimming, or playing volleyball. For the rest of the month of May, Lieutenant Lynn was still listed as Company C officer even though the designation of his unit was changed to "Fleet Marine Force, Pacific, In the Field" after the ship's arrival in New Caledonia.

On May 28, 1944, Private First Class Sledge and Lieutenants Lynn, Dearmore, and Butler joined hundreds of other Marines embarking on the USS *General R. L. Howze*, a naval transport ship crewed by the U.S. Coast Guard. All the Marines on board were slated to join the First Marine Division.

USS *General R. L. Howze* (AP-134)
(Wikipedia photograph in the public domain)

The *General R. L. Howze* supported the buildup in the Pacific with eleven tours of duty transporting troops and supplies throughout the combat area. This time, the ship was headed over a thousand miles north-northeast to the island of Pavuvu in the Russell Islands group of the British Solomon Islands Protectorate.

The *General Howze* was built specifically as a troopship and was consequently much nicer than many of the converted troopships like the *Robin Doncaster*. It was clean and freshly painted, and Sledge reported that even the enlisted Marines had well-ventilated compartments, each holding only about twelve men. The ship had a library where troops could get more books and magazines. It was also stocked with thousands of atabrine tablets, the bitter little yellow tablets that prevented malaria. As the ship headed north, each Marine was required to take one tablet every day. The Marine Corps had learned its lesson about malaria the hard way on Guadalcanal.

Lieutenant Lynn was on the *General Howze* roster as "Heavy Artillery Officer." For the period from April 3 to June 1, 1944, he received a stellar officer fitness report. He was rated especially high in "handling enlisted men," "training troops" (aboard ship), "attention to duty," "using good judgement and common sense," "leadership," "loyalty," "cooperation," "physical fitness," and "intelligence." Was this the same officer who sat in the Naval Gunfire Liaison School back in California reading novels and sleeping in class? Maybe he was just where he wanted to be, or maybe, he felt he'd better buckle down and show the Marine Corps what he was capable of doing. Major R. D. McAfee, USMC, wrote in the fitness report that he would be glad to have Lieutenant Lynn serving under his command in combat.

The *General Howze* landed at Pavuvu, the temporary home of the First Marine Division, on June 1, 1944. While still on board the *General* in Macquitti Bay, the clear water inlet of the island surrounded by groves of coconut palms, Sledge wrote that the ship's deck provided a view of "coral-covered roadways and groups of pyramidal tents."[6] He also noted that the Marines on the docks "appeared hollow-eyed and tired."[7] As he and his fellow Marines disembarked the next morning, they passed a line of Marines waiting to go aboard the *General Howze*. They were heading home after spending more than two grueling years on Pacific jungle islands fighting a determined and capable Japanese army.

Private Sledge was assigned to Company K, Third Battalion, Fifth Marines, an infantry assault unit. Lieutenants Lynn, Dearmore, and Butler were assigned to the Eleventh Marines, the artillery regiment of the First Marine Division. Specifically, Lieutenant Lynn was assigned to Battery A of the First Battalion; Lieutenant Dearmore was assigned to the Headquarters and Service Battery of the First Battalion.

In two-months' time, Lieutenant Lynn had been transported from a cushy classroom in Coronado, California, to the isolated tropical island of Pavuvu in the Pacific Ocean. He was assigned one of the most dangerous jobs in the Marine Corps, that of an artillery unit's forward observer.

*June 8, 1944*

*Dear Necie,*

*We arrived at our new station a week ago, and I've been so busy dealing with it all that this is the first time I've been able to write. We're busy from dawn to dark, and there's no electricity at night so it's almost impossible to read or write then.*

*I can't say where I am, but want you to know that I'll appreciate any food packages you and your Mom can send. Some clean socks would be nice, too. It rains nearly every day here, and it would sure be nice to be able to put clean socks on before I try to sleep. Books and magazines would be swell, too, even though there's not too much time for reading.*

*I can't say too much about what we're doing here, but we are training hard getting ready for some action somewhere in the Pacific. Is that specific enough?*

*Say hi to everyone there, and let me know what you decide to do about working in Washington. Like your Mom, I'll be a bit worried about your traveling there by yourself, but I know you can handle it...*

*Steve*

In the storied annals of First Marine Division history, the memory of Pavuvu, where Lieutenant Lynn disembarked on June 2, 1944, carries with it considerable scorn. Perhaps George McMillan, in his book *The Old Breed: A History of the First Marine*

*Division in World War II*, best provides the background needed to understand why.

After first being recruited at the Tun Tavern in Philadelphia in 1775, the skill and reputation of U.S. Marines grew as the decades passed. McMillan reports that in France during World War I, Captain John Tomason said about the Marines fighting there that they were an *"old breed* of American regular, regarding the service as home and war an occupation, and they transmitted their temper and character and viewpoint to the highhearted volunteer mass."[8]

After the Great War, as World War I was known at the time, America plunged into isolationism and generally neglected its military readiness. The so-called Old Breed Marines, however, used the limited resources they were given to develop techniques for amphibious landings—that is, landings against defended beaches. They were testing the techniques as early as 1933, in part because a few Marine planners had foreseen as early as 1921 the probability of a war with Japan for the islands in the Pacific. During the 1930s, too, the Marine Corps recruited the pick of Naval Reserve Officer Training Corps honor graduates to strengthen its cadre of company commanders and flight leaders.[9] Its operations and training exercises in the Caribbean and North China during the interwar years provided the Old Breed Marines experience that proved invaluable during the early World War II campaigns. By 1940, the First Marine Brigade was calling itself the "Raggedy-Ass Marines" in recognition of their "tradition of hard, dirty service."[10] Before the war even broke out, they had "tested and perfected many of the most important modern innovations in amphibious warfare, not the least of which were the (use of the) amphibian tractor (amtrac) and the Higgins landing boat."[11]

On February 1, 1941, the First Marine Division was created from the First Brigade. Training at Guantanamo, Cuba, the division had three infantry regiments (the First, Fifth, and Seventh) formed from Old Breed regulars and the organized Marine Corps reserves called up in late 1940. The artillery regiment, the Eleventh Marines, had been disbanded in 1929 but was reconstituted in 1940 at Quantico and arrived at Guantanamo to join the rest of the Division in late 1940. According to McMillan:

> The First [Division] was not only the first division in the Marine Corps but it was also the first integrated

amphibious striking force of such size formed in the United States armed forces. ... To an unarmed and unprepared United States already at war in the spring of 1942, 15,000 trained and disciplined Marines meant just about the only ready striking force the nation possessed.[12]

In mid-April 1942, the First Division was ordered to travel from Norfolk, Virginia, to Wellington, New Zealand—a trip that took almost a month. Most of the division's artillery regiment, the Eleventh Marines, traveled with their equipment by train across the United States to San Francisco, where they boarded the USS *John Ericcson* on June 22 and sailed for Wellington. Major General A. A. Vandegrift, the division commander, thought he would have six months to train his Marines in New Zealand. Instead, he was told that seven weeks after docking on June 20, the First Division would be expected to land against the Japanese at Guadalcanal to provide forward areas for offensive action.

The Battle of Guadalcanal was long, complex, costly, and brutal. It began in August 1942 and didn't end until early February 1943. The fighting had depleted the First Division by mid-November when, as McMillan quoted the division's final action report, the First Division "was no longer capable of offensive operations. The cumulative effect of long periods of fatigue and strain, endless labor by day and vigilance by night were aggravated to an alarming degree by the growing malarial rate."[13] McMillan added:

> When the [First Division] Marines departed [Guadalcanal], many of them were so weak they could not climb the cargo nets [onto the ships]. Sailors who fished them out [of the water, where they had fallen] and helped them into the ship openly wept upon seeing their emaciated bodies and otherwise poor condition.[14]

During its time at Guadalcanal, the First Division suffered 650 Marines killed in action, 1,278 Marines wounded in action, 31 missing in action, and 8,500 Marines contracting malaria and/or dysentery.[15] For its valor, the First Division was awarded the first of three Presidential Unit Citations it would earn during World War II.

The First Division was relieved on Guadalcanal in early December by the Second Marine Division reinforced by two Army regiments, Army artillery, the Second Raider Battalion, and elements of two Marine defense battalions, all of which fought on until the final U.S. victory was declared February 9, 1943. For many reasons, historians consider the Guadalcanal victory a major turning point in the Pacific war. At the end of World War II, the Japanese naval planner Captain Ohmae told U.S. interrogators, "After Guadalcanal I knew we could not win the war. I did not think we would lose, but I knew we could not win."[16]

Among other consequences of the Battle of Guadalcanal, the victory prevented the Japanese from invading Australia.

**1st Marine Division insignia**
(Wikipedia photograph in the public domain)

The First Division Marines were sent to Melbourne, Australia, to recover and regroup. Replacements were incorporated into the depleted units of the division, and the sick men who could be treated there were. Others returned to the United States.

The Marines loved Australia. The climate was ideal for restoring the health of the malaria-ridden Marines, and the Australians were kind, caring, generous, grateful, and fun-loving. In fact, it was during their stay in Australia that the First Division adopted the traditional Australian folk song "Waltzing Matilda" as its battle hymn. First Division Marines still ship out to this song today.

By late December 1943, the First Marine Division was engaged in another debilitating campaign—Operation Backhander. The immediate target was the Japanese-held airfield at Cape Gloucester, New Britain, in Papua New Guinea and part of an Australian mandate at that time.

They landed the day after Christmas and fought until the last division personnel left May 4, 1944. The crescent-shaped island was among the wettest that U.S. troops would ever have to fight upon. McMillan summarized the battle this way:

> Rainforest, jungle, continual rain, mud ... everything disintegrated including letters, photos, wallets ... pocket knives rusted ... socks and uniforms and boots rotted.[17]

Thigh-deep mud and fallen trees inhibited the movement of men and artillery, and the Japanese opposition was fierce. Marine losses have been calculated at fourteen hundred killed and wounded, and the Japanese killed and wounded are estimated to have been at least thirty-nine hundred.[18]

Even with the respite in Australia during 1943, more than two-thirds of the First Division Marines who left New Britain in 1944 had been in the Pacific for more than two years, and as George Garrand and Truman Strobridge wrote in *Western Pacific Operations*, volume 4 of *History of U.S. Marine Corps Operations in World War II*:

> Two strenuous jungle campaigns had sapped their reserves of energy. Alternately racked by malarial chills or burning up with its fever, weakened by poor rations, and rotten with a variety of fungus growths in various parts of their bodies, these Marines were both physically and mentally exhausted.[19]

Officially promised "rest and rehabilitation" and led to believe that many of the "twenty-four month" Marines would be relieved by replacements, the weary Marines leaving Cape Gloucester in late April and May were optimistically hoping for a rest camp where they could relax and recover from their harrowing experiences. Where would they be taken? Back to Melbourne? New Zealand? Either would be like a trip to heaven after what they'd been through. Maybe even Hawaii? Or the States? Rumors among the Marines ran rampant.

Imagine their disgust and disappointment when they were sent instead to Pavuvu in the Russell Islands, about sixty miles north of Guadalcanal—yet another steamy tropical jungle island. A small portion of the island had formerly been a coconut plantation but was now deserted and covered with rotting coconuts. Most of the island was covered with dense impenetrable jungle like the jungles on Guadalcanal and Cape Gloucester.

A Navy Seabee unit was supposed to begin preparing the island for the division before its arrival but was shipped back to the United States after having completed only a pontoon pier and one primitive road. Pavuvu had no mess halls or recreation buildings. It didn't even have cleared areas where tents could be set up to escape the tropical rain showers. It did have plenty of mud, quicksand, rotting coconuts, crocodile-infested swamps, biting black gnats and red ants, huge scampering rats, skin-sucking tree leeches, scorpions, skin-inflaming centipedes, diving bats, slithering snakes, crawling land crabs, swarms of flies, malaria-carrying mosquitoes, and monsoon rain. The Marines learned to especially despise the huge land crabs because they crawled into the Marines' boots and other personal belongings at night.

Rather than settling into an established camp in New Zealand, Hawaii, Australia, or even on Guadalcanal, as other regrouping units had done, the bone-tired First Division Marines found themselves on an island where they had to build their own rest camp from the ground up. Daily work details carried buckets and sometimes helmets full of coral for tent decks and roads. Many tons of rotten coconuts had to be collected, often by hand, to clear areas for the molding canvas tents and cots that had been delivered to the island for their use. There was initially no electricity, so there were no lights or refrigeration. There was no beer for the first few weeks and precious little after that for men who'd had none since they left Melbourne nine months before. Even fresh water was in short supply, so Marines had to wait for afternoon rain showers to bathe—quickly—and rinse off before the rain stopped.

When Second Lieutenants Lynn and Dearmore arrived on Pavuvu with hundreds of other replacements, the Old Breed Marines of the First Division had already been there about a month. They had made enough progress building a camp that straight lines of pyramidal cotton tents could be seen through the coconut palms that lined Macquitti Bay, as Sledge noted. It was easy to pick out the Cape Gloucester veterans from the new replacements. Sledge wrote that the veterans were "thin, some emaciated, with jungle rot in their armpits and on their ankles and wrists ... some had to cut their boondockers [boots] into sandals, because their feet were so infected with rot they could hardly walk."[20]

**1st Division Marines laying a concrete deck for a mess tent on Pavuvu, June 1944**
(United States Marine Corps photograph, U.S. National Archives (#127-GW-791))

Monotonous and unappetizing B rations (canned and other preserved food) and occasional hot C rations (dehydrated eggs and potatoes and Spam) were served to officers and enlisted men alike in outdoor chow lines, often in the rain. Fresh meat (primarily old mutton from Australia) was available for only one meal a week on average, and fresh eggs were served only twice during the division's four-month stay.[21] This meager food rationing existed in spite of the fact that because the men were in such poor shape after the Cape Gloucester campaign, their rations were supposed to be increased by 25 percent.[22] Sledge wrote about a four-day period after he and Lieutenant Lynn arrived when all the Marines had to eat was oatmeal morning, noon, and night.[23] Some Marines tried hunting crocodile and fishing in lagoons with gunfire, TNT, and hand grenades, but both activities had to be forbidden because of ensuing casualties. The men also started butchering some of the six hundred cows that had been abandoned on the plantations at the beginning of the war, but the Australian government, which officially controlled the islands, insisted they stop.[24]

The jungle rot and ringworm that so many Marines had acquired at Cape Gloucester were exacerbated by the dirty tropical conditions. Even as Lieutenant Lynn arrived at Pavuvu on June 2, more and more Marines were becoming sick because of the hard work and inadequate rations. Historian Frank Olney Hough reported that "morale plummeted to the lowest point it ever reached during the Pacific service of this elite unit."[25]

Pavuvu was isolated, and the boredom was stifling. It was also cramped; most of the roughly fifteen thousand Marines lived and trained in a former plantation area of less than one square mile. Entertainment was initially limited to old movies watched out in the open, and they were often interrupted by tropical rain showers. It was lonely. It was miserable. For some of the Marines, it was too much to bear and resulted in suicide.

To make matters worse, the Marines on Pavuvu resented the conditions on Banika, the nearby island with a large naval base. It had lights; Navy nurses; PXs stocked with chocolate, cigars, and dry socks; good food; and thousands of rear echelon troops who had never seen combat but still complained about the stateside commodities they were lacking. Banika was hard for Marines to get to unless their jungle rot developed into cellulitis and they had to be transported to the naval hospital there. Even then, Marines were often treated disdainfully, especially by naval officers.

Why send the First Marine Division to Pavuvu? Until the end of the Cape Gloucester battle, the First Marine Division had been under the control of General Douglas MacArthur (U.S. Army). Following what Rottman called a "brief (inter-service) battle" which Admiral Chester Nimitz (U.S. Navy) won, the division was attached to the Third Amphibious Corps under the control of the Navy in May 1944.[26] General Roy S. Geiger, the commanding general of the Third Amphibious Corps, wanted to find a place for the First Division to rest, refit, and train that was not under the control of General MacArthur but was still in the vicinity of where the Marines would need to prepare for their next campaign. After the Third Marine Division had returned to Guadalcanal "to rest and retrain" after the Battle of Bougainville in January 1944, MacArthur had demanded that the Third Division provide an average of a thousand Marines a day for work details.[27] This obviously interrupted both the "rest" the Marines needed and their training program before they headed out to fight the Battle of Guam in July. General Geiger wanted to avoid a repeat demand performance with the First Division.

General Geiger chose Pavuvu after checking it out only by flying over it. He assumed the Seabee battalion on Pavuvu could prepare adequate facilities before the Marines arrived, and he assumed Pavuvu's proximity to the developed naval station on Banika would ensure the delivery of the provisions the First Division needed. Neither assumption proved to be correct. Furthermore, the terrain of Pavuvu was unsuitable for training, which became problematic in the run up to Stalemate II, the First Marine Division's next campaign designed to invade and occupy the south Palaus (Peleliu and Angaur) as well as the islands of Yap and Ulithi.

Morale building was additionally challenged by the fact that not all of the "24-month Marines" could be replaced with new personnel. Some of them were specialists for whom no replacements were available. Some nonspecialist infantrymen had to stay because at that point in the war, there just weren't enough available trained Marines to relieve them. By the end of July, 4,860 replacements (including Lieutenant Lynn and 259 other officers) had arrived on Pavuvu. When the division left for the Peleliu operation in late August, about 40 percent of its Marines were replacements with varying degrees of training and experience. About 30 percent were Guadalcanal and Cape Gloucester campaign veterans; the other 30 percent were Cape Gloucester veterans having joined the division back in Australia in 1943.[28]

Some new replacements began complaining about the conditions on Pavuvu within just a few days after arrival but were soon brought into line by the Old Breed veterans. Until they had been in combat, the new guys were told they should quit whining. The transmission of these veterans' "temper and character and viewpoint to the high-hearted volunteer mass" began early on Pavuvu, just as Captain John Tomason had described it happening in France during World I.[29] The inculcation of the Old Breed values of fortitude, resilience, loyalty, and esprit de corps began immediately upon the replacements' arrival in spite of the rotten conditions everyone was enduring.

As a newly minted replacement officer, Lieutenant Lynn had to step right in to help supervise building the "rest" camp on Pavuvu. When he arrived, the enlisted men's area was still under construction, and officers' "country" was makeshift tents in the mud. Washing up was done out of his helmet or during one of the frequent tropical downpours. Work parties were still picking up rotting coconuts and palm fronds by hand when the available bulldozers and other vehicles got stuck in the deep mud. At the same time, he and the other artillery officers were trying to come up with some way to train their new replacements with no good target areas for firing practice.

Pavuvu was a hellish introduction to the jungle islands of the South Pacific. Lieutenant Lynn could only follow the lead of experienced Old Breed officers and keep himself and the men he supervised moving forward.

*June 25, 1944*

*Dear Necie,*

*People who have never been anywhere near them always imagine how beautiful the South Pacific islands are, but I can now truthfully look them in the eye and say those people are full of bull crap. If I began listing all of the horrible features and creatures of this place, you'd think I was exaggerating. The Marines here complain a lot but everyone is doing their job, and we're getting it all put together faster than anyone else could—given the circumstances.*

*Thank you for the food packages. They are a god-send because the chow here is really boring and bad, and there's not enough of it. If rationing allows, send more socks, too—as many pairs as you can get a hold of. Our feet rarely stay dry, and new clean socks are like gold here.*

*Missing you…*

*Steve*

# 10
# Vernice
## Champaign, Illinois, and Washington, DC
## April–June 1944

> These women came from all over the country, every conceivable background, and for widely varying reasons. Yet, each one knew that moving to wartime Washington would be an adventure they couldn't quite conceive and probably wouldn't forget.
>
> —Cindy Gueli, *Lipstick Brigade*

*June 29, 1944*
*Dear Stevie,*

*I'm leaving for Washington tomorrow! I can hardly believe it! Everything has happened so quickly. Mother is nervous about my leaving but everything has been arranged for me—even the housing. I'll find out the exact address when I get there, and I'll send it to you as soon as I have it...*

*Necie*

During early 1944, the Cryptanalytic Branch of the Signal Security Agency (SSA) was aggressively seeking out and recruiting qualified college-educated women to work as part of its exponentially growing Arlington Hall Station staff just outside Washington, DC. After long, contentious debate over the inadequacy of the civil service employees foisted upon the unit, the branch was finally given the go-ahead to do its own recruiting. Specifically, the SSA was given permission to expand its recruiting efforts to women graduating from universities and teaching colleges in the Midwest.

Vernice Milleville was just the kind of candidate they were looking for: a native-born, intelligent woman with a broad college education and negligible security risk. She had no training in cryptography, but she was conscientious, diligent, patriotic, trainable, and at least academically knowledgeable in history and foreign affairs. She had experience with two foreign languages, French and German, and her successful employment with the telephone company as a local and long-distance switchboard operator indicated she had the mechanical aptitude to master code-managing equipment. Most important, she had no apparent skeletons in her closet. Excellent character and integrity were critically important.

How Vernice and the Cryptanalytic Branch recruiters specifically touched base with each other is unknown. Perhaps it was a referral by her brother-in-law, Norman "Mac" McQuown, who was doing classified work in New York City for the War Department at the time. (She listed him as a Department of War employee on her application.) Perhaps the SSA recruiters contacted her personally as the type of candidate they were looking for. Maybe she was just curious when she saw an announcement on a bulletin board or in the newspaper about recruiters on campus looking for candidates willing to work in Washington. Recruiting announcements were plastered nearly everywhere; they would be hard to miss.

In any case, after she quit working for the Illinois Division of Child Welfare (DCW) in May 1944, Vernice completed a War Department Civilian Questionnaire, which was sent directly to Lieutenant Wilford Trinkle in the War Department. She received a letter dated June 12, 1944, asking her if she would accept an appointment as a "Cryptanalytic Aide, SP-5," pending satisfactory performance on an aptitude exam, medical clearance, and appropriate security clearance. On June 19, she replied that she would accept the position if offered and sent back to the chief signal officer her application for federal employment as required by the Civil Service Commission. She also sent her personnel security questionnaire, a certificate of medical examination stating she was "capable of performing duties involving *arduous* physical exertion," and a completed housing form. Only four days later, the U.S. Army Signal Corps at Arlington Hall Station, Arlington, Virginia, requested a personnel security check for Vernice Marilyn Milleville for the purposes of determining suitability for "Classified Administrative Work."

Her DCW supervisor was contacted by the FBI investigators conducting her secret "loyalty and character" evaluation for the War Department. Her former employer rated her qualifications as "average to excellent" but rated her emotional stability "poor." More specifically, she said, "Miss Milleville was unable to adjust to a work situation which included relationship to people and absence from her family home." Was a personality conflict between Vernice and her supervisor to blame for this unflattering assessment? It's impossible to know, but everyone else the investigators contacted gave sterling accounts of Vernice's abilities and character.

Mildred Johnson, her supervisor at the telephone company, highly recommended Vernice for "employment in the War Effort" and stated that Vernice would be eligible for reemployment if she wished to return to the company. Hilda Alseth, her supervisor at the University of Illinois Engineering Library, and Essie LeSure, a former teacher, both rated her qualifications for the work as "excellent."

Only a week after the investigation was initiated, Vernice was issued an employment agreement signed by Lieutenant Trinkle and travel authority from the War Department. It specified that she should travel to Washington in a lower standard berth of a Pullman car at the U.S. Army's expense and then proceed to Arlington Hall Station.

After a brief whirlwind of preparation and good-byes in Champaign, Vernice climbed aboard the Illinois Central Railroad's orange and brown Panama Limited headed to Central Station in Chicago. She could only take what she could carry or wear, so she folded her clothes and camera into two small suitcases; stashed her money, travel vouchers, and makeup in her purse; and carried one coat over her arm.

**Photo Vernice took of her parents before she left for Washington, DC, 1944**
(Photograph in family collection)

Her parents anxiously watched and waved from the train station platform as the train whistle blew. The engine then pulled the Limited out of Champaign with their youngest daughter on board. It must have been heart-wrenching for them.

In Chicago, Vernice made her way from Central Station near Michigan Avenue and Roosevelt Road north to Grand Central Station at 201 W. Harrison Street. There she maneuvered her way through the wartime crowds to catch her assigned Baltimore & Ohio (B&O) Railroad train, the royal blue, silver, and gold all-Pullman Capitol Limited that would carry her on to Washington, DC. The train was scheduled to leave Chicago at 4:30 p.m. as train number 6.

If the train didn't have to stop on the sidings to allow priority military trains to pass through, the ride to Washington took about seventeen hours. It was a thrill for Vernice. Excited and naturally outgoing, she undoubtedly spent time in the lounge seating cars watching the landscape fly by and chatting with her fellow passengers. Maybe she skimmed through the magazine library's offerings as well. Although her mother packed her a lunch for the train ride, Vernice spent some of her own hard-earned cash in the dining car sitting with other passengers and perhaps trying the "all-you-can-eat" salad bowl the B&O was famous for. The B&O line was the first to have air-conditioned cars, which on a packed train in the early summer heat was much appreciated. Authorized to travel in a lower standard berth of a Pullman car, she slept fitfully in one of the several ten-roomette five-bedroom sleeping cars added to the Capitol Limited in 1941 to accommodate the increase in wartime travel.[1]

The Capitol Limited rumbled into Washington, DC's Union Station late in the morning the next day. As the train slowed to a stop, Vernice watched everything and everybody she could see out the window in the bustling station. She was told to be in Washington by July 1, 1944, and she made it there on time.

(Route map photograph from Wikipedia in the public domain)

From the day she filled out the War Department Civilian Questionnaire to the day she arrived in Washington, DC, less than six weeks had passed. Traveling to the capital to work for the government, Vernice Marilyn Milleville of Champaign, Illinois, was about to become one of the thousands of women referred to as Government Girls in the Lipstick Brigade. She knew she was being hired to be a "cryptanalytic aide" at Arlington Hall Station, but she didn't know what she would really be doing. She wasn't even sure where she would be living, although she had been told it would be arranged for her. Vernice was on her way to becoming one of the seven thousand women who served in the U.S. Army's cryptography services during World War II.[2]

## 11
## Steve
## Pavuvu in the Russell Islands
## July–August 1944

**Don't just look. See!**
—Steve Lynn to his children

*July 7, 1944*
*Dear Necie,*

*We're training like crazy here even though it's still tough conditions. At least now, the officers' area is looking better. We have ten good size tents with strong coconut log backs to provide some shelter from all of the rain, and the electricity was finally rigged up so there's more to do at night. We even have an officers' mess with a bar so we can eat by ourselves and give the enlisted guys a break during meal times. I heard the engineers are working on digging more wells and running more pipe for showers, so the lines for the cold showers won't be quite as long.*

*We all pitched in to build a theater so we can watch the old movies we occasionally get without getting rained on, and a big shipment of ASE books was delivered earlier this week to stock our "library." That was a real bonus because I think I'd traded for just about every ASE on the island before this shipment came in. I never knew so many Marines read so much! Of course, there's not that much else to do here other than read and play cards when you're not training.*

*A bunch of letters caught up with me a few days ago—several from you, some from my sisters and mother, a couple from your sisters Norma and Dolores, and even one from Pat. They definitely improved my mood! Tell your Mother I really appreciated the food package she sent, too. I'm working hard to learn a lot of new stuff out here before our Division's next operation, and sometimes I'm not sure I'm taking it all in just the right way. It's great to know you all are thinking of me...*

*Steve*

The Eleventh Marines on Pavuvu was typical of all Marine artillery regiments in mid-1944 in that it comprised 2,639 Marines serving in the following capacity:[1]

> 229 Marines in Headquarters and Service Battery (command, executive, communications, and support personnel)

> 1,204 Marines in two 105 mm Howitzer Battalions, each with three batteries of four 105mm howitzers and one Headquarters and Service Battery
>
> 1,206 Marines in two 75 mm Pack Howitzer Battalions, each with three batteries of four 75 mm pack howitzers and one Headquarters and Service Battery

This configuration would change as the war progressed. The number of 75 mm pack howitzers would be reduced in number, and 155 mm howitzers would be added.

The First Battalion of the Eleventh Marines to which Lieutenant Steve Lynn was assigned upon his arrival on Pavuvu was a 75 mm pack howitzer unit. The unit had been instrumental in the Cape Gloucester campaign, supporting the Fifth Marines who were trying to cut off Japanese withdrawal routes around a place called Natamo Point. As an entire unit, the Eleventh Marines performed admirably in the campaign, and it was the only unit to receive a unit award, the Navy Unit Commendation, in the New Britain fighting.[2]

Like all untested replacements joining the First Division, Lieutenant Lynn had a lot to learn from the Old Breed Marine veterans on Pavuvu. As an officer, he had to learn it while at the same time trying to earn the respect of the enlisted men who served under his command.

As the battalion's forward observer, Lieutenant Lynn was responsible for accurately requesting indirect artillery, mortar, and naval gunfire onto enemy targets from a forward position—that is, from a location closest to the enemy target. It was critical that he not just look at a situation; he had to really see what was there and what was happening or about to happen. "Don't just look. See!" was the observers' training mantra.

Stationed between the target area and the firing guns, Lieutenant Lynn had to accurately plot target coordinates and relay them by radio or field phone to the fire direction control center responsible for sending "fire" onto the targets. He worked with a team of six to eight enlisted men who carried the wire, telephone, and radio equipment used to maintain communication. Since he was trained to call for and direct fire onto targets that artillerymen, mortar teams, or naval ships could not see themselves, he was essentially the "eyes" for the gunners.

After the guns were fired, he also had to observe the shell bursts and call for adjustments in the fire to more effectively hit the targets. In combat, he was a prime target for enemy forces who knew the critical role he was playing, and he was easily identifiable as the Marine carrying the map and field glasses.

In calling for fire, Lieutenant Lynn first identified himself using a code name or some other method agreed on with the fire direction center. He would also report his position and then the *azimuth* to the target, which is the direction from which he was looking at the target (the horizontal angle or direction of a compass bearing). This was especially important if he was at an angle to the direction of fire from the guns.

Next Lieutenant Lynn would provide the target location as accurately as he could. The location might be communicated using coordinates on a mutually shared map or grid, or by using the range and azimuth from a known location, or by using the range and direction from Lieutenant Lynn to the target, or perhaps by the shift from a previously fired-upon target—among other possibilities. The specific circumstances dictated the method used to communicate the target location.

Finally, Lieutenant Lynn needed to identify the type of target so that artillery officers in the fire direction center could order the firing of the proper shell and fuse type.

To be an effective forward observer, a Marine has to be quick-thinking and decisive. He needs to have stellar map-reading and plot calculation skills, and he needs to know all about the equipment available for firing at a target. He needs to be able to communicate clearly and concisely, and he needs to have a comprehensive working knowledge of his communication equipment. He has to understand what a good target is in tactical terms, and he has to be aware of the target's proximity to advancing Marines to avoid "friendly fire" on those men by their own troops. He has to be able to keep calm in combat conditions, and he has to earn the trust of his fellow Marines.

During his first month of training with the First Battalion, Eleventh Marines on Pavuvu, Lieutenant Lynn impressed his commanding officer, Major J. H. Moffatt Jr., with his competence. Apparently, the twenty-three-year-old redheaded second lieutenant from southern Illinois was able to meet Major Moffatt's high expectations as the younger officer worked to gain the confidence of his fellow Marines during the training exercises and help them endure the hardships on Pavuvu. Major Moffatt stated in his monthly fitness report that he was glad to have Lieutenant Lynn under his command.

Training on Pavuvu was difficult for the entire division, including the Eleventh Marines, for three reasons: limited time, limited equipment, and limited space. Time spent building the camp from the ground up took away from time for rest, rehabilitation, and training.

New equipment was slow in arriving, which delayed training. Because of the short turnaround time before the next campaign and the delays in equipment arrival, the artillery battalions had very little time to even practice loading and unloading the 75 mm pack howitzers and the 105 mm howitzers into the vehicles that would be carrying them into battle … much less firing them. At least when it did arrive as the summer went on, the new equipment was painted Marine Corps green (rather than Army colors), which was morale boosting.

DUKW (or Duck), an amphibious truck, 1944
(U.S. Marine Corps photograph, U.S. National Archives)

Finally, the island itself was too small for realistic training scenarios. Until two full-scale training rehearsals were held on Guadalcanal in late August, the artillerymen of the Eleventh Marines had to fire at targets on one small island and into the water offshore. Lieutenant Lynn and the other observers (spotters) called in target locations from a boat, or a DUKW (a 2.5-ton, six-wheeled amphibious truck known as a Duck), or an OY-1 plane overhead if they were going to be serving as an aerial artillery spotter in a Marine Observation aviation squadron in the upcoming operation.

The first Marine Observation aviation squadron, VMO-1, was activated on October 27, 1943. Marine aerial observers were first used, however, in August 1942 at Guadalcanal when regular missions were flown from Henderson Field by U.S. Navy pilots flying Douglas SBD Dauntless airplanes.

When the First Marine Division prepared for the Cape Gloucester campaign, it organized its own ad hoc air observation group consisting of two Piper Cub airplanes for each artillery battalion in the regiment. The Piper Cubs were flown by twenty-two volunteer officers and enlisted men who happened to have flying experience. Most of the pilots were corporals and privates first class from a wide variety of division units who received no flight pay or advancement in rank.[3] The small planes and their crews proved their worth as an essential component of an artillery regiment, and before the Cape Gloucester campaign ended, trained Marine Aerial Observer artillery officers were available for assignment.

In total, seven VMO squadrons were formed by the Marine Corps to fight in the Pacific. Each VMO squadron (Marine Observation squadron) had twenty-eight crewmen for each nine-pilot squadron. VMO-2 and VMO-4 were the first designated observation squadrons to go into action, supporting the Second and Fourth Marine Divisions, respectively, over Saipan in June 1944; VMO-1 first went into action over Guam in July 1944 with the Third Marine Division.

Unlike the Army, the Marine Corps chose to use aviation personnel for flying, and ground-based field artillery officers for observation (or "spotting"). The field artillery officers chosen to be observers (or "spotters") were generally from near the top of their field artillery class.[4]

The Marines began using Stinson OY-1 Sentinel aircraft instead of Piper Cubs in October 1943. The OY-1s were thought to be more powerful and sturdier. Each two-seater OY-1 carried a pilot and an observer. The observer sat in the backseat, often using field glasses to look for and identify enemy positions and targets. There he also managed the radio equipment, which was securely attached to the back of the pilot's seat. The planes were often referred to as "Grasshoppers" because they could land on short grassy airstrips if need be.

The fuselage and wings were fabric-covered; the frame was aluminum and wood. The plane had a high-wing design, which allowed maximum visibility for the pilot and spotter. Sometimes cameras were attached to the wing struts for aerial photography of terrain.

As the war progressed, the OY-1s were used not only for artillery spotting but also for reconnaissance, liaison, light transport, and medical evacuation work.

VMO-3 Stinson OY-1 Sentinel on Pavuvu, August 1944

(U.S. Marine Corps photograph #94728, U.S. National Archives #127-G-1146)

Lieutenant Lynn then began training with VMO-3, the "Bird Dogs," commanded by Captain Wallace J. Slappey. Originally commissioned on December 1, 1943, at Quantico, Virginia, the squadron arrived in the Russell Islands (Pavuvu and Banika) via Espiritu Santo, New Hebrides, and Guadalcanal on May 17, 1944, just a couple of weeks before Lieutenant Lynn arrived at Pavuvu on the USS *General Howze*. Its pilots and ground crew spent the next three and a half months preparing for the invasion of the Palaus (Peleliu and Angaur) in coordination with the Eleventh Marines, the artillery regiment the squadron would be supporting.

Stinson OY-1 control panel and extension cables to the backseat

Artillery spotter's view (without radio pack, which would sit on blue box)
(Displayed in Flying Leathernecks Aviation Museum; photographs by M. Vieregg)

VMO pilot and observer flying gear

(Displayed in Flying Leathernecks Aviation Museum; photograph by M. Vieregg)

After disembarking on Banika, the ground crew and pilots of VMO-3 tried to move to Pavuvu to join the Eleventh Marines for training. They set up a tent area with the Eleventh Marines where they stayed for five nights, but there were no operating facilities available for their planes, so they received permission to return to Banika Island. Given the horrible living conditions on Pavuvu at that early date (especially compared to those on Banika), they were undoubtedly relieved to be leaving Pavuvu even though their quarters on Banika consisted only of a tent area they themselves assembled out near the airstrip, Renard Field. The ground crew began assembling the squadron's planes, which had been shipped across the Pacific Ocean in crates, and Captain Slappey flew over to Pavuvu on May 29 to draw up plans for artillery practice with the Eleventh Marines.[5]

Captain Slappey landing on Pavuvu, May 1944
(U.S. Marine Corps photograph #91893, U.S. National Archives #127-GW-1146)

All the day-to-day operations for VMO-3 are recorded in Captain Slappey's monthly reports.[6] The first half of June was used for engineering flights to check out the planes after they were reassembled on Renard Field. On June 14, one of the squadron's ten planes (number 60495) was lost when the squadron's engineering chief crashed it into Macquitti Bay near Pavuvu on an unauthorized flight. The injured pilot was recovered and then confined in a medical unit. A new engineering chief was appointed by Captain Slappey the next day.

On June 16, the squadron began a regular training schedule carrying Eleventh Marines' artillery spotters over firing and impact areas. The landing strip where the VMO-3 pilots picked up the spotters on Pavuvu was a dirt roadway right by the shoreline. Captain Slappey described it as "dangerous for operations." These training flights continued through July as observers were assigned to the squadron from the artillery regiment.

Each battalion in the artillery regiment had at least one aerial observer. Lieutenant Lynn was the aerial observer for the First Battalion; fellow FAC classmate Lieutenant Frank McCalpin was the aerial observer for the Second Battalion; Lieutenants Charles Aldrich and Gene McDonald, who had also attended FAC with Lieutenant Lynn (as well as Aerial Observers' School), were the aerial observers for the Fourth Battalion.

VMO-3 Grasshopper about to land on Pavuvu airstrip, June 1944
(U.S. Marine Corps photograph #91788, U.S. National Archives #127-GW-1171)

By all accounts, July was a crucial month for the entire First Division. E. B. Sledge, George McMillan, and others reported that by the end of the month, the Old Breed veterans and the new replacement Marines had started to fuse into an organized elite combat unit. McMillan described it this way:

> Old men snapping in the new ones, the replacements ... the new men, in turn, helped lift Pavuvu's gloom. They could not feel Pavuvu as oppressive a place as did the men who had served at Gloucester and Guadalcanal. And their unsureness made the veterans more sure of themselves.[7]

McMillan also gave considerable credit to the junior officers of the First Division like Lieutenant Lynn who he said were of "unusually high caliber" because the division had a reputation for ruthlessly relieving incompetent officers.[8] New equipment was arriving in Marine Corps green. And, of course, they all had in common the miseries of Pavuvu itself. Maybe it just made them all so mad to be there that they decided to collectively buckle down and prepare ferociously to fight the next battle. McMillan recalled:

> Some common instinct [directed] a new seeking of cohesion, a new consciousness of their outfit, a new evaluation from within the Division. ... They knew they stood or fell together ... in an elite outfit ... that could "take it" and "dish it out."[9]

An elaborate Field Day was held on Pavuvu on the Fourth of July. Units within the division competed in a track meet complete with high jump, long jump, running races, and discus throws. There were boxing matches, softball and baseball games, tug-of-wars, sack races, volleyball competitions, a fishing tourney, and pie-eating contests. The Marine engineers even built a six-foot tall "firecracker" to celebrate the event.

**Marine engineers lighting and getting ready to run from Fourth of July "firecracker"**

(U.S. Marine Corps photograph #86271, U.S National Archives #127-GW-1183

By August 1944, Lieutenant Lynn was officially listed as the First Battalion's air observer on the unit's roster. He had proven his talents as an aerial artillery spotter to the commanding officer of the battalion, Lieutenant Colonel R. W. Wallace. He had learned how to adjust field artillery fire from the air "on the fly." He had spent much of July listening to the formally-trained air observers' advice and flying with the VMO-3 pilots over Pavuvu, "learning adjustment and registration field artillery fire, basic aerial photography, and the elements of dead reckoning navigation. In addition, he received instruction in methods of aerial survey, and air/ground communications."[10]

Adding to the learning curve for Lieutenant Lynn in August was the introduction of a different kind of plane for artillery spotting that would be used during the earliest days of the next campaign, the Douglas SBD-5 Dauntless. It was a much larger, faster naval scout plane and dive-bomber. The VMO-3 squadron received one of the SBDs on August 2 to use for training Lieutenant Lynn and the other aerial spotters in the heavier aircraft. The squadron pilots were also checked out in the SBD.

**SBD-5 Dauntless flying over Midway, October 1943**
(U.S. National Archives photograph)

August 7, 1944, was a banner day for all the First Division Marines on Pavuvu, and VMO-3 played a starring role. The squadron pilots ferried the Bob Hope Troupe to and from the division area on Pavuvu in their OY-1 aircraft. Every Marine who has written about his time on Pavuvu raves about the show that day. It was the outstanding highlight of their miserable stay on the island. The show arrived on Pavuvu only because of the personal effort of the famous comedian and "at considerable inconvenience to his troupe, who managed to sandwich in a morning performance between rear echelon engagements (at Banika and elsewhere) shortly before the Division shoved off for Peleliu."[11] E. B. Sledge wrote the following about the show:

> Probably the biggest boost to our morale about this time on Pavuvu was the announcement that Bob Hope would come over from Banika and put on a show for us. Most of the men in the division crowded a big open area and cheered

as a Piper Cub (OY-1) circled over us. The pilot switched off the engine briefly, while Jerry Colonna poked his head out of the plane and gave his famous yell, "Ye ow ow ow ow ow." We went wild with applause. ... Bob Hope, Colonna, Frances Langford, and Patti Thomas put on a show on a little stage by the pier ... really boosted our spirits. It was the finest entertainment I ever saw.[2]

Bob Hope (*center*) and Jerry Colonna (*right*) teasing a Marine on Pavuvu, August 7, 1944

Film star Frances Langford singing for the Marines on Pavuvu, August 7, 1944
(U.S. Marine Corps photographs)

After the war, Bob Hope declared that the most emotional show he ever did was the one he did for the First Division on Pavuvu. He would get choked up talking about it.[13]

August 12 was the last day of artillery practice on Pavuvu. The VMO-3 pilots, Lieutenant Lynn, and the other Eleventh Marine aerial artillery spotters flew observation flights in their OY-1s and the borrowed SBD. After that, the artillery equipment and the Eleventh Marines' artillerymen were loaded onto ships for transport to Cape Esperance, Guadalcanal, where two full division rehearsals for the next amphibious landing took place August 27–29.

After the rehearsals, the artillery was loaded onto twenty "new Marine-designed and built amphibian trailers with a watertight top and two wheels underneath," which would be towed ashore onto the landing beaches by amtracs (amphibious tractors)[14] The larger 105 mm howitzers were loaded onto DUKWs, which would be launched from LST (Landing Ship, Tank) vessels.

Marines loading a 105 mm howitzer, Pavuvu, August 1944

(U.S. Marine Corps photographs, U.S. National Archives #127-GW-791)

For the next week, the VMO-3 squadron limited its flight time to ferrying runs between Banika and Pavuvu. Those flights ended August 20. After that date, some of the planes had to be prepared for loading aboard LSTs, and the other planes underwent engineering flights so they could be checked out before the ground echelon left Banika for Guadalcanal. Two crated OY-1s were loaded onto an LST for transport to the combat zone on August 23.

On August 25, Lieutenant Lynn and the other aerial artillery spotters for the Eleventh Marines were officially assigned to the VMO-3 squadron for temporary duty, which meant they would travel into the combat zone with the VMO-3 pilots instead of with the other artillerymen of the Eleventh Marines. On the same day, the VMO-3 ground echelon traveled to Guadalcanal on two ships and an LST. On August 27, Lieutenant Lynn traveled from Banika Island to Kukum Field on Guadalcanal along with the other aerial observers and the pilots of VMO-3 in the remaining eight OY-1 aircraft. Immediately after they landed, the dismantling and crating of the remaining OY-1s began so the planes could be shipped to the combat zone.

The rest of the men in Lieutenant Lynn's home unit, Battery A, First Battalion, Eleventh Marines, boarded the USS *Fayette* (APA-43) at Guadalcanal on September 1. They left the area on September 8 along with Steve's friend Lieutenant Jack Dearmore, who traveled in one of the other divisions' APA transports up "combat lane."

Very few Marines knew for sure where the next battle would be until they left Pavuvu and were on their way to the rendezvous area. Captain Slappey received operational orders from the headquarters of the Third Amphibious Corps on August 30 and then waited anxiously on Guadalcanal with Lieutenant Lynn and the other Marines in VMO-3 to board the escort carriers that would take them all into battle.

Marines assembling to leave Pavuvu for Guadalcanal and then Peleliu, August 1944
(U.S. Marine Corps photograph, U.S. National Archives #127-GW-791)

*August 28, 1944*
*Dear Necie,*

*I got your letter describing your apartment in Arlington and telling me about some of your new friends. It sounds like you're working long hours, but you're safe and settled and enjoying Washington when you have some free time. Fill me in on all the details because it's wonderful to hear about what's going on there.*

*We've been getting the news about the fighting on Saipan and Guam. Sounds like the Japs can really target their mortars and artillery accurately. We think we can do better. Sounds like progress is being made in Burma, too. All of this seems more real to us than what's going on in Europe even though my brother Joe is over there now.*

*I'm waiting with some other guys for transport off this island so we can head out to the next campaign. I have to admit I'm pretty nervous about this first combat assignment but I've taken all of the training seriously, and I feel like I'm as ready as I'll ever be ... so here goes...*

*Steve*

## 12
## Vernice
## Arlington, Virginia
## July–August 1944

**The recruitment of these American women—and the fact that women were behind some of the most significant individual code-breaking triumphs of the war—was one of the best-kept secrets of the conflict. The military and strategic importance of their work was enormous.**

—Liz Mundy, *Code Girls*

*July 15, 1944*
*Dear Steve,*

*When you left Champaign last year, did you imagine you would be flying over the Pacific Ocean in a small airplane? I remember your saying one time you'd rarely seen an airplane until you got to Champaign, and now you're in one just about every day. I hope the pilots aren't daredevils—any more than they have to be.*

*Since I got here, we've all been attending daily lectures about the work. It feels a little bit like being back in school. When I'm not at a lecture, I do mostly filing and other clerical work. My job responsibilities should get a little more interesting in a week or so, though. It doesn't really matter, I guess, except that we work really long hours and the time goes faster if the work is interesting to think about. As long as it somehow gets you and the other men home sooner, I'll be happy...*

*Necie*

When Vernice Milleville arrived at Union Station in Washington, DC, it was jam-packed with bustling throngs of people, many in uniform and some in civilian clothes. She jostled her way out to the curb and waited in a long line outside the station in the midday summer sun until it was finally her turn to take the next taxicab. The driver loaded her two suitcases into the trunk, and Vernice gave him the address she had been given in her travel documents. Then she sat back in the seat, took a deep breath, and stared out the car window. She didn't want to miss any of the sights to be seen as the cabbie drove west and then southwest across the Arlington Memorial Bridge over the Potomac River. The Capitol Building was off to the left; then the White House was visible to the right. She almost missed the Washington Monument on the left as she stared at President Franklin D. Roosevelt's home. The road formed a semicircle around the Lincoln Memorial just before passing over the bridge. Excited to be where all the action was, Vernice didn't worry too much about the rising summer heat and humidity.

After crossing the Potomac, Vernice grew concerned about the address she had been given. Was it correct? The area was filled with trees except where new residential homes were being built. She was about to ask the cabbie if they were in the right place when he pulled over in front of a high hedge interrupted only by a wrought iron gate. It was nearly impossible to see the building beyond. After assuring her that he had driven her to the right address, the cabbie accepted the fare money she handed him and drove off. Fortunately, three other women walking along the sidewalk toward the gate reassured her, and through the gate she walked.

What Vernice saw in front of her was the impressive main building of what had formerly been an idyllic private women's junior college. Six three-story ionic columns framed each side of the main entrance of her new employer's administrative headquarters. She paused for a moment to take it all in and then approached the uniformed guards just inside the gate. After one of the guards found her name on a list of newly arriving employees, she walked up the stairs onto the building's portico, entered through the door, and reported for work at Arlington Hall Station as a "Cryptanalytic Aide, Grade SP-5," with an annual salary of eighteen hundred dollars (plus overtime). It was July 1, 1944.

On that first day, Vernice and several other women beginning their job with the Signal Security Agency (SSA), were sworn into service by Jo Palumbo, who greeted all new employees and helped them navigate the logistics of their arrival.[1] Gathered into a former finishing school parlor transformed into a meeting room, Vernice and the other women raised their right hands and solemnly swore "to support and defend the Constitution of the United States against all enemies, foreign and domestic....SO HELP ME GOD" (caps included).[2]

She signed an affidavit swearing that she was not "a member of any political party or organization that advocates the overthrow of the Government of the United States by force or violence."[3] Then she had to certify that she had not "paid or offered or promised to pay any money or other thing of value to any person, firm or corporation for the use of influence to procure" her appointment.[4] She also signed a secrecy oath swearing she would *never* speak about her work, and she understood that if she did, she would be subject to prosecution under the 1917 Espionage Act.

**Arlington Hall Station Administration Building, 1943**
(National Security Agency photograph)

The identification photos taken that first day—both a front view and a profile—became part of her official badge. In the photos, she looks young, intelligent, happy, confident, and maybe a little saucy with her dark hair fashionably waved and rolled back in a *U*-shaped cut. In the profile view, her hair clip bedecked with six small flowers is visible just behind the top roll of her hair. Mostly hidden by the mug shot sign with her name and identification number is what might be the new dress she had chosen to wear for her first day on the job.

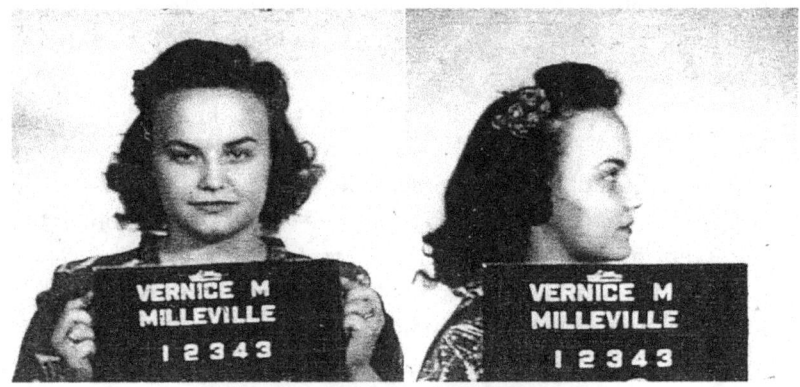

**U.S. Army Personnel File ID photos**
(Photographs reproduced with family permission)

After the first-day's tasks were completed, Vernice was given the address for her housing accommodations and told to report again first thing the next morning. Carrying her two suitcases, purse, and coat in the late afternoon heat, Vernice walked about twenty minutes to her new home at 400 South Glebe Road in the Alcova Heights neighborhood of Arlington, Virginia.

Homes were springing up in the Arlington Hall area as the Washington metropolitan area boomed during the war years. Many of them were designed with boarders in mind. They were often two-story brick homes with three or four bedrooms and three or four bathrooms. Many of the Arlington Hall neighborhood homes built in the 1940s are no longer there, but at the time, they provided many Government Girls a new, clean place to sleep in one's own bed in a room shared with a roommate.

Housing in the Washington, DC, area during the war years was extremely difficult to find, and it was expensive. Prior to World War II, the metropolitan area had already been filling up with people flooding into the capital to work in Depression-era government jobs. The war accelerated the crunching of people into limited space. At the war's height, more than one thousand people arrived in Washington every day.[5] The number of federal employees tripled between 1939 and 1943.[6] The City's Defense Housing Registry processed up to ten thousand requests every month.[7] Government Girls received V-cards (*V* for *victory*) which supposedly gave them priority as war workers, but almost everyone had a V-card. Some women housed in crowded private boardinghouses in the capital itself even had to "hot-bunk," which meant sharing the same bed with someone who worked a different work shift.

To address the housing shortage, First Lady Eleanor Roosevelt spearheaded the drive to build Arlington Farms, a complex of ten dormitories for female government workers built on the grounds of the old Custis-Lee estate close to Arlington National Cemetery in Arlington, Virginia. Completed in October 1943, the complex was dubbed "28 Acres of Girls," and it accommodated as many as eight thousand female government workers through the end of the decade.[8] Arlington Farms and other government dorms accommodated about 20 percent of the Government Girls who traveled to Washington to work during the war, but the overall supply of rooms never kept up with demand.

By the time Vernice arrived in July 1944, Arlington Farms was full. Wanting to keep its workers close by, the security-conscious SSA arranged for their housing with the owners of the newly built homes nearby. SSA agents actually made the rounds of nearby neighborhoods knocking on doors seeking rooms to rent for the hundreds of women being hired to work at Arlington Hall Station. The home at 400 S. Glebe Road had a room waiting for Vernice.

When Vernice reported for work the next morning, she knew she had a lot to learn, but first her new employers needed to get a better handle on where in the organization she would best fit. A proctor carefully watched over the new arrivals as they took a series of aptitude tests. Vernice received high scores on cryptography, reasoning, mechanical skills, and word meaning—not quite as high but still good scores on number coding and digital reversal. She definitely had the aptitude to learn the skills the U.S. Army Signal Corps needed in its Cryptographic Unit.

Until her security clearance came through for classified work, Vernice was assigned to the Signal Service at Large. She spent the first few weeks working on general clerical tasks and attending orientation sessions which included stern lectures about security. The indoctrinating lectures about the necessity of maintaining physical and operational security stressed:

> You simply did not talk about what you were doing except with persons in your own section, and the time even for that was limited. ... If anybody outside of Arlington Hall happened to ask you what your duties were, you were supposed to say that you worked in filing.[9]

And another perspective:

> Women accepted into the cryptologic field were sworn to secrecy. The penalty for discussing the work outside of approved channels could be death, as it was considered an act of treason during a time of war. One WAC [Women's Army Corps member] still recalled more than fifty years later, the first lecture she received: "Don't talk." The Army informed her and her fellow WACs that no one was to know of their work. Anyone caught discussing it would be treated as a spy and shot.[10]

Meanwhile, FBI investigators continued their investigation of Vernice. They confirmed her birth date, family associations and education; searched confidential government files for her name and activities; interrogated her mother about whether or not Vernice had contracted contagious childhood diseases like mumps and measles; and examined the Champaign, Illinois, police records for any criminal activity. The summary conclusion: "There appears to be no reason to question loyalty of Subject." By the last week in July, Vernice was cleared to actually begin working in the security-sensitive role of cryptographic aide in the Cryptanalytic Branch of the SSA.

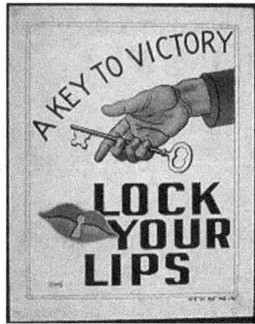

One of the many security posters at Arlington Hall
(U.S. National Archives photograph)

Understanding a bit of the history of the SSA prior to 1944 helps set the stage onto which Vernice walked when she began working for the agency. It reflects the political undulations of the previous three decades and the efforts of several fascinating characters, only a few of whom will be introduced here.

Prior to America's entry into World War I in 1917, no U.S. government department carried out cryptanalytic activities; that is, no government agency was responsible for breaking either diplomatic or military codes and ciphers of other governments. (A *code* is a method of secret writing involving the substitution of words and phrases in a message; a *cipher* is a method of secret writing involving the transposition or substitution of individual letters or syllables in a message.) The best cryptanalytic work was being done as a personal patriotic effort by George Fabyan at his own expense at Riverbank Laboratories in Geneva, Illinois.

Before the war, Fabyan had hired a small group of cryptologists including Elizebeth Smith to work on the Bacon Cipher. The Bacon Cipher was a notion held by some people at the time that at least some of Shakespeare's work had been written in cipher by Sir Francis Bacon. Fabyan also hired William Friedman to work as a geneticist at Riverbank Labs, but over time Friedman became more interested in the codes and ciphers work ... and Elizebeth Smith, who later became his wife.

Beginning in June 1916, Fabyan redirected his cryptanalytic team's efforts to working on the codes and ciphers of the countries fighting against the Allies in World War I.[11] The enemy's intercepted coded messages were forwarded to the Riverbank team by the War, Navy, State, and Justice Departments.[12] Part of the responsibility the Riverbank team took on was training military personnel in the use of codes, and William Friedman became the lead instructor. Friedman actually invented the term *cryptology* to embrace the whole field of secret communications, to include cryptanalysis, cryptography, and intercept.[13]

After the U.S. Congress declared war on Germany on April 6, 1917, William Friedman served as a lieutenant in the cryptology unit of the American Expeditionary Forces, and the government began to plan its own official cryptographic efforts, forming the Code and Cipher Bureau within the Military Intelligence Section of the War Department. The bureau was partially funded by the State Department.

By November 1918, the Code and Cipher Bureau (redesignated MI-8), employed 18 officers, 24 civilian cryptographers and cryptanalysts, and 109 typists and stenographers.[14] It was led by Major Herbert O. Yardley. The bureau was successful in providing the cryptologic services influencing military, diplomatic, political, and economic phases of conducting the war and the uneasy peace that followed. In 1920, Major Yardley hired both William and Elizebeth Friedman to work for the bureau via the War Department.[15]

**Elizebeth Smith Friedman**
(Undated National Security Agency photograph)

**William F. Friedman, 1919**
(Wikipedia photograph in the public domain)

As the United States retreated into isolationism after World War I, the Code and Cipher Bureau's budget was cut significantly—in half in 1920 and a bit further every year after that. Yardley and William Friedman persevered in their cryptologic efforts with ever-shrinking staff numbers and resources, but the bureau was still supported by both the War Department and the State Department.

Herbert Hoover was elected president in 1928, and he appointed Henry L. Stimson secretary of state. As reported by James Gilbert and John Finnegan in their book *U.S. Army Signals Intelligence in World War II*, when the activities of the secret bureau were brought to Stimson's attention for funding consideration, Stimson characterized the activity as being highly unethical and declared it would cease *immediately* so far as the State Department was concerned."[16] Secretary Stimson went so far as to say, "Gentlemen do not read each other's mail."[17] As a result, Yardley's Code and Cipher Bureau was discontinued, and all bureau cryptologic files were transferred to the U.S. Army Signal Corps. William Friedman became the first head of the Army's Signal Intelligence Service (SIS).

What happened next helps explain the atmosphere in the Cryptanalytic Branch of the Signal Security Agency when Vernice began working there in July 1944, and it explains the promise she would have to make when she left the SSA late in 1946.

Herbert Yardley was so embittered by Stimson's dismissal of both him and the important clandestine work the Code and Cipher Bureau had done with limited resources throughout the

1920s that he wrote a book revealing the most secret bureau techniques. It explained in detail the methods the bureau had developed to invent codes for U.S. use and to analyze foreign codes and ciphers. Published in 1931, *The American Black Chamber* provided information that the Japanese, Italians, and Germans then used to develop their own codes and ciphers during the 1930s that proved extremely difficult to break well into World War II. According to Gilbert and Finnegan, after its release, "about 30,000 copies of the Japanese translation of *The American Black Chamber* were sold in Tokyo in a period of less than a month."[18] In addition, the book understandably increased the distrust America's allies had in the country's ability to keep secrets—a distrust that vastly reduced cooperation between the British and Americans even after the United States entered the war in Europe in 1942.

After the bombshell of *The American Black Chamber* hit, cryptologic efforts gradually regained their footing during the 1930s, primarily because of William Friedman's stolid perseverance. His funding continued to be sparse, but he was able to hire a small talented staff of cryptologists (seven people in May 1936) who continued to study and develop the field of cryptology. They also pioneered the use of machine ciphers to safeguard U.S. Army communications, implemented training courses for reserve officers, and established a small network of radio intercept stations. By 1939, the SIS had received funding to employ forty-five people.

The greatest prewar SIS accomplishment under Friedman's direction was deciphering the machine cipher used by the Japanese foreign office, code-named Purple by the United States. Genevieve Grotjan, a former math teacher and railway annuity statistician, discovered the breakthrough patterns on September 20, 1940, when she was working with Frank B. Rowlett's team.[19] The SIS was then able to build a copy of the Japanese machine and read decrypted Japanese foreign office dispatches, code-named Magic, as quickly as they were written and sent out. (Unfortunately, the messages did not include Japanese military planning details and therefore did not forewarn the United States about the Pearl Harbor attack.)

The importance of Magic can hardly be overstated. As Japanese diplomats in Germany and elsewhere shared their thoughts with their colleagues and superiors around the world, and until the war's end, their words were being simultaneously read by SIS personnel in Washington and analyzed by the American intelligence community. According to author Liza Mundy:

The Purple cipher didn't just give the Allies insight into Japanese thinking. As Friedman pointed out, the ability to read messages produced by the Purple machine provided "the most important source of strategically valuable, long-term intelligence" available to the Allies as World War II unfolded, including the thinking of fascist and collaborationist governments around all of Europe.[20]

Part of a Purple cipher machine recovered from Berlin's
Japanese Embassy at the end of World War II
(United States National Security Agency's National Cryptologic Museum photograph)

It was not until the war drums started beating louder and more grimly in Europe in 1939 that funding for the Signal Intelligence Service began to slowly but significantly increase. Special permission from President Roosevelt had to be obtained to suspend civil service regulations allowing the SIS to hire the specific people it needed, but the permission wasn't obtained until June 1940 and then only for the twenty-six people budgeted for the previous year. As Magic decrypts and difficult verbal negotiations forewarned of the deteriorating relationship with Japan, budgeting for forty-eight more SIS employees was approved in January 1940; forty-two more employees, including Japanese translators, were approved in October 1940.

By December 7, 1941, Pearl Harbor Day, seven radio intercept monitoring stations were in operation picking up messages that needed to be decoded, deciphered, translated, assessed, and shared with appropriate diplomatic and military personnel including the president. (One monitoring station in the Philippines was soon overrun by the Japanese army.) There were only 106 civilian employees in the SIS at the time, and even after dividing the Magic diplomatic work with the U.S. Navy, the cryptology personnel shortage was severe as the country now involved itself in a two-front war. Add to the *number* of people needed the *kind* of people needed, and it was a daunting challenge to ramp up as quickly as circumstances required.

Ironically, it was President Roosevelt's secretary of war, Henry L. Stimson, who was given the responsibility for addressing the problem—the same man who under President Hoover in 1929 had defunded and discontinued Herbert Yardley's Codes and Cipher Bureau because "gentlemen do not read other men's mail." Stimson had the good sense to call on Alfred W. McCormack, a well-respected Chicago lawyer, to study the situation and make recommendations for improving the handling of signals intelligence. According to Parrish, McCormack was "very quick, very perceptive, very hard-working," and in two months' time, he returned with a report stating, "there was a very large job to be done all along the line."[21]

McCormack himself was commissioned as a colonel and made deputy head of the newly organized special branch within the Military Intelligence Service called the Signal Security Agency (SSA). For the rest of the war, McCormack and the chief of the SSA, the "linguistically colorful" Colonel Carter W. Clarke, fought their own war to get the personnel they needed to address the cryptology challenges faced by the nation.[22] The Civil Service Commission's refusal to prioritize qualified personnel continued to be an ongoing frustration, and the archival records are full of memos from Colonels McCormack and Clarke justifying, demanding, pleading, and begging for more personnel.

To get an idea of the SSA's workload and McCormack's constant pleas for additional staff, consider the situation described in a memo he wrote in April 1943:

> During the month of March [1943] we (G-2 [military intelligence unit]) received 4,500 deciphered messages from Arlington Hall. This was still only a fraction of the available material—114,085 messages intercepted. The bottleneck ... lies in the processing and translating facilities of Arlington Hall, which are largely a problem of civilian

> personnel. ... It is estimated that the volume of material coming in will at least double by the end of June. ... Leaving out of account the Japanese Army traffic, the total volume could easily increase four-fold by the end of the year.[23]

Emphasizing the need for a particular kind of employee, he went on:

> Manpower cannot be built up by writing a T/O [a personnel request form] and filling the places with what personnel happens to be available. To do the work well, a man [or woman] must have not only a broad education and background of information, but must have more than his [or her] share of astuteness, skepticism, and desire to solve puzzling problems; and he [or she] must have capacity for laborious detail work that very few people have.[24]

He also emphasized the need for the utmost security:

> Only persons of the greatest good sense and discretion should be employed on this work. This consideration is basic, since intercept information involves a different kind of secrecy than does most other classified information.[25]

On January 3, 1944, McCormack sent out yet another urgent plea for more civilian personnel, just as Vernice was finishing up her college degree:

> On the verge of definitive breakthrough in deriving intelligence from Japanese Army messages. Critical need for at least 2,000 persons. Upwards of 200,000 Japanese Army messages have piled up on the shelves at Arlington Hall, unread.[26]

The huge problem for the SSA was having too few people working in the agency to decode, decipher, translate, manage, analyze, and share the flood of information now coming into Arlington Hall Station. They desperately needed Vernice and other college-educated women to help carry the load.

Over the course of the war years, Colonels McCormack and Clarke fought for an increase in SSA personnel, from 106 civilians on Pearl Harbor Day in December 1941 to a total of 10,731 people, including the 5,661 civilians and 2,187 military personnel at Arlington Hall Station *and* the 2,523 people in the field on V-J Day in August 1945.[27] Each one of these people had to be chosen with specific attributes in mind: some with translating skills, some with cryptanalytic aptitudes and skills, some with clerical and supervisory skills, some with recruiting and personnel management skills, some with counterintelligence and surveillance skills—all with an uncompromising commitment to remain completely silent at all times about the work they did. Alfred McCormack wrote in a letter to Colonel Clarke on April 5, 1943, stating that "only individuals of first-rate ability and suitable training should be taken into the work."[28]

By the time Vernice began working for the SSA in July 1944, its headquarters had moved from the Munitions Building in downtown Washington, DC, to Arlington Hall in Arlington, Virginia. The new location was more secure and had more room for expansion. The three-story, yellow brick building set in one hundred acres of woods was seized by the U.S. Army under the War Powers Act in early 1942. All SSA personnel were at Arlington Hall by August 1942 and were soon working on the codes and ciphers of twenty-five countries.

By spring 1943, two additional "temporary" wooden buildings, Building A and Building B, had been built to house all the operating units, and the original building was then used for administration. Arlington Hall was officially renamed Arlington Hall Station during the summer of 1943.

**Buildings A & B, Arlington Hall Station, 1944**
(National Security Agency photograph)

When Vernice transitioned into classified cryptographic work after receiving her security clearance in late July 1944, she was already familiar with the double, heavy steel fencing topped with barbed wire that completely surrounded the Arlington Hall Station grounds. There was also an accompanying alarm system in place around the perimeter. To enter the grounds, she had to show her distinctive badge with its photo identification to the armed guards at one of the four entry gates. As she stepped through the gate, she was joining a workforce of about fifty-one hundred civilians and two thousand military personnel on duty at Arlington Hall that summer.[29]

Vernice had also begun to know her way around "station." In addition to the administration and two operations buildings, there were barracks and mess halls for enlisted personnel, a station dispensary, a theater, a post exchange, a motor pool, a firehouse, and warehouses. She knew where the cafeteria was, too. It provided food service around the clock, and she would be working at least forty-eight hours a week, often more. Additional fencing surrounded each of the two operations buildings, which also could only be entered by authorized personnel wearing official ID badges via security checkpoints. She definitely had learned where she could and couldn't go.

The two-story operations buildings, A and B, were rectangular and designed with a long hallway running each building's length. Extending off of the long hallway at right angles were multiple rooms. Each room had a center aisle running through it. The workers in some rooms, the majority of whom were women, sat occasionally at desks but mostly at tables covered with paper, rulers, pencils, cards, graph paper, notebooks, and sometimes thin paper strips hanging from strings. Wooden file cabinets and boxes stood against the walls, and large fans cooled the women as they worked in the stifling summer heat and humidity. Apparently, mice moved in as quickly as the cryptographic aides and clerks, and they became legendary.[30]

In the rooms receiving encrypted messages from listening stations around the world, women worked on a variety of machines. Some machines were hooked up to multiple cables; others looked more like adding machines or typewriters.

**Machine operator in Building B at Arlington Hall Station, 1944**
(National Security Agency photograph)

During Vernice's first full month of cryptographic work, August 1944, more than one hundred thousand new intercepted enemy messages flowed into Arlington Hall Station every week. Every one of them needed attention because any one of them might contain information that could save American lives—including the life of U.S. Marine Corps Second Lieutenant Steve Lynn.

*August 25, 1944*
*Dear Stevie,*

*I got the idea from your last letter that you'd be changing station soon. I hope this reaches you before you leave.*

*I'm working as many as sixty hours a week now, and we still can't get all of the work done. The days fly by quickly and I fall into bed exhausted at night.*

*Know that I'm thinking of you constantly...*

*Necie*

# 13
## Steve
## Peleliu in the Palau Island Group
## September–October 1944

None of us would ever be the same after what we had endured. To some degree that is true, of course, of all human experience. But something in me died at Peleliu.
—E. B. Sledge, *With the Old Breed at Peleliu and Okinawa*

I feel strongly that only a Marine who was on the scene at Peleliu can understand what took place during that period of time. It was a nightmare, to say the least. Every man there deserved a medal.
—Arthur Jackson, USMC

*September 13, 1944*
*Dear Necie,*
*This will probably be the last chance I'll have to write for a while since we'll soon fly into combat from the ship we're on. The cruise to the combat zone hasn't been too bad. The Navy officers haven't given us any more grief than we've given them in return, and the food has been wonderful compared to what we had on island. I've had plenty of time to read, and we've kept a profitable poker game going at night.*

*We get radio news from the States in the officers' ward room. Sounds like the push across France is still going well. Hope it continues as the weather there turns colder. Here in the Pacific, MacArthur sounds like he's anxious to get back to the Philippines. Supposedly this operation we're about to begin is going to help him do that. We'll see how it works out.*

*Thanks again for all of the letters. Regular mail service has been promised during this next campaign, so keep them coming. Do you have any pictures of you taken in Washington? Sure would be special to see them...*

*Steve*

What was it like on Peleliu during September, October, and November 1944? Reading the official battle summaries and the firsthand accounts in the memoirs of veterans who were there evokes intense sadness, horror, and grief. From the first hour of landing to the last day of hostilities, the campaign involved combat at extremely close quarters in extremely hostile conditions. The cost in American lives was so shocking, the battle was controversial even at the time the American public first became aware of it, and it continued to be debated for years.

The Peleliu campaign (and Saipan before it) did not initially receive much notice from the American public because the nation's focus was on Europe. As Americans listened to the news during the summer of 1944 about Rome's liberation, the Allies' June 6 invasion at the beaches of Normandy, the subsequent fighting across France, and the liberation of Paris, events in the Pacific received less attention. Saipan was assaulted on June 15; Guam was retaken in July, and the Peleliu campaign began on September 15. The airborne Market Garden landing in the Netherlands began the same day as the Peleliu landing. In addition, the press corps had been led to believe the Peleliu campaign itself would be so short in duration that their involvement was unnecessary; consequently, it didn't get much initial coverage. While the ferocious battle for Peleliu was still going on in mid-October, the American media were focused on General Douglas MacArthur's return to the Philippines. For all practical purposes, Peleliu remained unknown—except to the men who fought there and the families of the soldiers and Marines who died there.

Traveling the twenty-one hundred miles north-northwest from Guadalcanal to the small island of Peleliu on the escort carrier USS *White Plains* (CVE-66), Lieutenant Steve Lynn could not have known what horrific experiences he would endure there. None of the 24,234 First Division Marines traveling across the Pacific could know—including the Old Breed veterans who had fought so valiantly at Guadalcanal and Cape Gloucester.[1] Even the First Division commanding general, Major General William H. Rupertus, didn't really have a clue. Shortly before the Marines landed, he predicted that the Peleliu campaign would be "tough but short, lasting not more than four days."[2] He was very wrong.

How could there be many surprises left for American planners after nearly three hard years of fighting the Japanese in the Pacific—especially since they had detailed intelligence about the Japanese troop strength and disposition in the area from code breakers at Arlington Hall Station? Basically, the answer is a lack of knowledge about two critical issues: the terrain on Peleliu and the major change in Japanese army tactics Japan's leaders had officially adopted in July 1944.

Peleliu is only six miles long and two miles wide. It's located in the Palaus, a group of more than one hundred islands encircled by coral reefs lying just south of the equator. It's about five hundred miles east of the Philippines and about two thousand miles due south of Tokyo. The climate is hot and humid with a rainy season in the fall when the battle was fought.

**Location of Peleliu and Pavuvu in the South Pacific**
(Map in the public domain modified by M. Vieregg)

Formerly held by Germany, the Palaus were acquired by the Japanese at the end of World War I. The Japanese first used the islands militarily as a jumping-off point for taking the Philippines. Later, the islands were used by the Japanese as both a staging base and a supply depot for subsequent offensive drives and in the struggle to hold on to Guadalcanal.

The Palaus had never had much economic value beyond the phosphate mining operation on Angaur, one of the islands in the group, and they were quite far off the traditional Pacific shipping routes. There were no Australian coast watchers or trading captains who knew enough about the islands to share information, and there had been no information gathered by the Americans or their allies before the war because the islands were too heavily fortified to send in land-based scouts. Consequently, the few available maps were old and inaccurate. Additionally, the islands had never been a tourist destination (although they are a diving destination today), and consequently, there weren't any tourist photos to consult (a source of information relied on heavily to plan European operations). In those presatellite days, the U.S. military had to rely solely on aerial photographs and submarine reconnaissance.

The aerial photographs taken by military photographers were woefully unrevealing because of the frequent cloud cover during the season in which they were taken and because the heavy jungle growth concealed the geological formations of the islands.

Additionally, the Japanese military had occupied the major islands in the group (Peleliu, Babelthuap, and Angaur) since shortly after World War I, and they had expertly camouflaged strategically important island features such as ridges and cave openings. The camouflage made the rugged island of Peleliu look flatter than it really is on the few aerial photos that could be taken before the Marines landed.

Submarine reconnaissance and "frogmen" landings about a month before the Peleliu invasion focused on the beaches. Their observations provided some useful information on the landing approaches to Peleliu but did not improve the overall island terrain maps. Once they "hit the beach," the Marines had very little accurate knowledge about the physical terrain of the island itself.

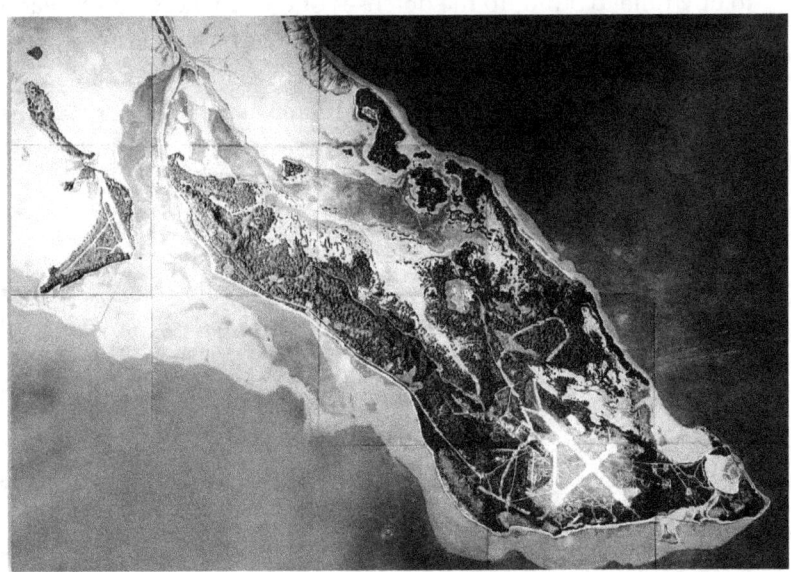

**Aerial photo montage of Peleliu and Ngesebus, 1944**
(U.S. National Archives photograph)

Noteworthy, too, is the fact there is essentially no surface freshwater on Peleliu: no lakes or rivers, just swampy areas. Inhabitants depended primarily on rainwater stored in cisterns. The Japanese stored water in a system of concrete water storage tanks. Many of these storage tanks were destroyed in the preinvasion bombardment to deny the Japanese access to water or because they were mistaken for military bunkers. The drinking water shortage would be a major challenge for the U.S. Marines during the first phase of the battle.

Perhaps even more important than their ignorance of terrain was the military planners' incomplete understanding of the shift in tactical response to American amphibious landings formally adopted by the Imperial Japanese Army leaders in July 1944. Instead of defending the beaches with banzai attacks by large numbers of infantry swarming the landing Marines, the Japanese now chose to substantially prolong the fighting by digging into fortified positions and forcing a long, costly campaign to secure the island. This "defense-in-depth" strategy combined with the "defense-to-the-death" tradition of the first-line Japanese troops on Peleliu was designed to delay American use of the airfields and cause large enough American combat losses to delay the units' deployments in future campaigns. The ultimate Japanese goal was to buy time to build up the defenses of the Japanese home islands.

Nearly a year before the battle for Peleliu began, the Imperial General Headquarters in Tokyo decided the Palaus would be part of the "zone of absolute defense where each Japanese soldier would fight to the death."[3] Consequently, first-line, combat hardened troops from Manchuria reinforced the rear echelon troops in the Palaus in March and April 1944. The Fourteenth Division was one of the oldest and best military units in the Japanese Army. Because they had several months to build defenses capitalizing on the tortuous coral topography of the island, and because they had excellent leadership by Colonel Kunio Nakagawa and Lieutenant General Sadae Inoue, the Japanese on Peleliu developed a very well-organized, strong, and deadly defense. It would take a heart-breaking toll on the Americans who fought there.

The core of the Japanese defensive system was in the Umurbrogol Ridges just north of the airfield. The natural caves in the Umurbrogol were developed, fortified, interconnected, and well camouflaged. Using the expertise and assistance of professional miners, new interlocking caves were blasted out of the soft coral of nearly vertical cliffs. In all, there were more than five hundred caves used by the Japanese troops on Peleliu. The largest cave held a thousand Japanese troops along with the food, water, ammunition, and other supplies they needed to sustain themselves. Another cave had nine levels of living quarters and could house two hundred men.

There was a mutually supporting system of pillboxes (low concrete emplacements for machine guns and antitank weapons) and riflemen positions. Some caves with artillery and naval gun emplacements had steel doors that could be rolled open to allow firing and then quickly closed again to protect the artillery pieces and personnel inside. Steel-reinforced concrete blockhouses had as many as sixteen mutually supporting automatic weapons.[4] Fallback defensive positions were established across the island's defensive zone. Many defensive positions were too deeply buried for American naval bombardment and air bombing to destroy.

American military planners did have a good read on the identity of the Japanese forces they would be facing. Just a few months before, an incredible fifty tons of documents captured in the Marianas were delivered to intelligence officers in Hawaii.[5] Combined with the information derived from Japanese radio intercepts decoded at Arlington Hall (code-named Ultra), the battle planners knew essentially every detail of every Japanese unit on all the islands in the Palaus. Unfortunately, knowledge about who the enemy is cannot by itself defeat him.

In total, Colonel Nakagawa had approximately 13,700 combat troops, service troops, and noncombatants (not including those in later landing units and failed raids) to defend the small island.[6] They received all the supplies they would have for the battle before July 1944. After that time, they received very little because Japanese shipping was strangled by American submarines and aircraft. For this reason alone, many historians and strategists have argued that the island could have been bypassed as other islands had been. The crack troops on Peleliu would have then gradually degenerated to a state of combat ineffectiveness, as garrisons on other bypassed islands did. The Japanese had no hope of reinforcements or more supplies.

Why the decision to assault Peleliu, then? The story is complicated and interesting and involves strong personalities (General MacArthur, Admiral Chester Nimitz, Admiral William

"Bill" Halsey, Admiral Ernest King, and President Franklin D. Roosevelt) as well as disagreements over strategy in achieving the ultimate goal of defeating Japan in the Pacific. Suffice it to say that Admiral Nimitz and General MacArthur insisted that Peleliu and other sites in the Palaus be taken. Among other considerations, they regarded the islands as a serious threat to MacArthur's flank as he attempted to mount a successful amphibious campaign to retake the Philippines.

Admiral Halsey was commander of the Western Pacific Task Forces and had overall command of Operation Stalemate II, the Palaus campaign and the capture of Ulithi. He first opposed the Peleliu landing as early as June 1944 after 168 Japanese aircraft were destroyed in March 1944 by the Fifth Fleet's carrier-based plane attacks on the Palaus. He then repeated his opposition to the landing after his carrier-based aircraft struck several islands in the Marianas as well as those in the Palaus again between August 31 and September 10. Admiral Halsey argued that these later attacks essentially destroyed all the remaining aircraft on the ground on Peleliu, leaving it isolated and impotent to interfere with the Philippines campaign. By this time, too, he reasoned that Japan was incapable of replacing the planes or pilots lost in these raids. Halsey also noted in a dispatch he sent to Nimitz that enemy air resistance to his raids was surprisingly weak, and therefore, "the Palau and Yap-Ulithi operations were unnecessary to support the seizure of the Philippines."[7]

Nevertheless, Admiral Nimitz, Admiral King, General MacArthur, and President Roosevelt made the decision to go ahead as planned. In retrospect, there is nearly total agreement now that Admiral Halsey was right about Peleliu and the rest of the Palaus. Many historians agree that the islands could have been bypassed and contained as others had been in the Pacific island-hopping campaign, just as Admiral Halsey recommended. (Ulithi in the Caroline Islands, however, was extremely useful later in the war effort. Fortunately, it was taken unopposed as part of the Stalemate II operation. It provided excellent anchorage and a seaplane base for the U.S. Navy, and it was a primary staging area for the Okinawa campaign. Lieutenant Steve Lynn would fly onto the Ulithi Atoll during March 1945.)

On Peleliu's southern lowlands, the primary military objective was the airfield, with two good runways surfaced with hard-packed coral suitable for both bombers and fighters. A scrub jungle flanked the field on the west and south; a dense mangrove swamp lay to the east. To the north, the sharp, steep ridges of the Umurbrogol mountain system provided the ideal holdout for the island's defenders. Because the highly developed Umurbrogol defensive system was so close to the airfield, Lieutenant Lynn and the other Marines, Seabees, and soldiers stationed there were under intermittent lethal fire until nearly the end of the campaign in November.

Stinson OY-1 Sentinel view of Umurbrogol ridges under fire just north of airstrip on Peleliu, October 1944
(U.S. Marine Corps photograph, U.S. National Archives #127-GW-696)

Also of military value was a fighter runway being constructed on the island of Ngesebus just north of Peleliu. Angaur, another nearby island, was a military target because it was thought to be suitable for a heavy bomber airfield potentially useful for launching airstrikes against the home islands of Japan. (It was, however, never used for that purpose. The fields on Guam, Tinian, Saipan, Ulithi, and Yap were used instead.) Nearby Babelthaup is the largest island in the group and was the headquarters for the commander of the Japanese Fourteenth Infantry Division, Lieutenant General Inoue. He remained on the island and did not take part in the fighting on Peleliu even though he was ultimately responsible for the troops there. Babelthaup itself was not a military target for the American planners. The only goal for Babelthaup was to isolate it using American aircraft and ships so General Inoue could not send reinforcements to Peleliu, Angaur, or Ngesebus.

The two American assault units given the task of taking Peleliu, Ngesebus, and Angaur operated under the umbrella of the Third Amphibious Corps commanded by U.S. Marine Corps Major General Roy S. Geiger. The First Marine Division commanded by General Rupertus would land on Peleliu and Ngesebus; the U.S. Army's Eighty-First Infantry Division commanded by U.S. Army Major General Paul J. Mueller was slated to take Angaur and act as the reserve for the First Marine Division on Peleliu. The Eighty-First was a new, untested unit first organized in Hawaii and then transported to Guadalcanal for the final rehearsals of the landings. Incidentally, the practice landings on Guadalcanal resulted in several casualties with broken bones. Major General Rupertus broke his ankle and was in considerable pain during the Peleliu landing. Both assault units left Guadalcanal on September 4 for the twenty-one-hundred-mile trip over smooth seas.

Lieutenant Lynn had left Guadalcanal three days earlier with the Peleliu Fire Support Unit commanded by Rear Admiral Jesse B. Oldendorf and the Escort Carrier Group commanded by Rear Admiral Ralph Ofstie. Admiral Oldendorf's ships would be responsible for the prelanding bombardment of Peleliu as well as the underwater demolition of artificial obstacles in the water along the landing beaches. The eleven escort carriers in Admiral Ofstie's group would provide combat air support, fly antisubmarine patrols, and deliver the VMO-3 pilots and artillery observers to Peleliu.

*Escort* carriers were smaller and slower than *fleet* carriers, and they outnumbered the fleet carriers during World War II by a ratio of about four to one. Many early escort carriers were built on commercial ship hulls because they could then be constructed relatively quickly. Such speed was critical after the attack on Pearl Harbor destroyed so much of the Pacific Fleet. In the Pacific theater, the squadrons of planes on the escort carriers provided air cover for troopships, aerial antisubmarine patrols, and bombing and strafing attacks on enemy beach fortifications during amphibious landings. At Peleliu, Admiral Ofstie's eleven escort carriers flew 328 sorties in support of landing Marines.[8] Additionally, the carriers flew sorties attacking the airfield on Babelthaup and bombing enemy ships in the islands' harbors. As Admiral Halsey predicted, no Japanese aircraft responded.

Lieutenant Lynn traveled to the combat zone on the USS *White Plains* (CVE-66), a Casablanca class escort carrier built in 1943. For the totality of its action during the war, the ship was awarded a Presidential Unit Citation and five battle stars. Lieutenant Lynn spent much of the time on the ship reviewing the battle plans, but he also had time during those two weeks to play cards, talk with the few other Marines on board (and maybe a few sailors, too), look out over the ocean horizon, and anticipate what was ahead of him. The OY-1 spotter planes were secured in crates on the hanger deck of the ship, and carrier personnel were assigned to assemble the planes under the direction of each pilot when the time came for their use.

**USS *White Plains* (CVE-66), March 8, 1944**
(U.S. National Archives photograph)

The battle plan going into the Peleliu campaign was for the First Marines (one of the three infantry regiments of the First Division) led by Colonel Lewis B. "Chesty" Puller to land on the beaches closest to the airfield, drive inland, secure the airfield, and then turn left to attack the Umurbrogol high ground. The Fifth and Seventh Marines (the two other infantry regiments of the division) led by Colonel Harold D. Harris and Colonel Herman Haneken, respectively, would land on the beaches south of the First Marines. The Eleventh Marines (the artillery regiment), reinforced by two Army 155 mm gun and howitzer battalions and two battalions of Third Amphibious Corps artillery, would land after the infantry and then set up to support the infantry. Four hours after the first landings, these artillery units were supposed to have their fires massed on the Umurbrogol ridges. Lieutenant Lynn's VMO-3 unit (Marine Observation Squad) was operationally a part of the Eleventh Marines but would call in fire targets to all the artillery battalions and to naval gunships as well.

The battle didn't work out as planned.

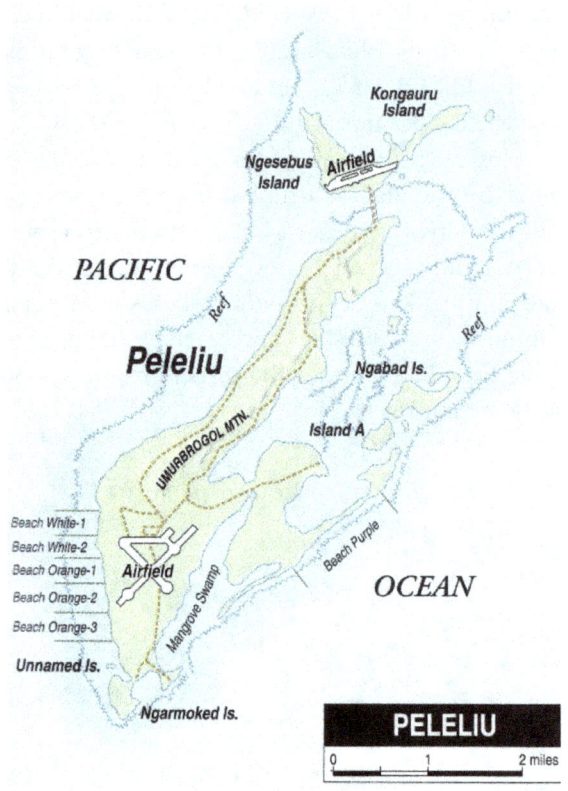

**Peleiu, September, 1944**
(Map first printed in *War in the Western Pacific* by Eric Hammel, reproduced by permission)

In spite of three days of intense preinvasion naval bombardment accompanied by very heavy aerial bombardment, the Japanese-prepared defenses were not destroyed. Admiral Oldendorf's Peleliu Fire Support Group (five battleships, five heavy cruisers, three light cruisers, and fourteen destroyers) bombarded pre-selected targets and blew off most of the jungle growth on the Umurbrogol ridge, but the Japanese had skillfully camouflaged their artillery positions and did not fire back during the bombardment, which would have given away their positions. In keeping with their new defensive strategy, the Japanese heavy artillery and troops were sheltered behind steel doors and in underground caves. Essentially unscathed by the prelanding bombardment, the Japanese were able to vigorously engage the landing Marines from their prepared positions.

The first American Marines touched shore at 8:32 a.m. on September 15 after crossing the reef under a clear sky on a calm sea. They were immediately hammered mercilessly by enemy artillery, mortar, machine gun, and rifle fire as they ran across the mined beaches. Much of the fire came from concealed concrete casements, and some came from a tiny island offshore. Enemy fire on landing vehicles carrying both men and equipment into shore was intense, and the landing beaches were constantly and heavily raked with gunfire. In the First Marines' zone, for example, only one tank escaped being hit during the trip ashore.[9]

**Marines taking shelter under a DUKW at Peleliu, with amtrac burning in the background, September 15, 1944**
(U.S. Marine Corps photograph #95249, U.S. National Archives #127-GW-1070)

More than half of the DUKWs (wheeled amphibious trucks) were knocked out of action.[10] Japanese soldiers attacked from tank traps, from reinforced pillboxes with cannon and heavy machine guns, from caves, and from dug-in positions. First Marine casualties were extremely high, and the regimental reserve and even headquarters personnel and engineers had to form a second line of defense to keep the unit from being driven back into the sea the first night. Marine Corps Major Frank O. Hough wrote that the first eight hours on the left flank of the beachhead on Peleliu saw "some of the fiercest and most confused fighting of the Pacific war."[11]

The Fifth and Seventh Marines south of the First Marines were able to make more progress than the First but still ran into stiff resistance and were unable to secure the airfield. The Fifth Marines did advance to the airfield's western edge to set up a defensive line. In the early evening, they had to defend their position against a Japanese tank and infantry assault that began at the airfield's north end. With the help of a U.S. Navy dive bomber and a few of the regiment's tanks, which had arrived on scene just a few minutes before, the attack was repulsed.

Casualty figures for the First Marine Division on Peleliu's D-day reflected the severity of the fighting and the ferocity of the Japanese defense. The division staff had predicted a first-day loss of 500 casualties, but the total figure was 1,111 killed and wounded, not including heat prostration cases.[12]

Yet in spite of the landing difficulties and tragic casualty rate, nearly 6,000 Marines were ashore by 11:30 a.m. As they had been trained to do, the Marines formed up into their fire teams and squads and pressed the attack against very heavy resistance.

Most of the Eleventh Marines' artillery battalions were set up by nightfall (not noon as originally planned). Some equipment had been lost to enemy fire coming into shore. Some units found their assigned firing positions still in enemy hands and had to search for new sites where they could set up and register their guns.

An Eleventh Marine veteran of Peleliu, Warner Pyne, recalled:

> What I saw and went through during my short stay on that butcher shop so overshadows anything else that I can't even remember how we got there. ... I was not in the first wave—the artillery never is—but I wasn't far behind. I landed with our (ground) observation group because part of my job was to locate places where we could set up guns as they arrived. ... We could see from shipboard that the riflemen were having a brutal time, but we didn't realize how brutal it really was ... [and] we were told to keep our heads down ... until we landed. Oh, my God, what a sight! You could see Marines lying all over the place, some dead and others wounded, wrecked landing craft of all types,

abandoned equipment everywhere … just a gruesome mess. It looked as if we were getting the hell knocked out of us and we were. But we were still there. … I'll never forget that sight.[13]

First 75 mm gun to fire on Peleliu—Lt. Lynn's 1st Battalion, 11th Marines, September 15, 1944
(U.S. Marine Corps photograph #95050, U.S. National Archives #127-GW-703)

Throughout the first night, all four regiments were tested with minor counterattacks, Japanese infiltration through their defensive lines, grenades tossed into their foxholes, sniper fire, and harassing fire. The U.S. Navy cruiser USS *Honolulu* and three destroyers remained in the fire support area all night to provide star shell illumination so the Marines could more easily see encroaching Japanese soldiers.[14] Adding to the chaos, many skilled radio operators and much equipment had been lost when enemy fire scored direct hits on the landing craft carrying them ashore. The messages sent and received were: "Heavy casualties … Need ammo, reinforcements … pretty grim outlook."[15]

Men in the support shore parties, including cooks and bakers, and the Second Marine Air Wing's forward ground echelon personnel had to pitch in to operate small boat platoons to unload equipment and evacuate the wounded while others served as stretcher-bearers, ammunition carriers, and even riflemen and grenade throwers in the front line. Sometimes small groups of Japanese, some wearing helmets of dead Marines, infiltrated behind the frontline positions, and furious life-and-death struggles occurred in the rear. As a group, the shore party Marines suffered twice the number of casualties on Peleliu than had been the case in any previous First Marine Division operation.[16]

For the first three days of the campaign, Lieutenant Lynn flew off the *White Plains* deck as an aerial spotter in a Douglas SBD Dauntless (a carrier-based torpedo bomber). It could return to land on the carrier after each flight; the Stinson OY-1s (nicknamed Grasshoppers) could not. The small Grasshopper observer planes couldn't take off from the escort carriers until the Peleliu airstrip was secure enough to land on. Back at Banika, Pavuvu, and Guadalcanal, Lieutenant Lynn had honed his skills observing from a loaner SBD. (By September 1944, the Navy had replaced many of its SBDs with Curtis Helldivers, but Marine squadrons continued to fly SBDs until the end of the war.)

On the second day of the battle, four battalions of Company K, Fifth Marines, began taking the airstrip. As they advanced several hundred yards out into the open, they came under an intense artillery and mortar barrage. About the experience, Private E. B. Sledge later wrote:

> Everyone was visibly shaken by the thunderous barrage we had just come through. When I looked into the eyes of those fine Guadalcanal and Cape Gloucester veterans, some of America's best, I no longer felt ashamed of my trembling hands and almost laughed at myself with relief.
>
> To be shelled by massed artillery and mortars is absolutely terrifying, but to be shelled in the open is terror compounded beyond the belief of anyone who hasn't experienced it. The attack across Peleliu's airfield was the worst combat experience I had during the entire war. It surpassed, by the intensity of the blast and shock of the bursting shells, all the subsequent horrifying ordeals on Peleliu and Okinawa.[17]

Amazingly, the Marine riflemen still advanced against withering fire from the dug-in Japanese. Working in tandem with Sherman tanks, and using flamethrowers and demolition charges, they eliminated enemy positions. Lieutenant Lynn and the other aerial observers, along with the forward ground artillery observers embedded within infantry units, called in supporting artillery fire and naval gunfire targeting difficult fortifications only identifiable when the enemy fired from them.

There was "furious hand-to-hand fighting" as the Marines ground their way forward.[18] Casualties escalated, and the number of Marines dropping from heat prostration onto the sharp coral mounted as well. The Marines gained ground but had to fight tenaciously to hold it. Sometimes they could not hold it, and then they would have to fight for the same coral rock all over again.

Marines working in tandem with a tank crew to move forward on Peleliu, 1944
(U.S. Marine Corps photograph #97253, U.S. National Archives #127-GW-759)

Add to this miserable scene the "sickening stench of decaying bodies which added to the difficulties under which the troops fought."[19] Not enough men could be spared during the first few days of the battle to collect and bury the dead whose bodies lay where they had fallen, exposed to insects and to the heat. The Marines recovered their dead as soon as possible, but the Japanese generally left their dead on the battlefield and sometimes booby-trapped them to kill Marines checking their condition or seeking water canteens, ammunition, or other items. Field sanitation protocol fell apart rapidly since no holes could be dug in the hard coral, compounding the almost unbearable smell. Pilots reported that the nauseating stench was perceivable from as high as fifteen hundred feet in the air, so Lieutenant Lynn and the other Marines of VMO-3 who flew as low as a few hundred feet above the ground seeking targets couldn't escape it, either.

The VMO-3 squadron ground personnel spent the first two days of the battle assisting the corpsmen in caring for the wounded coming aboard the ships. They also passed ammunition to the landing parties. On September 17, the VMO-3 ground personnel were transported onto Peleliu itself and immediately began building a small (five-hundred-foot-long) coral airstrip just south of the main airfield. They also set up shop to reassemble the crated planes that would be delivered by the amtrac (amphibious tractor, also known as an LVT) drivers on September 19. By the afternoon of the eighteenth, they were ready to receive the first two OY-1s flying from the escort carriers offshore onto the small runway they had built.

Naval log records indicate the weather was perfect for flying on September 18, the day Lieutenant Lynn flew onto the Peleliu airfield. The sky was mostly clear, with scattered cumulus at two thousand feet. Except when the pilot had to look directly into the bright sun, the visibility was unlimited. During the morning, the two Stinson OY-1s on board the USS *White Plains* were reassembled. Second Lieutenant Lynn's plane took off from the ship at 5:00 p.m. and landed on the small newly built airstrip at 5:30 p.m. It was the first planned landing of an American plane on Peleliu. He was in the rear observer seat of the tiny single-engine plane named Baby Buck. Piloting the plane in the front seat was Marine First Lieutenant James H. Buckalew of Meridian, Mississippi. According to the news release sent to Lieutenant Lynn's hometown newspaper, the northern section of the field was under mortar fire when the plane landed. The airfield would remain under fire for almost the entire time Lieutenant Lynn was stationed there.

### Lt. Steven A. Lynn On First Plane to Operate on Peleliu Island

Peleliu Palau Island (Delayed)---First American plane to operate from Peleliu's airdome was a paperweight, 90-mile-hour Stinson used for aerial observation of enemy lines.

The pilots were Marine Second Lieutenants James H. Buckalew, of 1521 25th Avenue, Meridian, Miss., and Stephen A. Lynn Jr., of Brookport, Ill.

The two lieutenanes were observing from a carrier-based torpedo bomber until the fourth day of the battle when they based themselves on the still embattled Island.

(Lt. Lynn is the son of Mr. and Mrs. S. A. Lynn of Route 1.)

*Metropolis (IL) News,* October 19, 1944
(Clipping in family collection)

Lt. Steve Lynn's Stinson OY-1, named Baby Buck
(U.S. Marine Corps photograph #97371, U.S. National Archives #127-GW-708)

A second VMO-3 OY-1 landed a half hour later. According to the commanding officer's report, one of the two planes landing on the primitive field had the tail wheel sheared off, and it hit the loose coral runway. The scattered coral flew up and put holes in one of the wings and the horizontal stabilizer.[20] Apparently, the coral "pavement" was soft and rough, and the planes' landing wheels loosened it. Captain Wallace J. Slappey didn't record which one of the two planes had the problem, but it was quickly repaired. It might have been Baby Buck because Steve later in life said his leg and hip were badly bruised upon landing. Both planes were secured for the night at the end of the strip. Lieutenant Lynn took cover in a shallow foxhole among the other Marines holding the airstrip and spent a sleepless night listening for Japanese infiltrators in the dark.

## Lt. Lynn Still In There Fighting

Peleliu, Palau Islands---(Delayed)---First operating plane to land on the captured airstrip here was a tiny grasshopper piloted by Marine First Lieutenant James H. Buckolaw, of 1521 25th Avenue, Meridian City, Miss., who set his plane, named "Baby Buck," down on the runway at 6 p. m. on the fourth day of the landing.

With him in the observer's seat was Second Lieutenant Stephen A. Lynn. of Brookport, Ill. The northern section of the field was still under mortar fire when the tiny piper cub set its wheels on the earth.

Article from local newspaper (possibly *Brookport (IL) Independent*), October 1944
(Clipping in family collection)

The next day, September 19, Lieutenant Lynn spotted for both artillery and naval gunships. The first flight went out at 6:00 a.m., and the observer began calling in firing coordinates immediately. The remainder of the OY-1s on escort carriers flew onto the small makeshift airstrip that morning. One of Lieutenant

Lynn's friends from Field Artillery Class, Second Lieutenant Charlie Aldrich, flew onto the airfield in the OY-1 piloted by First Lieutenant Robert Pauly. They had taken off from the escort carrier USS *Saginaw Bay* (CVE-82).

One of the three OY-1s lost from the squadron during the battle crashed into the ocean trying to take off from an escort carrier on the nineteenth. The winds were inadequate for the heavy load the plane carried. The crew was rescued by a nearby destroyer and returned to active duty with the squadron a few days later. Other landing OY-1s blew out tires running over shrapnel on the improvised airstrip. Another one shattered a propeller. The VMO-3 ground crew rapidly repaired them all, and the planes were sent up for aerial spotting missions the same day.

All flights on September 19 averaged about two-and-one-half hours in length, and three airplanes were in the air at all times by midday. The last flight landed at 6:00 p.m.

The reality of battle wasn't like the VMO training. Pilots had been taught to stay at a reasonable altitude in front of enemy lines to observe and find suitable targets for the spotters to call in. Instead, Captain Slappey wrote the following in his unit report for September 19:

> They [the pilots and observers] fired missions while flying through air strikes, creeping naval gun fire, our own artillery fire, and enemy small arms fire at extremely low altitudes. Many enemy positions would not have been located had they not come down to a tree-top level and searched. Whenever targets were found at these low altitudes, the planes would retire to a thousand to fifteen hundred feet and [call] fire on them until they were destroyed.

The report goes on to describe the artillery observers calling in fire "with good effect" on several targets, including enemy troops running back and forth between caves, three enemy-occupied buildings, a small oil dump, a gun position on the northern tip of the island, caves, and mortar positions. The effect of fire on other targets such as hidden caves and mortar positions was harder to evaluate, and repeated firing on an enemy radio station seemed to have no effect at all. The pilot/spotter teams also registered the artillery battalions on prominent island landmarks throughout the day.

Captain Slappey reported that "morale was excellent" and everyone was healthy.

The VMO-3 ground crew kept busy not only fueling and servicing the planes arriving from the escort carriers but also reassembling the planes brought onshore and to the airfield by amphibious vehicles. In his book *Peleliu: Tragic Triumph—The Untold Story of the Pacific War's Forgotten Battle,* Bill Ross shares the following anecdote about the rest of the small spotter planes arriving at the airfield in crates:

> Just after 3:00 p.m. [on September 19], three grime-covered amtracs roared, throttles wide open, over a ridge from White Beach Two. "Hey, you guys!" the driver of the lead vehicle yelled. "We got some fuckin' big crates for you. I think they're airplanes. Unload 'em quick so we can get the hell outta here." Captain Wallace J. Slappey had been sweating out the arrival of the "fuckin' big crates" since slogging across the field nearly twenty-four hours earlier. He was commanding officer of VMO-3, the official designation of the 1st Division's own "air force" of seven small unarmed artillery spotter planes.
>
> The "Piperschmitts" and "Messercubs" [nicknames for the OYs] made the voyage from Pavuvu aboard an LST [Landing Ship, Tank]. Mechanics had removed the wings, tail assemblies, and landing gear from the two-seater fuselages and then carefully packed them in wooden containers for the long trip to Peleliu. VMO-3 ground crewmen had done the job to perfection. The planes were undamaged, not even a slight tear in the fabric covering, and were reassembled and ready for flight in a matter of hours.[21]

The Dauntless torpedo bombers Lieutenant Lynn and the other observers had flown in the first few days of the campaign were too fast and too high to effectively do the "low and slow" flying job Captain Slappey's Marine pilots and spotters had trained for in the OY-1s. The smaller planes could circle a few hundred feet above the ridges, and the number of times supporting fire hit the wrong targets dropped substantially after Lieutenant Lynn and the other spotters started flying in the OY-1s.

In their slow (90 miles an hour), unarmored planes, Lieutenant Lynn and the other observers in his squadron supported the ground troops not only by calling in targets for mortar, artillery, and naval gunfire but also by flying at extremely low altitudes along and across the front lines looking for enemy gun positions ahead of the advancing Marines. They would then warn the infantry teams of those enemy positions ahead of them. At times, Lieutenant Lynn and the other spotters would even lob grenades and mortar shells into enemy positions from above. The pilots would also fly at low altitudes by fortified cave openings so Lieutenant Lynn and the other observers could see directly into the caves to find good targets. The Grasshoppers were low, slow targets for Japanese soldiers who knew they would call in their positions, but the Japanese soon learned there was substantial risk in firing at them. Retired USMC Colonel Joseph Alexander later wrote in *Storm Landings* about the VMO-3 pilot/observer teams:

Grasshopper flying low overhead directing artillery fire onto enemy positions on Five Sisters Ridge in Horseshoe Valley, Peleliu, September 1944
(U.S. Marine Corps photograph, U.S. National Archives #127-GW-697)

So effective were the pilots and their observers that Japanese gun crews eventually ceased firing at the first sight of the Bird Dogs [OY-1s] overhead, knowing from painful experience that accurate counterbattery fire would be called down on their heads in short order.[22]

At other times, the Grasshopper flights would maintain patrols over the enemy-held islands to the north looking for troop-carrying barges attempting to reinforce Japanese positions on Peleliu itself. (Only about five hundred Japanese troops of the twenty-five thousand troops General Inoue had on Babelthaup made it to Peleliu during the battle or thereafter. The rest surrendered in 1945 along with General Inoue after having been isolated there by American air and sea superiority for nearly a year.) Sometimes, the spotters directed amtrac patrols to enemy troops trying to escape the island.

Both landing and taking off from the airfield were perilous adventures as the pilots tried to avoid tire blowouts caused by running over shrapnel or potentially fatal accidents caused by running into bomb craters. On many occasions, the spotter planes returned with holes from small arms fire and shell fragments. The excellent VMO-3 ground crew immediately repaired the damaged planes and returned them to the flight line.

It wasn't until the morning of September 19, the fourth day of the battle, that the Seabees could start clearing the main airfield of land mines, debris, and shell fragments. Lisle Shoemaker, the United Press correspondent, was the first journalist on the scene, and he counted more than 150 demolished Japanese planes in and around "the barely recognizable skeletons of burned-out hangars."[23]

**Grasshoppers on the Peleliu airstrip among Japanese wreckage, September 1944**
(U.S. Marine Corps photograph #96198, U.S. National Archives #127-GW-708)

The Seabees continued working under intermittent mortar and rifle fire, and within seventy-two hours, they had cleared and leveled an operative airstrip complete with runway lights. Occasionally, hidden high-velocity guns in fortified Japanese positions in the Umurbrogol pocket would bombard the airstrip, and sometimes Japanese suicide squads armed with high explosives would wreak havoc on the runways. Then rifle squads of Marines would have to assault each Japanese emplacement individually under continuing Japanese artillery and mortar fire. The fire-blanketed airfield Lieutenant Lynn's small plane had to land on and take off from became known as Mortar Valley. No planes other than VMO-3's OY-1s could be brought onto the field until September 24, a week after Lieutenant Lynn had landed.

On the second day of VMO-3 operations, September 20, an operating schedule was adopted. It called for three of the OY-1s to be up in the air at all times between 6:00 a.m. and 4:30 p.m. In addition to periodically reregistering artillery battalions as battle conditions changed, the pilots and spotters scoured the island for new targets. They called in fire on a large enemy ammunition warehouse and watched it erupt into flames. They also called in fire onto enemy troops exposed in the hills and along roadsides. They constantly kept their eyes open for puffs of light blue smoke indicating possible mortar positions. They called in fire on pillboxes, caves, enemy oil dumps, enemy bivouac areas (not only on Peleliu but also on nearby smaller islands), enemy observation posts, and enemy-held buildings hidden in trees. Unfortunately, the first signs of dysentery broke out in the squadron the same day.

Dysentery is a bacterial disease spread through contaminated food and water. During the first week of the Peleliu campaign, clean water was a rare commodity, and in the unsanitary conditions of the battlefield, the dysentery-causing bacteria flourished. The bacteria penetrate the lining of the intestine and cause swelling, sores, abdominal pain, and severe diarrhea containing blood and pus. Symptoms can also include fever, fatigue, vomiting, headaches, and dehydration. In some cases, it can be fatal. With proper care, mild cases may last four to eight days. Serious cases may take up to six weeks to resolve. While conditions for the disease to flourish were ideal on Peleliu, conditions for its treatment were not, and it became a major problem as blowflies landing on corpses and feces picked up the bacteria and then landed on C rations as soon as they were opened. To fully recover, the Marines needed rest and constant rehydration with clean water. Two days after Captain Slappey noted the first dysentery case in his unit report, the majority of the squadron, including Lieutenant Lynn, had come down with the disease. It remained a major problem for all of the Marines and soldiers on Peleliu for as long as they were there.

Peleliu's airfield under attack from the Umurbrogol heights, September 1944
(U.S. Navy photograph)

The VMO-3 pilots and observers persisted in maintaining the ambitious aerial observation flight schedule as much as possible. The daily reports paint a picture of the ongoing target finding both on Peleliu and other nearby islands—concentrations of enemy trucks, antiaircraft mounts, warehouses, more enemy troops, enemy observation posts, more fuel dumps. In an effort to find hidden enemy gun positions along the Marines' front line, one pilot and observer intentionally exposed their OY-1 at low altitude on September 21 to draw fire in order to locate enemy guns that had been holding up the infantry advance. The pilot/observer team did indeed find the guns, which were in turn destroyed, but the OY-1 returned to base with many holes in its wings and fabric-covered fuselage; fortunately, the pilot and spotter were not injured.

That same day, the USS *White Plains*, which had carried Lieutenant Lynn to the Palaus from Guadalcanal, and three other escort carriers sailed away full of casualties. After transferring the casualties to hospital ships, the escort carriers participated in the unopposed seizure of Ulithi.

Forward ground observers and Lieutenant Lynn and his fellow aerial artillery observers called the coordinates for the targets they spotted into an assigned Fire Direction Center (FDC). There the coordinates were given to the men at the mapping tables who "computed" the exact location and transmitted the information to the artillery units responsible for firing.

**"Computers" in a Peleliu FDC, September 1944**
(U.S. Marine Corps photograph #96137, U.S. National Archives #127-GW-703)

In all, Marine artillerymen fired 133,000 rounds of shells during the thirty-five days their guns were in action. Calculated on a minute-by-minute, twenty-four-hours-a-day basis, lanyards were pulled at a rate of one every twenty-three seconds.[24]

As the Eleventh Marines First Battalion surveyor, Lieutenant Lynn's good friend Lieutenant Jack Dearmore was constantly surveying in gun positions to effectively target rapidly changing Japanese positions.

**2nd Lt. Lynn's good friend 2nd Lt. Jack E. Dearmore
surveying in a gun position on Peleliu, September 1944**
(U.S. Marine Corps photograph #102070, U.S. National Archives #127-GW-703)

On September 22, VMO-3 lost the use of another one of its OY-1s when direct hits from enemy fire in the engine mount and accessory section of the engine rendered it unrepairable. Fortunately, the pilot and observer were still able to land safely.

By the same day, a week after landing on the island, the First Marine Division had taken control of the entire airfield and all of the island south of the Umurbrogol pocket. There was ample room now for the artillery to be properly deployed, and the beaches had been sufficiently organized to more efficiently provide supplies and reinforcements. By First Marine Division estimate, about two-thirds of the original Japanese garrison had been incapacitated. Most of the terrain of strategic value had been seized, but the cost in American lives had been extremely high. In one week there had been 3,946 casualties in the First Marine Division.[25]

Also on September 22, units of the U.S. Army's Eighty-First Division began relieving the survivors of the woefully depleted First Marine Regiment. The regiment suffered 56 percent casualties, eliminating it as an effective assault unit. Among the nine rifle platoons of the regiment's First Battalion, not one of the original platoon leaders remained, and there were only seventy-four riflemen left. Seventy-one percent of the battalion had become casualties.[26] There has been considerable debate over the years about whether the First Marines should have been relieved by reserve troops earlier in the battle. The First Marine survivors left Peleliu for Pavuvu on September 30 aboard the hospital transport ships USS *Pinkney* (APH-2) and USS *Tryon* (APH-1). Two of the three DUKWs overturned as they approached the ships, dumping the men into the sea. Fortunately, no one drowned.[27]

The first VMO-3 plane crews flying out on September 23 caught sight of enemy barges trying to bring in reinforcements from Babelthaup and called in fire to destroy them. The planes were also used that day for aerial photography flights and for reconnaissance flights by commanding officers. Fire was called in on two critical enemy pillboxes to "good effect," allowing the infantry to advance to new positions. Flights to constantly patrol sea channels where the Japanese could bring in reinforcements were specifically scheduled after a small group of enemy troops arrived on Peleliu overnight.

On September 24, VMO-3 pilots and observers in the first flights of the day attacked twenty-five Japanese soldiers swimming ashore from barges sunk during the night. From the backseats of their planes, Lieutenant Lynn and the other spotters threw hand grenades at the enemy soldiers and shot them with M1 carbines and pistols stowed in the small rear seat compartments before taking off.

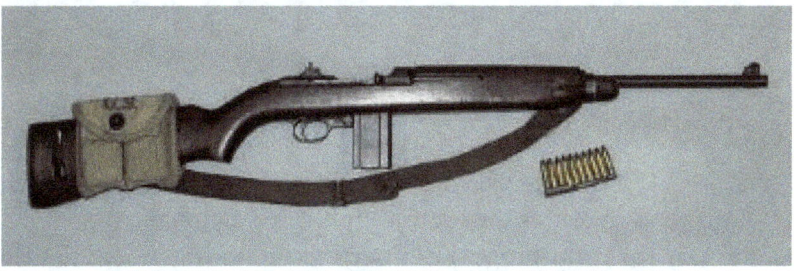

**Inland M-1 carbine in original World War II configuration**
(Reproduced with permission from Curiosandrelics, Own work, CC BY-SA 3.0, https://commons.wikimedia.org/w/index.php?curid=9489414)

The attacks from the small planes continued off and on all day during lulls in artillery spotting. When they ran out of ammunition, the observers directed a naval scout plane to strafe the swimming Japanese soldiers. All but five Japanese soldiers were killed.

By September 24, too, the Seabees had fully restored a short runway on the Peleliu airfield, allowing a large number of Second Marine Air Wing aircraft to land even though heavy fighting was still under way only fifteen hundred yards north of the airfield. The six remaining small planes of Captain Slappey's VMO-3 squadron were now joined by three cargo planes (two C-46s and a C-47), four seaplanes (PBYs), and eight fighters (Hellcats) which could be used for night operations. By September 25, the control tower was ready for around-the-clock operation. Shortly thereafter, the rest of the Second Marine Air Wing—some sixty aircraft—flew in from Guam.

**Peleliu airfield operations base and tower, 1944**
(U.S. Marine Corps photograph #97471, U.S. National Archives #127-GW-696)

The Marine Corsairs arrived on September 26 and began close air support for the ground troops trying to take Bloody Nose Ridge in the Umurbrogol just fifteen seconds away from the airfield by air. Lieutenant Lynn and everyone else on the airfield were regularly shaken by the impact of the half-ton bombs the Corsairs dropped onto the nearby ridges.

**Second Marine Air Wing Corsair, carrying 1,000-lb. bombs, taxiing before takeoff from Peleliu airstrip, September, 1944**
(U.S. Marine Corps photograph #98233, U.S. National Archives #127-GW-638)

As the Marines on the ground reduced the enemy-held territory, the target area for calling in fire was reduced as well. There was too much danger of hitting the attacking Marines themselves. This meant the spotters had to be in close communication with ground units who could specifically locate caves and enemy positions in the Umurbrogol pocket. Sometimes fire was called in to provide cover for the ground troops so they could destroy the caves. Lieutenant Lynn and the other spotters also fired on caves and enemy soldiers directly from their OY-1s using grenades, mortar shells, and their M1 carbines.

**Peleliu airfield looking west from the control tower, September 26, 1944**
(U.S. Marine Corps photograph #96566, U.S. National Archives #127-GW-696)

During the second and third weeks of operations, the demanding observation schedule was still being maintained, but there were also an increasing number of reconnaissance and photography flights around the island and at low altitude over the front lines for Division Intelligence staff. More enemy troops were found in the water at the north end of the island by spotters overhead who directed artillery fire onto them. They also called in amphibious tractors to track them down. Lieutenant Lynn called in fire on more warehouses and more mortar positions. He dropped more grenades, antitank grenades, and mortar shells on enemy positions from the backseat. These actions sometimes didn't directly destroy the positions, but they provided the cover ground troops needed to approach and eliminate the enemy positions holding up forward advances.

Occasionally, Grasshopper crews dropped surrender leaflets behind enemy lines, but few Japanese troops ever did surrender.

The third OY-1 lost during the battle went down behind enemy lines on September 25 "while searching for an enemy supply depot at extremely low altitude." The pilot and observer were rescued by an infantry patrol under cover of a tank while a second OY plane directed the patrol from overhead. Before they took cover to await the arrival of the patrol, the crew destroyed the IFF (Identification Friend or Foe) equipment in the downed plane to prevent its capture by the enemy. The pilot of the downed plane, Clare Vincent VandenBroek, suffered a head injury in the crash; the observer suffered a back injury. Both were evacuated from the island. Was Lieutenant Lynn the spotter in the plane overhead? He never talked about it, and the names of the two crew members in the plane overhead couldn't be found in the archived records.

Two VMO-3 ground personnel were also evacuated during the campaign. Both had "accidental self-inflicted knife wounds to their wrists." Combat fatigue was taking its toll in all the Marine Corps and Army units on the island. The sleepless nights, noise, stench, and constant deadly attacks were unrelenting.

Pfc. Arthur Olivero from Chicago, 2nd Battalion, 11th Marines, Peleliu, September 1944
(U.S. Marine Corps photograph #132252, U.S. National Archives #127-GR-1070)

During the early evening of September 25, Lieutenant Lynn and every other spotter flying overhead registered all the artillery battalions on Peleliu to target the barge channel between the islands to stop enemy reinforcements from moving onto Peleliu during the night.

During the following two days, the VMO-3 squadron turned more of its attention to the other islands in the Palau group because the artillery firing area on Peleliu was becoming so constricted. Enemy pockets of resistance were small, and massed artillery fire was too dangerous to Marines on the front lines. Artillerymen of the Eleventh Marines not needed on the guns actually became infantrymen ("infantillery") filling gaps when the infantry units took heavy casualties.[28]

Lieutenant Lynn and the other aerial spotters were still able to call in fire on a large Japanese pocket directly north of the Peleliu airfield, but its effectiveness was hard to assess. They each continued to personally fire on enemy positions from the backseats of their OY-1s as well.

When the Fifth Marines landed on Ngesebus on September 28, Lieutenant Lynn spotted artillery fire onto the island to support the Marines on the ground. While one VMO-3 Grasshopper crew was directing Marines on the ground to an enemy machine gun position, it received enemy fire in the engine. It was forced to make an emergency landing onto a coral reef. Amazingly, the pilot and observer were unhurt and were able to fly the plane back to the airfield after quickly dispatched ground crew members made emergency repairs on the coral reef. Some of the OY-1 crews scouted the islands north of Ngesebus and dropped hand grenades onto small buildings and mortar positions to "good effect." Another crew dropped propaganda leaflets over Japanese positions on Peleliu.

By the same date, the First Marine Division had lost 843 killed, 3,845 wounded, and 356 missing, a total of 5,044 casualties. An estimated 9,076 Japanese had died, and only 180 Japanese had been taken prisoner.[29] Even so, it would be nearly two more months of bitter fighting before Peleliu was "secured." It would be several months longer before all isolated pockets of Japanese soldiers would be captured or killed.

Cape Gloucester Marine veteran Pfc. John M. Smith with head wound, being guided off the front lines back to an aid station by a corpsman on the right and a Marine guard on the left, Peleliu, September 1944
(U.S. Marine Corps photograph #95024, U.S. National Archives #127-GR-1070)

To add to the misery on the ground, heavy rains began falling late on September 28. More severe weather would soon follow. The rain allowed the Japanese to replenish their diminishing water supply, and the resulting mud slowed down the Marines' advance. They would have to assault cave after cave with rifles, bayonets, and flamethrowers in the wind and torrential rain and often without tank or artillery support. Heroically, artillerymen dragged 75 mm pack guns up muddy slopes by hand in an effort to support the infantrymen with direct fire. The bad weather grounded the VMO-3 squadron on September 29 and most of the next day.

In the first two weeks of the battle for Peleliu, the pilots and spotters of VMO-3 had flown 184 flights, spending nearly 363 hours in the air supporting the Marines on the ground. They had all been shot at repeatedly and daily either in the air or on the airfield where they were based. They had all experienced numerous emergency landings in their planes shot through with enemy fire. They had directly killed many enemy soldiers, and they had through their "calling in fire" killed innumerable others. They had also saved the lives of countless fellow Marines on the ground. Every pilot and ground crewman of VMO-3 and every artillery observer now had dysentery, and the squadron itself still had three more weeks left on the island.

Except for the Umurbrogol pocket less than one mile north of the airfield, Peleliu was in American hands by September 30. It is a major understatement to say the ridge system was much easier to defend than to take. To control the Peleliu airfield, though, the Umurbrogol pocket could not be ignored. The only way to neutralize it was for rifle squads, tanks, and artillery to systematically work together to seal or "cure" each cave one by one. It was a debilitating, agonizing battle of attrition. The hellish conditions in the Umurbrogol pocket for the Marines and soldiers on the ground were described by E. B. Sledge. Comparing them to the battlefields he would personally experience later on Okinawa and those he had read about in Europe, he wrote:

> They [the other battlefields] were nothing like the crazy-contoured coral ridges and rubble-filled canyons of the Umurbrogol Pocket on Peleliu. Particularly at night by the light of flares or on a cloudy day, it was like no other battlefield described on earth. It was an alien, unearthly, surrealistic nightmare like the surface of another planet.[30]

**Terrain north of the airstrip heading into the Umurbrogol pocket, October 1944**
(U.S. Marine Corps photograph #108389, U.S. National Archives #127-GW-760)

By September 30, too, it was apparent another First Marine Division assault regiment was finished as a fighting force. Dysentery, high casualties, and combat fatigue had decimated the ranks of the Seventh Marines. The regiment had landed on Peleliu with 3,217 men. By October 3, 1,486 of them were dead, wounded, or missing.[31]

It was a high price to pay, but by October 1, much of Peleliu and all of Ngesebus was under U.S. control, and so the daily schedule for artillery spotting maintained earlier in the operation was canceled. Lieutenant Lynn and the remaining artillery spotters were placed "on call." The pilots flew several reconnaissance flights with infantry officers over enemy positions on Peleliu to help the officers direct the Marines on the ground.[32]

On October 2, three VMO-3 mechanics and three of the remaining OY-1s were loaded onto an LST for transport back to Pavuvu. The destroyer-escorted convoy also included elements of the First Division Headquarter and Service, First Medical, First Motor Transport, First Service, and First Tank Battalions as well as the First and Second Battalions of the Eleventh Marines. Lieutenant Lynn was detached from the VMO-3 squadron, and he rejoined the First Battalion, Eleventh Marines to return to Pavuvu on LST 121. Lieutenant Lynn would serve with many of the same VMO-3 pilots and crewmen again on Okinawa. Lieutenant Lynn disembarked from LST 121 at Pavuvu on October 12 after a tempestuous sea voyage through typhoon-strength winds and waves.

Back on Peleliu, strong winds intermittently grounded all of the remaining planes of VMO-3 for the first few days after Lieutenant Lynn left, and Captain Slappey reported that "dysentery is causing the men a great deal of anguish." Registering artillery battalions was an ongoing daily responsibility for the pilots and remaining spotters when weather allowed.

By October 4, the typhoon-scale winds had disrupted the supply chain onto the island so severely that the amount of available food dropped down to four days' rations. All the Marines on the island were then limited to two meals a day. An emergency call was made to Guam to supply not only food but also socks, boondockers (boots), and dungarees (pants).[33]

The ninety survivors of the First Battalion, Seventh Marines were relieved by the last remaining assault regiment of the First Division, the Fifth Marines, on October 5 and 6. They and the two remaining depleted battalions of the Seventh Marines had the responsibility of continuing the drive into the Umurbrogol pocket until they in turn were relieved by units of the Army's Eighty-First Division later in the month.

Poor weather, the poor condition of the battle-weary planes, and the poor health of the squadron's crew reduced the VMO-3 squadron's activities as the month dragged on. One VMO-3 pilot received shrapnel wounds in the neck and head on October 7 while flying one of the remaining spotters over the Umurbrogol pocket to direct artillery fire. His wounds were treated back at the base and he returned to duty. One of the ground crew injured earlier with an "accidental knife wound" returned to the unit for duty the same day. Only a few flights for reconnaissance, checking new maps, photography, monitoring Japanese troop movements, and registering artillery battalions were flown daily between October 10 and 17.

The remaining units of the Fifth Marines and Seventh Marines were still spending their haunted nights on the ground in the Umurbrogol watching for snipers, enduring enemy mortar blasts, and fighting Japanese infiltrators carrying knives and grenades into their positions. They were finally relieved by units of the Army's 321st Infantry on October 15, but they couldn't be transported off the island until October 30. Some were so weak that they needed help climbing the cargo nets onto the USS *Sea Runner*, the ship carrying them back to Pavuvu.

On October 17, Captain Slappey received the much-awaited news that the VMO-3 squadron was to prepare for immediate departure from Peleliu. The remaining planes were immediately disassembled on October 18, and the camp area was cleaned and then inspected by the Second Marine Air Wing medical officer. The remaining observers, pilots, and ground crew boarded a ship (probably an LST) during the evening. The gear remained on the beach under guard.

The last two battalions of the Eleventh Marines left for Pavuvu on October 20, leaving the remaining artillery responsibilities to U.S. Army units. VMO-3 personnel left Peleliu the morning of October 22. According to Captain Slappey, "the conditions aboard the ship were crowded, dirty, and very poor food. Morale of men low." After ten days aboard ship, the VMO-3 enlisted Marines disembarked at Pavuvu, rejoining Lieutenant Lynn and the others who had left earlier in the month, and the officers went on to Banika.

At noon on October 30, General Geiger passed Marine Corps command over the Palaus (including Peleliu) to General Mueller, the commander of the U.S. Army's Eighty-First Division.

All four regiments of the First Marine Division had left Peleliu to return to Pavuvu by mid-November, leaving the final Peleliu "mopping up" to the Army's Eighty-First Division units. During the night of November 24–25, 1944, Japanese Colonel Nakagawa and his cocommander, General Murai, committed suicide, and on November 27, Colonel Arthur P. Watson of the Army's Eighty-First Division reported organized resistance on Peleliu had ended.

At the time, it was reported that the battles for Peleliu, Ngesebus, and Angaur had been won at the cost of 1,658 American Marines' and soldiers' lives (killed in action or died of wounds). In addition, there were 7,504 wounded or injured Marines and soldiers and 73 missing Marines. The figures were later revised upward. The First Marine Division suffered 6,786 casualties, with more than 1,300 killed in action. Casualties in the division's three infantry regiments averaged more than 50 percent of their total reinforced strength of about 3,000 men apiece at the time the fighting started.

The U.S. Army's Eighty-First Division suffered another 3,278 casualties, including those sustained on Angaur.[34] When all is said and done, the battle had the highest casualty *rate* (about 40 percent) of any amphibious assault in American history.[35] U.S. forces suffered about one casualty for every Japanese serviceman killed—a ratio much higher than the average loss ratio in Pacific war battles.[36] It's estimated there were at least 10,900 Japanese lives lost; the Marines alone buried 10,695 Japanese dead. On average, 1,589 rounds of heavy and light ammunition were used to kill each *one* Japanese serviceman on Peleliu.[37] Only nineteen Japanese army and navy troops and 202 Korean and Okinawan laborers from the Japanese forces were taken prisoner.[38]

After the war ended, Japan's Lieutenant General Sadae Inoue officially surrendered the remaining Japanese forces in the Palaus to General F. O. Rogers of the U.S. Marine Corps aboard the USS *Amick* on September 2, 1945.

The last official surrender of World War II occurred on April 22, 1947, when a Japanese lieutenant emerged from the mountains and swamps of Peleliu along with twenty-six Japanese Second Infantry soldiers and eight Japanese Guard Force sailors. A Japanese admiral was taken to Peleliu to convince the Japanese troops that the war was truly over and it was acceptable to give themselves up with honor.[39]

The official postbattle summary for the Peleliu operation stated:

> Air spotting for deep [naval] supporting fire was used extensively in neutralizing enemy reserves, gun positions, supply and ammunition dumps, and observation and communication points. *Air spotting proved to be one of the best and most effective means of fire control.*[40]

In his book *The Assault on Peleliu*, Frank Hough wrote:
> Also notable ... was the effect on the enemy of the ubiquitous aerial observers. So promptly were weapons positions spotted and brought under attack that the Japanese exposed themselves as little as possible, thereby reducing their volume of fire during a crucial stage of the operation.[41]

Additionally, Hough noted:

> The 1st Division's own observation planes [VMO-3] ... continued skillful direction of artillery fire until the enemy-held pocket became so constricted as to bar massed fires as dangerous to friendly troops. The Marine fliers [and observers] ... continued to display daring, ingenuity, professional skill, and an eagerness to cooperate that raised the morale of the ground troops immeasurably.[42]

Ground crewman Cpl. Frank R. Karpinski servicing a VMO-3 OY-1 on Peleliu, September 1944
(U.S. Marine Corps photograph, U.S. National Archives (#127-GW-708))

Official records indicate that while the VMO-3 operated on Peleliu, approximately 120,000 rounds of ammunition were fired by the artillery units on the island. The number of rounds fired through the use of aerial observation was estimated to be between 85 and 90 percent, or around 102,000 to 108,000 rounds.

Having sustained 6,786 casualties, the First Marine Division returned to Pavuvu with one infantry regiment lost as an effective fighting unit and two others severely depleted. U.S. Marine Corps Second Lieutenant Steve Lynn returned to Pavuvu needing time to personally come to grips with the brutality and violence of the unspeakable sights, sounds, and smells he had endured in battle. His mental and physical abilities to confront the utter blackness of the darkest sides of human experience had been tested. He needed to mourn the deaths of fellow Marines. He had to deal with, or bury, the terror he had experienced while being attacked and nearly dying many times daily. He needed to recover from dysentery and gain back the substantial amount of weight he had lost during the battle. He had done the job he had been trained to do to the best of his ability. Somehow, he had survived the battle while so many other Marines had not.

Lieutenant Lynn may not have realized then that the time he'd spent at Peleliu had forever changed him and all the other soldiers, sailors, and Marines who fought there.

The First Marine Division (Reinforced) was awarded a Presidential Unit Citation "For extraordinary heroism in action against enemy Japanese forces at Peleliu and Ngesebus from September 15 to 29, 1944."

(Copy from Steve Lynn's personal papers in family collection)

**THE SECRETARY OF THE NAVY**
WASHINGTON

The President of the United States takes pleasure in presenting the PRESIDENTIAL UNIT CITATION to the

FIRST MARINE DIVISION (REINFORCED)

consisting of FIRST Marine Division; First Amphibian Tractor Battalion, FMF; U.S. Navy Flame Thrower Unit Attached; Sixth Amphibian Tractor Battalion (Provisional), FMF; Third Armored Amphibian Battalion (Provisional), FMF; Detachment Eighth Amphibian Tractor Battalion, FMF; 454th Amphibian Truck Company, U.S. Army; 456th Amphibian Truck Company, U.S. Army; Fourth Joint Assault Signal Company, FMF; Fifth Separate Wire Platoon, FMF; Sixth Separate Wire Platoon, FMF,

for service as set forth in the following

CITATION:

"For extraordinary heroism in action against enemy Japanese forces at Peleliu and Ngesebus from September 15 to 29, 1944. Landing over a treacherous coral reef against hostile mortar and artillery fire, the FIRST Marine Division, Reinforced, seized a narrow, heavily mined beachhead and advanced foot by foot in the face of relentless enfilade fire through rain-forests and mangrove swamps toward the air strip, the key to the enemy defenses of the southern Palaus. Opposed all the way by thoroughly disciplined, veteran Japanese troops heavily entrenched in caves and in reinforced concrete pillboxes which honeycombed the high ground throughout the island, the officers and men of the Division fought with undiminished spirit and courage despite heavy losses, exhausting heat and difficult terrain, seizing and holding a highly strategic air and land base for future operations in the Western Pacific. By their individual acts of heroism, their aggressiveness and their fortitude, the men of the FIRST Marine Division, Reinforced, upheld the highest traditions of the United States Naval Service."

For the President,

*[signature: John L. Sullivan]*
Secretary of the Navy

# 14
# Vernice
## Arlington, Virginia
## September–October 1944

**Pencil-pushing-mammas sank the shipping of Japan...**
—A line from the poem written on the one-year anniversary of the cracking of Japanese code 2468 by code breakers Marjorie Miller and Ann August

**Don't just look. See!**
—Steve Lynn

*Ultra* and *Magic*—two words representing two of the best kept World War II secrets—didn't become public knowledge until F. W. Winterbotham's book *The Ultra Secret* was published in 1974. Vernice Milleville learned what they were all about when she began working for the Signal Security Agency (SSA) at Arlington Hall Station thirty years earlier. *Magic* represented the American ability to decipher Japanese diplomatic codes. *Ultra* referred to the American and British ability to decipher Japanese and German army, navy, and air force codes.

In 1939, William Friedman and Frank Rowlett led the team that reverse-engineered a machine, nicknamed Purple (illustrated in chapter 12), providing important clues about the Japanese diplomatic code. By 1942, the intercepted code could be read fairly quickly and accurately, and the information it provided was referred to as Magic. It provided critical insight into internal political and external diplomatic Japanese thinking.

The vital importance of Magic can be conveyed by quoting a letter written by General George C. Marshall to New York governor Thomas Dewey on September 27, 1944:

> Our main basis of information regarding Hitler's intentions in Europe is obtained from Baron Oshima's [the Japanese envoy's] messages from Berlin reporting his interviews with Hitler and other officials to the Japanese Government.[1]

The Japanese Ultra codes took longer to decipher. The British and the U.S. Navy had helpful but still limited success in deciphering Japanese military codes as early as spring 1942, but the U.S. Navy code breakers didn't truly succeed in breaking the Japanese naval codes until later that year. The toughest nuts to crack were the multiple codes used by the Imperial Japanese Army. Deciphering them was the responsibility of the U.S. Army. As U.S. military forces began their island-hopping offensive campaigns in the Pacific, it was essential that the Japanese army codes be cracked.

The critical breakthrough occurred in early 1943 when U.S. Army code breakers at Arlington Hall and MacArthur's Central Bureau in Australia caught two fortuitous breaks. First, a coded directory of forty thousand Japanese officers listed by rank and assignment was captured by Allied forces. The directory gave the code breakers a way to track the location of any given Japanese unit by tracking the officers assigned to it.

Second, when a Japanese plane crashed in Burma (now called Myanmar), the British found message templates with some of the code groups filled in. Wilma Berryman, Ann Caracristi, and their mostly female colleagues at Arlington Hall Station painstakingly worked with this new information comparing it to Japanese navy code groups and other small pieces of information they were able to pull together. By late summer, they had broken the Japanese army's address code system enough to be able to provide intelligence analysts with copious and useful military information from the Japanese radio intercepts flowing into Arlington Hall. Arlington Hall was now able to produce a daily order-of-battle summary.[2]

The address code breaking was never completely finished because the Japanese periodically changed their codebooks and their methods. Every time the Japanese changed their encryption, the team led by Berryman and Caracristi had to figure out a way to unlock it again.

The main Japanese army codes remained an unsolved mystery. Working meticulously and thoughtfully during spring 1943, the code breakers next unlocked the exceedingly complex Japanese shipping code, the massive water transport code 2468. It was used by the Japanese army to route all of its many types of supply ships *(maru)*. That success led in turn to unlocking the Japanese administrative codes used for troop movements, promotions, battle casualties, and sickness reports, and finally the codes for tactical information including battle plans. By September 1943, the code breakers at Arlington Hall could read it all—if they could hire enough qualified people to decode and manage the intercepted messages flooding in.

By the time Vernice arrived in mid-1944, more than one hundred thousand intercepted Ultra and Magic messages per week were forwarded to Arlington Hall Station from listening posts in the Pacific and elsewhere. There was also a large backlog of messages that had piled up beforehand. By that time, too, the British had again become confident enough in American security to share their success with Enigma and other German code and cipher systems. By 1944, the Signal Security Agency (SSA) had become the military's most important single source of intelligence. The agency provided 70 percent of the Japanese diplomatic intelligence (Magic) and 80 percent of the Japanese military information (Ultra).[3]

Ultra would dramatically change the course of the war in the Pacific. It provided the Allies with accurate estimates of Japanese army, navy, and air force orders of battle, including not only where the Japanese were but also how strong they were in any given location. With Ultra in hand, military intelligence officers were no longer "guessing" about enemy strength.

Now they could provide military planners with much more accurate information. General Marshall noted at the time:

> Operations in the Pacific are largely guided by the information we obtain of Japanese deployments. We know their strength in various garrisons, the rations and other stores available to them, and what is of vast importance, we check their fleet movements and the movements of their convoys.[4]

Most of that information came from Arlington Hall, and Vernice was there to help manage it. When coded or ciphered messages arrived at Arlington Hall, Vernice and the other cryptographic aides and clerks first had to log in the "traffic" and index it. Then they had to remove the American encryption added by the sender at the radio interception station. Following that process, the intelligence could only be derived if the messages were decoded, decrypted, and translated. After the translations were drafted, their accuracy had to be rechecked before they were typed for reproduction. The typed translations had to be proofread for accuracy yet again before clerks and aides prepared the required number of copies. Finally, the messages had to be logged out as they were forwarded to the appropriate military intelligence offices. When messages were considered extremely urgent, they were forwarded by special courier or by special electronic cryptographic circuits.

Although early versions of International Business Machines (IBM) computers were used to help break codes and ciphers, most of the work was done by Vernice and other women using typewriters, carbon paper, mimeograph machines, and other more specialized equipment.

Like most new aides at Arlington Hall, Vernice began as a "sorter." When radio intercepts came in, she sorted the messages by their American-added intercept source code at the beginning of each message. What radio station had intercepted the message? She couldn't just look casually at the source codes because mistakes in reading them could cost lives. She had to really *see* the source code and sort the intercepts accurately.

After she proved her competence at quickly and accurately sorting intercepts, Vernice was given more challenging tasks looking for and accurately detecting repeating patterns in the sequences of numbers and letters in the intercepted messages. She had to learn to really see the code patterns in each message...not just look at what appeared to be random sequential shapes.

Based on individual skills, interests, and aptitudes, Vernice and the other women working at the big tables around her gradually sorted themselves into the many varied jobs required for all of the work that needed to be done. Some women became typists and keypunch operators; others were taught Japanese for translating duties; some were selected to attend lectures on the Japanese military organization, code structures, and decryption in preparation for becoming code breakers. Others built files on Japanese place-names and specific ships. Other women joined units at Arlington Hall Station working on the code systems of other countries—for example, Italy, Brazil, Egypt, Turkey, and Portugal.

Still other women at Arlington Hall encoded American messages sent out to other Americans and their Allies. These women constantly needed to be sure their messages did not become predictably repetitive or contain other cryptographic errors that would make them easier for the enemy to decode or decipher. Other Arlington Hall workers created fake traffic to distract and confuse enemy code breakers.

After she received the required security clearance, Vernice worked in the B Operations Building in which Japanese code systems were studied and intercepted messages were decrypted. The Japanese army code work, designated B-II, was divided among seven sections. Each section concentrated on a different aspect of the work such as incoming traffic analysis, Japanese water transport messages, Japanese army ground messages, and Japanese air unit messages. Every section was further divided into subsections each with specific responsibilities. Generally, an entire subsection physically occupied one or more of the long rectangular rooms called *wings* branching off the main corridor of each floor of the building.

**Cryptologists working in Arlington Hall subsection B-II-g-5 (Indicator keys), ca. 1944-45**

(National Security Agency photograph)

Until V-J Day, August 14, 1945, Vernice worked in wing 4 on the second floor in Section B-II-G, the Japanese Air Section. This section was responsible for the cryptanalysis and decrypting of intercepted messages from the Japanese military air units.

Specifically, she worked in subsection B-II-G-4, the Cribbing unit. She and her coworkers searched for patterns in the decoded messages, identified any stereotypical patterns, kept track of the message originators, and then keyed in any patterns and stereotypes they found in their analyses so they could be used as *cribs* to help break the Japanese code systems.[5] Section B-IV, the Situation Room, also shared a corner of the same wing. Its personnel used the decoded information from the B-II sections to study current military operations as well as economic and diplomatic developments. A few people from the Japanese Army Translation Branch, B-I, were also nearby.

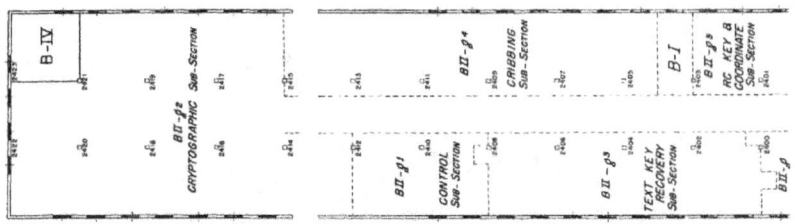

A portion of the wing 4 floor plan on the second floor of the B Operations Building, June, 1945. Vernice worked in the Cribbing Sub-section area.
(National Security Agency diagram)

Any message to be sent in code is first written in *plaintext*. Then it is coded into *ciphertext* to be sent out to its recipients. The intended recipients have the *key* (a sequence of letters and/or numbers) that allows them to translate the ciphertext back into plaintext. Vernice and her coworkers searched for *cribs*--the character sequences in ciphertext that might be coding for predictable or possibly repeating words or word patterns in coded messages. The cribs could then be tested by overlapping them onto other intercepted messages. If they passed the tests, the cribs could sometimes be used to deduce the encryption pattern or even determine the key for the code system being used. When used to break a code system, this strategy is called a *known-plaintext attack,* or KPA.

To search for possible cribs, Vernice consulted decoded Japanese Order of Battle reports, listings of Japanese officers, gazetteers, dictionaries, American battle summaries, weather reports, etc. as well as reams of decoded Japanese *Hatsu-chita* messages. (*Hatsu* is the where the message originated; *chita* is the destination of the message. For example, if an intercepted message was sent from Tokyo to Peleliu, Tokyo is *hatsu*; Peleliu is *chita*.) The volume of work depended on the number of decoded messages available for study, but usually the volume of messages was large. In June, 1945, the officer in charge of the air section stated that "approximately half of the available traffic" was being processed which he thought "represented an adequate sampling." At the same time, however, he stated "approximately 125 additional people are needed to fulfil the personnel requirements of this section."[6]

Cryptologists working in Arlington Hall subsection B-II-g-3 (Text keys), ca. 1944-45; Vernice worked in subsection B-II-g-4 (Cribbing) just across the aisle on the right-hand side of the photo.

(National Security Agency photograph)

Vernice and her coworkers worked at least eight hours a day, six days a week. They often worked ten or twelve hours a day and sometimes seven days a week. Section B-II-G operated twenty-four hours a day, with three shifts. Inadequate lighting made the night shift work particularly taxing until an adequate number of fluorescent desk lamps were requisitioned in June 1945.[7] Work was exciting, boring, stimulating, exhausting, important, and mind-numbingly detailed...and you couldn't talk about it.

All SSA personnel were required to attend repeated lectures on security and watch movies produced by Frank Capra (who would go on to direct *It's a Wonderful Life* in 1946) and others meant to inspire patriotic hard work in the war effort. High-level lecturers were brought in to educate the Arlington Hall workers on the geography of the war, the histories of the antagonists, the nature of the fighting in the European and Pacific theaters, and enemy sabotage efforts in America itself. For example, Major General Wilhelm D. Styer, chief of staff of the Army Service Forces, spoke on the topic "Fighting to Win." The assistant director of the Federal Bureau of Investigation, Hugh H. Clegg, presented a lecture entitled "The Enemy in Our Midst."[8]

"Silence Means Security" posters reminding employees to keep their mouths shut about their work hung on nearly every wall throughout Arlington Hall Station.[9] At the end of every workday, all trash cans would be emptied into large canvas containers. Then a supervisor would poke through all the rubbish with a wooden ruler to make sure no classified documents had slipped through.[10] All discarded classified documents were separated and burned.

**World War II–era poster**
(U.S. National Archives and Records Administration NSAID 515419)

By all accounts, most women at Arlington Hall Station had a passion for their work. They felt they were doing valuable, important, challenging work that was saving American lives. They were right. The work Vernice and the other Government Girls did at Arlington Hall was incredibly important in helping the Allies win the war.

These women provided the information enabling the U.S. Navy's submarines, surface ships, and planes to isolate Japan from its sources of raw materials; deprive Japanese soldiers of food, medicine, and ammunition; and prevent the delivery of spare parts for aircraft and other war weapons. Liza Mundy notes in her book *Code Girls*:

> At the end of the war, a U.S. naval report found that "more than two-thirds of the entire Japanese merchant marine and numerous warships, including some of every category, were sunk" as a result of the information derived from the code-breaking at Arlington Hall.[11]

Breaking the Japanese naval code also enabled the sinking of the mighty Japanese battleship *Yamato* at the beginning of the Okinawa campaign, which undoubtedly saved countless American lives.

Decryption and analysis of Japanese diplomatic, naval, army, and administrative codes—both Magic and Ultra—kept Allied leaders informed about changes in Japanese Army organization, the status of Japanese railroads, shipping losses, the numbers of Japanese battle casualties and illnesses, the sailing of Japanese troopships, the location of Japanese aircraft, the tactical and strategic goals of the Japanese army and navy, shifts in Japanese troop training techniques, diplomatic exchanges between Axis and collaboration leaders, and so on and so on and so on.

In his book *American Magic*, Ronald Lewin quotes the historian Thomas Carlyle to describe those many cryptologists working during the war on Ultra and Magic, including Vernice:

> The noble, silent men [and women], scattered here and there, each in his [or her] own department; silently thinking, silently working; whom no Morning Newspaper makes mention of! They are the salt of the earth. A country that has few or none of these is in a bad way.[12]

The excitement of learning and knowing what was going on out in the Pacific where Steve and the other "boys" were fighting kept Vernice working hard, long hours. In a way, it kept her close to Steve even though she could never specify what she was doing in the letters she wrote him. Later in her life, Vernice commented that she often thought she knew more about where he was in the Pacific and what he was up against than he knew himself.

*October 4, 1944*
*Dear Steve,*

*The letter you wrote as soon as you left Peleliu reached me today. The newspapers are only now reporting on the battle. It sounds like it was really horrible! People are shocked by the preliminary reports on casualties. I breathed a huge sigh of relief when I saw your letter in the mail because it meant you had survived. How are you feeling? Are they giving you time to rest and recover? Are they feeding you all right out there? Please let me know how you are, and send a photo if you can.*

*Work here is demanding. I never knew there could be so much work to do in one place ... and more every day. Most everyone is friendly, though, and when I hear the reports of what you and the other men have to endure, I don't complain about the long hours and the minor inconveniences of war time Washington...*

*Necie*

## 15
## Steve
## Pavuvu Revisited and En Route to Okinawa
## October 1944–March 1945

> Each night during the northward trip [to Okinawa] I had noticed the beautiful Southern Cross constellation slipping lower and lower on the starlit horizon. Finally, it disappeared. It was the only thing about the South and Central Pacific I would miss.
> —E. B. Sledge, *With the Old Breed*

*October 13, 1944*
*Dear Necie,*

There were lots of letters waiting for me when I got off the boat here. I've read them all once quickly, and now I'll go back and read them more slowly. I want to just take in everything that's normal and peaceful as much as I can. Besides, I'm pretty exhausted and have some recovering to do so reading the letters helps me relax and go to sleep.

The island isn't nearly as bad as it was when we were here before, but some things don't change. The land crabs and rats haven't disappeared. At least now there's screening in lots of areas to keep the insects out of our faces some of the time, and there's more fresh food and cold drinks. What really hit us when we got back, though, was the sight of thousands of new Marines on the island! As beaten up as we all are, we must have been a scary sight when we disembarked from the ships.

As soon as we got back on island, we each received six bottles of beer and a case of Coca-Cola. Some of the other officers spend a lot of their off time in the officers' club getting drunk, and I may join them later or maybe tomorrow, but now I need a little time alone. I guess you know me well enough to appreciate what I'm feeling...

*Steve*

Like most of the other exhausted and traumatized Peleliu veterans, Lieutenant Steve Lynn spent the first couple weeks back on Pavuvu resting and recovering. Conditions on the island had improved while they were away. They returned to find a network of hard coral-paved roads and a bona fide fifteen-acre parade ground built by Marine Corps engineers and Seabees. Their moldy, leaky army tents had been replaced with taut new tents equipped with wooden decks and electric lights. There were showers, laundries, and a well-stocked PX. A new Red Cross canteen was being built, staffed by female Red Cross workers; it was never a big draw perhaps because there were more than fifteen thousand men on the island and only six women, a rather lopsided ratio for mixed socializing.

**Artillerymen arriving back at Pavuvu from Peleliu greeted by the First Division band, October 1944**
(U.S. Marine Corps photograph, U.S. National Archives #127-GW-791)

The new screened mess halls provided a place where the men could read, write letters, play cards, eat, and talk without the incessant insect nuisance. Perhaps most appreciated by the returning Marines was the food. Occasional fresh meat, Coca-Cola, and ice cream were now available because refrigeration units had been brought onto the island. There was even a regular three-can-per-week beer ration. The men were happy to see the current movies and magazines as well as plenty of sports and recreation equipment, too.

The land crabs were still there, though. E. B. Sledge reported that he and his tent mates killed more than one hundred land crabs the first night they arrived as they went through the personal belongings they had left on the island when they departed for Peleliu.[1]

The really sad part about those first few weeks back on Pavuvu was having to realistically confront the beating the First Division had taken. Unless they had personally seen a fellow

Marine die on Peleliu, the survivors on Pavuvu could always hope wounded friends in their unit or other units might be waiting for them back on the island. All too often, they learned their friends just hadn't survived the battle. It was a tough reality to accept.

When their transports pulled up to the new steel pier on Pavuvu, the returning Marines were greeted by about forty-five hundred replacement Marines including many "green" recruits (including draftees) and "ninety-day-wonder" officers. Some Guadalcanal veterans were returning to the division after having served in the United States for a year, but the Peleliu veterans realized then and there that they would be the ones to play a large role in initiating the new replacements in the ways of the Old Breed. Just a few months before, they had been the untested Marines; now they were the "old men" with an average age in the very low twenties. This was especially true since many experienced noncommissioned officers with twenty-four months overseas were being rotated back to the States.

Their work was cut out for them, and they had to do it in a hurry. Operation Iceberg, the campaign to invade and occupy Okinawa and the surrounding islands, was already being planned, and the First Marine Division was slated to participate in just a few short months. Another 1,900 men and 45 officers arrived in November, and 2,500 men and 125 officers arrived in January 1945. They all needed to be absorbed into the depleted First Marine Division units and inculcated with the Old Breed tradition and esprit de corps. Two-thirds of the First Division Marines who would fight in the Okinawa campaign were veterans of at least one of the division's previous three Pacific campaigns—Guadalcanal, Cape Gloucester, and Peleliu; one-third were "green." All new replacements and the returning Guadalcanal veterans from the States had to be meshed with the Peleliu veterans to form a cohesive fighting force.

The First Division Marines were relieved to learn that Major General Pedro A. del Valle had replaced Major General William H. Rupertus as the division's commanding officer. There was and continues to be debate about General Rupertus's judgment during the battle of Peleliu, and many survivors had not forgotten his prediction of an engagement lasting only a few days.

Much credit for returning the mangled First Division to an elite fighting force in a short period is given to del Valle and his staff. General del Valle held the Legion of Merit for bravery on

Guadalcanal, where he had been the Eleventh Marines' commanding officer. He was a spit-and-polish kind of leader who placed great emphasis on divisional pride. While indigenous islanders were paid to do the labor around camp, the Marines concentrated on training and rebuilding unit esprit de corps.

**Major General Pedro A. del Valle, ca. 1944**
(U.S. Marine Corps photograph, U.S. National Archives)

By the time the Peleliu veterans returned to Pavuvu, the replacement Marines had already learned they would spend many hours on the newly built parade ground in close order drill. The "old" Marines joined them after a few weeks of recovery time. Sledge reported that during close order drill, the Marines dressed in "clean khakis which each man pressed under his mattress pad on his canvas bunk."[2] At many parades, medals and decorations were awarded for meritorious service at Cape Gloucester and Peleliu. It was a tremendous morale booster. The review for the Eleventh Marines' artillerymen was held on Pavuvu's parade ground on December 13, 1944. Lieutenant Lynn stood at attention with his battalion as General del Valle inspected the troops.

Commanding Officer Wilburt S. Brown reviews his regiment,
the Eleventh Marines, on Pavuvu, December 13, 1944
(U.S. Marine Corps photograph #1014147, U.S. National Archives #127-GW-1157)

In addition to regular close order drill of companies, battalions, and even full regiments, the entire division was soon engaged in a rigorous training schedule encompassing combat maneuvers, field problems, and practice landings. General del Valle emphasized coordinated tank/infantry training under supporting artillery fire, which would prove to be tremendously valuable on Okinawa.

Pavuvu's small size and deep mud still constrained training—especially for the artillery units. It wasn't uncommon to run field maneuvers through the bivouac area itself. Large scale exercises had to be held on Guadalcanal sixty miles away.

After a two-week recovery period in late October, Lieutenant Lynn continued his training as a forward and aerial battalion artillery observer. In his additional role as battalion motor transport officer, he trained and supervised enlisted men in the maintenance and logistical use of the First Battalion's vehicles and artillery equipment as well as in basic field artillery tactics.

As a field artillery–trained officer, Lieutenant Lynn trained new artillerymen—a role that was critical for the unit's success in the upcoming campaign. His First Division artillery regiment, the Eleventh Marines, would be working with the Sixth Division's artillery regiment, the Fifteenth Marines. Their activities would be coordinated with the Third Amphibious Corps' six artillery battalions and the U.S. Army's Twenty-fourth Army Corps artillery units.

All these artillery regiments had been depleted by recent engagements, and necessary replacement equipment was still being transported across the Pacific. Critically, too, there just were not enough field artillery–trained replacements available to fill in the gaps. Officers and enlisted men from seacoast defense and antiaircraft units were substituted into the field artillery units, and Lieutenant Lynn was one of the few trained field artillery officers available to teach them the basics of field artillery tactics and equipment operation.

In commenting on his regiment's personnel situation during the training period leading up to the Okinawa campaign when as a colonel he was the commanding officer of the Eleventh Marines', Major General Wilburt S. Brown later stated (in a letter dated October 10, 1954):

> The heavy casualties suffered at Peleliu, plus the rotation without immediate replacement of all officers and men with 30 months' service in the Pacific after that battle, posed a severe problem. Only one battalion commander remained of the four who went to Peleliu. There were only eight field officers in the regiment including myself and the (naval gunfire) officer. Fourteen captains with 24 months' Pacific service were allowed a month's leave plus travel time in the United States, and they left Pavuvu at the end of November and were not available for the training maneuver at first. I recall that the 4$^{th}$ Battalion (Lt Col L.F. Chapman, Jr.) had only 18 officers present including himself. He had no captains whatever. The other battalions and (regimental headquarters) were in very similar shape. The 3d Battalion had to be completely reorganized due to heavy casualties on Peleliu and was the only one with two field (grade) officers. But it had only about 20 officers of all ranks present.[3]

There were also new pieces of equipment Lieutenant Lynn needed to become familiar with and then train the other artillerymen to use. One was the LVT (A)-4, the Landing Vehicle Tracked (Armored), now equipped with a powerful 75 mm howitzer. It was also called an armored amtrac. It would be used for the first time on Okinawa. Because the LVT(A)-4 was essentially both a light tank and an artillery piece providing fire support for troops, its operators had to be taught field artillery methods, and the forward artillery observers needed to understand the machine's capabilities. Three hundred and sixty of the LVT(A)-4s were to lead another fourteen hundred unarmored LVTs and seven hundred DUKW amphibious trucks in the landings on Okinawa.[4]

Two other new artillery pieces supporting frontline infantry units were the M7 self-propelled 105 mm howitzer siege guns and the 4.5-inch rocket launchers fired by the so-called Buck Rogers Men. Additionally, the Marines would fight alongside the attached U.S. Army 4.2-inch mortar platoons. Lieutenant Lynn had to personally and quickly achieve proficiency with these new weapons so that he could in turn train the enlisted men who would fire them.

**LVT (A)–4, 1945**
(U.S. Marine Corps photograph, U.S. National Archives)

**Rocket launchers**
(U.S. Marine Corps photograph, U.S. National Archives)

Like everyone else during this training period, Lieutenant Lynn had to endure multiple inoculations—at least seven, including one for the plague that "burned like fire."[5] Everyone had sore arms; some had fevers from the shots.

The Marines on Pavuvu enjoyed a Corps-provided turkey dinner on Thanksgiving Day 1944. Lieutenant Lynn's battalion ate fifty-five large turkeys, fruitcake, California nuts, and candied almonds shipped directly to the island by one U.S. food distributor. Lieutenant Lynn received special holiday food packages from his mother, Necie, and Necie's mom. By then, he had recovered from the dysentery he'd picked up on Peleliu and could really enjoy the familiar food from home.

Picture sunburned, red-haired Steve leaning back in a chair after Thanksgiving dinner, smoking a cigarette and talking with his buddies. Because of the daytime tropical heat sometimes well over a hundred degrees, they're all shirtless and trying not to move any more than they have to. Maybe they're even nursing a cold beer or two as they talk about Thanksgiving at home and the food packages they received. The radio is on in the background. They'd pooled their resources and traded twelve quarts of liquor to get it from a Seabee. They just hope none of the vacuum tubes in the radio gives out. Some guys are talking about trading another quart of whiskey for a Seabee-made bed. The Seabees stretched strips of used tire inner tubes in both directions over wooden two-by-fours, creating a bed way more comfortable than the issued Marine field cots. As the sun sets, one of the guys suggests another game of poker to ward off the melancholy homesickness triggered by the holiday memories.

*December 22, 1944*
*Dear Necie,*

*Christmas packages are starting to arrive! Everyone has to open the ones with food in them right away or the ants will carry them away, so we're all gaining weight eating fruit cake, cookies, and fancy breads. It's not as good as being in your Mom's kitchen in Champaign where you get to eat them as soon as they're out of the oven, but I'm definitely not complaining. I'm saving the packages that aren't food for Christmas.*

*I've been busy every day trying to get the new artillerymen up to snuff. We haven't fired too much but I've been teaching a lot of artillery fundamentals and equipment operation. The greenhorns listen to the "veterans" pretty well. I guess we've earned a bit of respect by what we went through. There isn't a day that goes by that I don't think about some of the guys from our regiment killed on Peleliu. I guess I'll never know for sure why I wasn't one of them...*

*Steve*

Following orders, Lieutenant Lynn left his artillery battalion on December 16 and boarded LST 222 to travel the sixty miles to Guadalcanal. Arriving the same day, Lieutenant Lynn began more training as an aerial artillery observer. For the Okinawa operation, the Marine aerial artillery observers would not be temporarily assigned to a specific VMO unit, as Lieutenant Lynn had been assigned to VMO-3 at Peleliu. Instead, they would operate under the umbrella of the Third Amphibious Corps (also known as III Phib Corps, or III AC) and be assigned to one of the four VMO squadrons flying missions on any given day during the battle.

Initially, there were three VMO units at Okinawa: VMO-2, VMO-3, and VMO-6. VMO-7 began to transition into the battle late in the campaign. VMO-2 left two weeks after the invasion began and sat out the rest of the campaign on Saipan. Consequently, VMO-3 and VMO-6 would fly the majority of the observation missions over Okinawa.

Through December 1944 and January 1945, Lieutenant Lynn and the other Eleventh and Fifteenth Marine artillery spotters trained with the VMO-3 squadron on Guadalcanal. Lieutenant Lynn already knew the nine pilots in VMO-3; he had flown with them over Peleliu. All the VMO-3 planes surviving Peleliu had undergone extensive overhaul at Henderson Field, and new OY-1s had been shipped in to replace those lost in the battle. The unit's pilots and enlisted men had spent early November building a new airstrip at Tassafaronga, Guadalcanal. Then they resumed training with artillery observers from the Eleventh Marines, the Fifteenth Marines, and the Third Amphibious Corps Artillery units.

The Third Amphibious Corps Artillery commanders' goal was to provide three qualified air spotters per artillery battalion, and the training Lieutenant Lynn and the other air spotters underwent during this period was intensive.[6] It stressed uniformity in communication procedure because the spotters would share their information within the context of a large triservice (Army, Navy, Marine Corps) operation on Okinawa. Target Information Centers (TICs) were set up at every level from Tenth Army down to artillery battalion level. The TICs were designed "to provide a centralized target information and weapons assignment system responsive to both assigned targets and targets of opportunity."[7]

Liaison officers for artillery, air, and naval gunfire would also be aligned with target intelligence officers. Consequently, all of the artillery observers—both ground and aerial—needed to use the same terminology and sequence of information when calling "fire" in on targets.

Shortly after Lieutenant Lynn arrived on Guadalcanal on December 16, all Marine Corps artillery units held a series of combined field firing problems (simulated exercises) lasting from one to three days. He and the other aerial spotters "fired" the majority of missions during these rehearsals.

In addition to taking a one-week course on the identification of Japanese military installations, Lieutenant Lynn and every other III Phib Corps spotter was required to make two one-hour spotting flights every week over Sixth Marine Division training activities on Guadalcanal. They reported targets and "fired" simulated problems with a Fire Direction Center ground station.[8]

The spotters were also checked out in carrier-type aircraft and instructed in basic aerial gunnery in case battle conditions delayed the landing of the OY-1 aircraft on Okinawa's airfields. At Peleliu, Lieutenant Lynn had spotted from a Douglas SBD Dauntless for three days before the OY-1s could land on the airfield. Such an adjustment might be necessary again, depending on how the Okinawa landing played out.

Throughout this six-week training period, the IIIAC Artillery and the Eleventh and Fifteenth Marines worked closely together to coordinate their training programs. Colonel Frederick P. Henderson, who served on the IIIAC Artillery headquarters staff at the time, later explained (in a letter dated March 11, 1955), "Great care was given to ... the ability to rapidly mass fires of all available guns at any critical point."[9]

These artillery units all conducted another "combined problem" on Guadalcanal January 11–13 during which the majority of the firing missions were spotted by Lieutenant Lynn and the other aerial observers flown by the pilots of VMO-3. By the end of the training exercise, when a firing mission was called in, the Marines "were able to have all artillery present, laid, and ready to fire in an average of five minutes from the time it was reported."[10]

Training with VMO-3 on Guadalcanal would be Lieutenant Lynn's military focus through January 1945, but there was also time to relax with fellow Marine Corps officers. In his book *Pacific Time on Target: Memoirs of a Marine Artillery Officer, 1943–1945*, Christopher Donner shared what "down time" might have been like. Lieutenant Donner served as an Eleventh Marine forward ground observer embedded with the Seventh Marines at Okinawa.

All artillery officers were bivouacked together in "officer country." During December and January, Guadalcanal battle veterans and Peleliu veterans who had been given thirty-day leave in the States filtered back into the officer ranks. Officers who had gone through Reserve Officer Class and Field Artillery Class together reconnected and partied heartily. After rising early in the morning and training hard during the day, they spent several hours every evening in the bars. Donner reported "wildly enthusiastic" singing of "Waltzing Matilda" (the First Division's adopted song), "I've Got Tuppence," "Call Out the Army and the Navy," and other popular tunes. Hours and hours of poker and hot dice games and many rounds of the song "Alouette" filled in the gaps. Sometimes, fights broke out to release tension but they didn't last long. Colonel

"Big Foot" Brown, the commanding officer of the Eleventh Marines, didn't approve.[11]

Among some of the officers, there was great interest, too, in the musicals *Oklahoma!* (which had opened on Broadway in 1943) and *Porgy and Bess* (which was revived on Broadway in 1942). New Decca vinyl record albums of those musicals and the popular Benny Goodman and Glenn Miller bands found their way out to Guadalcanal and were listened to intently and repeatedly. The songs "Don't Sit under the Apple Tree (with Anyone Else but Me)" and "Wabash Cannonball" were among other musical favorites.

**Clarinetist Benny Goodman in the film *Stage Door Canteen*, 1943**
(Film screenshot, public domain, via Wikimedia Commons)

All the Marines stocked up on the newest Armed Service Edition "pocket books" (as illustrated earlier in chapter 9), reading them there and then trading them for new ones to have on hand during the upcoming battle.

Christmas 1944 was a big deal for Lieutenant Lynn and the other Marines training for the Okinawa campaign. The Corps provided a huge feast to celebrate the day:

> Turkey, tomato juice cocktail, green pea soup, giblet gravy, dressing, cranberry sauce, whipped potatoes, buttered peas and corn, apple pie, coffee, and fruitade.[12]

It was quite a change for everyone; both officers and enlisted men were usually issued only canned or dehydrated food rations. The only other days the Corps provided such a meal were November 10 (the Marine Corps' birthday), Thanksgiving, and New Year's Day.

On Christmas Day, too, every Marine received a mimeographed greeting signed by General del Valle:

> We are all conscious at this time of our loved ones at home, and all of us wish we could be with them. We can be with them in spirit by the exercise of our Christian faith on the anniversary of the birth of our Lord, and by resolving ... to work and fight harder than ever, to the end that our country's enemies may be quickly beaten, that peace may come on earth to men of good will, and that we may return to our loved ones in the assurance that we have done our duty.[13]

Back on Pavuvu, the Eleventh Marines fired an artillery salute at midnight on New Year's Eve.

Lieutenant Lynn's Officer Fitness Report for the period of October through December 1944 was stellar. Lieutenant Colonel R. W. Wallace, the commanding officer of his battalion, rated Lieutenant Lynn's performance as "excellent" or "very good" in all categories and noted he would "be glad to have him" under his command.

On January 29, 1945, Lieutenant Lynn boarded LST 945 at Guadalcanal and headed back to Pavuvu, where he was assigned to the Headquarters and Service Battery of the Eleventh Marines as a battalion aerial and forward observer. The VMO-3 personnel back on Guadalcanal had started to prepare their planes and equipment for transport to "the location of the impending operation," and the VMO-6 squadron had not yet arrived, so training flights for the observers ended in early February. Additionally, Lieutenant Lynn was needed to continue training the Eleventh Marine field artillerymen back on Pavuvu. They were preparing for two full-scale landing rehearsals on Guadalcanal with the other Marines and Army personnel in the area. The enlisted men of the VMO squadrons reported to attack-cargo ships after the planes and equipment were crated. They participated in the training maneuvers on Guadalcanal while the VMO-3 pilots stayed onshore back at the base.

While Lieutenant Lynn was back on Pavuvu during February, five VMO-3 pilots—including Lieutenant James Buckalew, with whom Lieutenant Lynn had first flown onto Peleliu—left the VMO-3 squadron to return home to the United States. They would be replaced with new pilots from VMO-1 and VMO-2 after the squadron's arrival in Ulithi. Lieutenant Lynn would have to meet these new pilots and learn to trust them over the skies of Okinawa.

At about the same time, all Marine Corps officers, including Lieutenant Lynn, received a book about the upcoming Okinawa operation. (Enlisted personnel were not officially told the destination until they were on their way to the island, but it wasn't a very well-kept secret.) The officers' book contained details about the landing, the ships taking part in the operation, how to treat captured civilians, the numerous poisonous snakes on the island including "the long, thick, dark snake called the habu," prevalent diseases on the island (lots of venereal disease and typhus but not much malaria), and so on.[14] It even included information about what curios were worth buying.[15]

Perhaps the only topic rivaling the time spent talking about the "habu" was the GI Bill of Rights, a law passed in 1944 to fund education and other benefits for World War II veterans. Many of the Marine Corps officers planned to go to college when the war was over … if they survived to go home.

**Deadly Okinawan habu snake being "milked" so an antivenom can be developed, 1945**
(U.S. Marine Corps photograph, U.S. National Archives)

For the period from January through March 1945, Lieutenant Colonel Wallace again rated Lieutenant Lynn highly in his Officer's Fitness Report, noting especially the "excellent" performance of his duties, physical fitness and military bearing, leadership abilities, intelligence, and loyalty.

On February 24, Lieutenant Lynn and five other Marine artillery officers on Pavuvu received orders directing them upon "competent authority" to proceed to Guadalcanal by "first available government transportation" and report to the commanding general, Third Amphibious Corps, for temporary duty as aerial observers. They had to wait a few days for transportation but reported for duty on Guadalcanal on March 3.

The aerial observers from the Eleventh Marines knew one another well. They had trained together as observers for their battalions on Pavuvu and Guadalcanal during the previous months. At Peleliu, Lieutenant S. Arthur Spiegel had been temporarily assigned from the First Battalion to VMO-3 along with Lieutenants Steve Lynn (First Battalion), Charlie Aldrich (Fourth Battalion), and Gene McDonald (Fourth Battalion). Captain Bob McClean was the reconnaissance officer for the Eleventh Marines' Third Battalion. Lieutenants Lynn, Aldrich, McDonald, and Frank McCalpin, had been in the same Field Artillery Class back at Quantico.

On March 4, Lieutenant Lynn was ordered with his five fellow artillery officers to fly via "first available government aircraft" to Ulithi atoll in the Caroline Islands. There they would "report to the Commander of Task Force 52.1 for water transportation to an orally designated destination."[16] They didn't leave until March 10, nearly a week later. They participated in daily one-hour communication drills designed to perfect communication procedure, but mostly they enjoyed free time on Guadalcanal.

On the same MAG 25 (Marine Aircraft Group 25) transport plane heading for Ulithi on March 10 were three of the VMO-3 pilots Lieutenant Lynn had flown with on Peleliu and trained with on Guadalcanal: Captain Wallace Slappey Jr., Lieutenant Jeremiah Riordon, and Lieutenant Laurence Stien. A fourth VMO-3 pilot on the flight, Captain Marion D. Boyer, had joined the squadron in late February. They had plenty of time to play cards and tell stories as they hopscotched across the Pacific Ocean. They flew about 1,060 miles the first day to spend the night on Manus in the Admiralty Islands north of Papua New Guinea. After traveling another 1,075 miles the second day, they spent the night on Peleliu before flying the remaining 400 miles to the Ulithi atoll on March 12. Consider the fact that a trip taking about six hours by air today took more than two days with two overnight stops in 1945.

During this same flight, Lieutenant Lynn had a chance to meet a few of the untested VMO-6 pilots he would fly with over Okinawa. VMO-6 had not arrived on Guadalcanal from San Diego until February 10, on the USS *Renville* (APA-227), so there had been no opportunity to get to know or train with its pilots and enlisted men. The unit had formed in November 1944 and trained at Quantico, Virginia, until December 26, when it left for San Diego. Upon its arrival on Guadalcanal, it was attached operationally to the Fifteenth Marines, the Sixth Marine Division's artillery regiment.

When they all arrived at Ulithi on March 12, Lieutenant Lynn and the other officers had five days before they were to report for assignment on the escort carriers. In total, Ulithi has only about 1.7 square miles of solid land spread out among forty small islets. The islets, though, enclose one of the largest deep-water lagoons in the world, which is what made it invaluable for staging the Okinawa armada.

The Ulithi atoll had been occupied by the United States in an unopposed operation during September 1944 as the battle for Peleliu raged. Within a month, the U.S. Navy began to build what became an immense floating naval base that could sustain naval operations throughout the western Pacific. The floating dry docks could lift a forty-five-thousand-ton battleship. Ships stationed there could distill water, supply metal alloys to fabricate any replacement part needed to repair a ship, repair optical equipment, refuel ships, make hundreds of gallons of ice cream, and bake thousands of loaves of bread every day—that is, do almost everything needed to sustain the Pacific Fleet in the Central Pacific campaign. By March 1945, it was said to be the world's largest naval facility. It had an estimated seven hundred ship capacity when it was first surveyed back in late September 1944 by the survey ship USS *Sumner*.[17] Fast carriers and their screening ships started using the anchorage in October 1944 after the indigenous Ulithians were persuaded to relocate to one of the islands in the southern part of the atoll. There the Ulithians were protected from U.S. personnel, who could not approach their island without permission. They were also provided with food, needed supplies, and medical care until the war ended.[18]

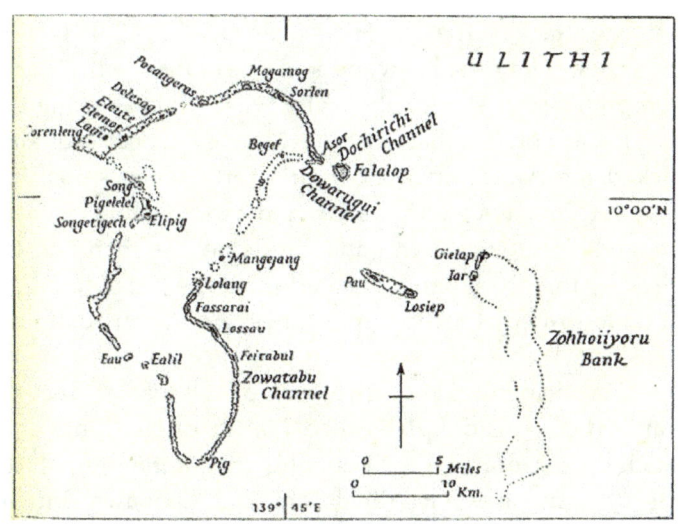
Ulithi atoll, 1943
(Public domain photograph of map in the University of Texas Map Library)

As they flew over the Ulithi lagoon and onto the airfield that day, Lieutenant Lynn and his companions would have been awed by the hundreds of ships anchored there in preparation for the upcoming Okinawa offensive—15 battleships, 29 carriers, 23 cruisers, and 106 destroyers, along with innumerable troopships, oilers, and supply ships. At its peak in preparation for the Okinawa campaign, there were 617 ships at anchor in the Ulithi lagoon in mid-March when Lieutenant Lynn flew overhead.[19]

Lieutenant Lynn's airplane landed on the twelve-hundred-foot runway built on the islet of Falalop. The runway ran the full width of the islet and then on another twenty feet past the natural shoreline. Seabees had lengthened and broadened the existing Japanese airstrip and built "coral taxiways, aprons, and hardstands."[20] Later that night, three Japanese kamikaze (suicide) planes appeared over Ulithi, and one plane struck that same runway. The other two crashed into the flight deck of the carrier USS *Randolph* (CV-15), tearing a one-hundred-foot hole in the ship, killing 35 crewmen, and wounding another 125. Amazingly, the *Randolph* was fully repaired within twenty-five days by U.S. Navy welders, carpenters, electricians, and other skilled workers at Ulithi.

The kamikaze attack on Ulithi was Lieutenant Lynn's first experience with Japan's "Divine Wind." Just after he returned to Pavuvu from Peleliu, Lieutenant Lynn had heard about the lone kamikaze attack on the USS *Franklin* on October 15, 1944. Like other Americans, he had wondered whether this seemingly incomprehensible suicidal behavior was a fluke. During the Battle of Leyte Gulf on October 25 and 26, however, scores of kamikazes attacked the American fleet, hitting forty-seven ships, including seven carriers. Four ships sank and twenty-three were heavily damaged. Lieutenant Lynn and everyone else then had to accept the reality that the Japanese had adopted the use of kamikazes as a workable strategy to stop the relentless American advance toward Japan.

Anticipating the invasion of Okinawa, the Japanese organized the suicidal plan called *Ten-Go,* or Heavenly Operation, to include not only *kikusui* (floating chrysanthemums), ten large raids of kamikazes on Allied forces at Okinawa, but also the sacrifice of Japan's remaining naval ships, including the mighty battleship *Yamato.* The goal was to destroy the American forces at Okinawa and force a negotiated settlement to the war, thus avoiding an invasion of Japan's home islands.

The Japanese had sixty-five airfields on Formosa and fifty-five airfields on Kyushu as well as several others in the immediate area of Okinawa from which they could launch *kikusui*. During the battle for Okinawa, they would successfully launch the ten major kamikaze raids on the American fleet and the airfields of Okinawa itself. The raids would claim hundreds of American lives and damage or destroy scores of ships and planes.

After finding temporary quarters at Ulithi, Lieutenant Lynn spent time at the recreation facilities built by the Seabees on Mog Mog islet. The facilities could accommodate one thousand officers and eight thousand enlisted men daily. Mog Mog had white sand beaches, a twelve-hundred-seat theater, and a five-hundred-seat chapel. Historian Samuel Morison, who was on Mog Mog at the time, described the "boogie-woogie" dance music, the crazy harmonica playing, and the inability to walk across the islet without kicking an empty beer can.[21] Gene Tunney, the former heavyweight boxing champion, had arrived to take charge of fleet recreation.[22] Free drinks at the crowded Crowley's Officer Bar and dances with the nurses from the three hospital ships *Solace, Relief,* and *Comfort* brightened the scene even more. (Sadly, six of those same nurses would die and four more would be wounded when a kamikaze plane blatantly violated the Geneva Convention and hit the brightly painted white hospital ship *Comfort* on April 28 as it steamed toward Saipan with battle casualties from Okinawa.)

**Ulithi beach, 1945**
(U.S. Navy photograph, U.S. National Archives)

At 4:00 p.m. on March 16, Lieutenant Lynn reported on board the USS *Admiral R. E. Coontz* (AP-122), a station (or administrative and service) ship in the fleet. He spent the night on the *Admiral R.E. Coontz*, and the next day boarded the escort carrier USS *Petrof Bay* (CVE-80). Five other Eleventh Marine artillery spotters accompanied him. They were joined on board by two VMO-6 pilots, First Lieutenant Thomas Alderson and Second Lieutenant Lester Bartels, who would fly two spotters onto the island of Okinawa. Two crated OY-1 planes were also loaded on board the *Petrof Bay* at Ulithi.

The *Petrof Bay*, called the "Mighty 80" by its crew, had dropped anchor at berth number 157 in the Ulithi anchorage on March 13, the day after Lieutenant Lynn arrived on the atoll.[23] Prior to arriving at Ulithi, the *Petrof Bay* had been at Guam, where it had picked up VC-93, a new squadron of U.S. Navy pilots to fly the new Wildcat fighters (FM-2s) and Avenger torpedo bombers (TBMs) hoisted aboard along with fuel oil and aviation supplies. By the time Lieutenant Lynn boarded the ship on March 16, the *Petrof Bay* had already been refueled and had a newly installed catapult system replacing one damaged in the Iwo Jima campaign.

USS *Petrof Bay* (CVE-80)
(U.S. Navy photograph)

At about the same time Lieutenant Lynn stepped aboard the ship, a "flash red," or bogey warning, triggered a general quarters alarm sending the ship's crew to their battle stations. A sighting of Japanese airplanes about fifteen miles out to sea triggered the alarm. The "flash red" only lasted about ten minutes, and the ship returned to normal operations. All the ships' crews were tense because of the kamikaze attacks earlier in the week on the USS *Randolph* and the Ulithi airstrip.

A few days after he boarded the USS *Petrof Bay*, Lieutenant Lynn heard the scuttlebutt about the March 18 kamikaze attack on the four separate carrier groups of Admiral Raymond Spruance's Task Force 58. At the time, the task force was carrying out a preinvasion military bombardment of Japanese ships near Japan and military installations on the Japanese home island, Kyushu. One-hundred-and-ninety-three Japanese planes, including sixty-nine kamikazes, damaged four U.S. fleet carriers in the task force. The USS *Franklin* almost sank, and the USS *Wasp* had to leave the battle for repairs. Carrier airmen, though, claimed to have destroyed 528 aircraft in the air and on the ground, and Japanese authorities later admitted the aircraft "losses were staggering."[24] These Japanese losses dramatically reduced the kamikaze participation through the first five days of the amphibious landings on Okinawa.

On March 21, the Japanese tried out a new suicide weapon on Task Force 58. They called it *ohka* (cherry blossom); the Americans called it *baka* (fool, or idiot). It was a forty-seven-hundred-pound bomb with rocket propulsion and a human pilot. It was carried under the belly of a "mother plane" and then cast off when it was near a target to be guided by its pilot in a suicide dive. The *ohka* would have been a devastating weapon because it was small and fast (up to 600 mph). Fortunately for the Allies, the weight of the *ohka* slowed down the bombers that carried them and the bombers' fighter escorts. The slow-flying planes became easy targets for the U.S. carrier-based Hellcat fighters.

Japanese *ohka* suicide bomb-plane found at Yontan Field, Okinawa, April 19, 1945
(U.S. Marine Corps photograph #120789, U.S. National Archives #127-GW-638)

By March 22, Lieutenant Lynn's fellow artillery observers and the VMO pilots had been dispersed among several escort carriers. The remaining seven VMO-6 pilots had been distributed among four other escort carriers (*Rudyard Bay, Tulagi, Saginaw Bay,* and *Chenango*). Several VMO-3 pilots had boarded the escort carriers *Fanshaw Bay, Makin Island, Lunga Point, Natoma Bay,* and *Sargent Bay* while their convoy was en route from Pavuvu to Ulithi. Captains Slappey and Boyer boarded the USS *Suwanee* (CVE-27) on March 22. Each of the crated OY-1 planes the pilot/observer teams would fly onto Okinawa had been carefully stored for safekeeping on the escort carriers with the pilots and observers on board.

On the *Petrof Bay*, Lieutenant Lynn and the other Marine officers spent their time exploring the ship, reading ASE pocket books, studying the officers' Okinawa briefing books, reviewing the information on the artillery units involved in the campaign, practicing communication procedures, and watching the growing and ever-changing armada in the harbor.

Ships arrived at and departed from Ulithi daily. Service ships refueled and replenished them all. The *Petrof Bay* itself continued to take on supplies, ammunition, and aviation fuel. Repair ships delivered and installed replacement parts. Admiral Marc Andrew "Pete" Mitscher's fast carriers and their accompanying service ships (Task Force 58) had left on March 14 to carry out the raids on Japanese airfields and naval vessels. The British Royal Navy ships that would be suppressing Japanese attacks from the islands between Okinawa and Formosa anchored in the lagoon's southern berths the same day. The minesweeper fleet tasked with clearing the transport shipping lanes and invasion routes to and around Okinawa left on March 19. (Leading up to landing day on April 1, the Task Force 52 minesweepers would clear twenty-five hundred square miles of ocean, discovering six enemy minefields and destroying 184 mines.) Fire support ships and their escorts straggled in from Iwo Jima needing immediate servicing before they would again fight in the battle for Okinawa with Task Force 54, the Gunfire and Covering Force. Additional fire support ships came into Ulithi from Pearl Harbor and the Solomon Islands. The Ulithi anchorage was a constantly changing panorama with hundreds of ships moving in orchestrated perpetual motion.

Finally, at 7:08 a.m. on March 21, the USS *Petrof Bay* departed Ulithi as part of Task Force 52, the Amphibious Support Force, commanded by Rear Admiral William H. P. "Spike" Blandy. More specifically, the ship was in Task Group 52.1, the Support Carrier Group, which included all the escort carriers with Marine pilots and artillery observers on board. The escort carriers provided the aircraft for antisubmarine patrols, combat air patrols, reconnaissance, and fire support for landing troops. Other ships in Task Force 52 included the all-important minesweepers, destroyer escorts and screens, and the ships supporting underwater demolition teams, gunboats, and mortar operations. The task force was only one element in "the largest military air, sea, and land operation ever conducted by America's military."[25] Nearly sixteen hundred ships would converge on Okinawa not only from Ulithi but also from Saipan, Guam, Tinian, the Philippines, Roi-Namur in the Kwajalein Atoll, Hawaii, and even the West Coast of the United States (San Francisco and Seattle).

USS *Shannon (DM-25)* on the move in the Ulithi anchorage, March 1945
(U.S. Navy photograph #80-G-K-3816, U. S. National Archives)

That same afternoon, the transports carrying the First Division Marines from Guadalcanal, Pavuvu, and Tulagi (in the Solomons) dropped anchor in the same berths formerly occupied by the escort carriers. They would leave Ulithi on March 27 in Task Force 53, the Northern Attack Force. Unfortunately, they would have to contend with the gale-force winds and heavy seas of a borderline typhoon as they made the trip northwest across the open Pacific Ocean toward Okinawa. Lieutenant Donner described the "gigantic waves" that tossed the Marines about like "twisting sticks" and "slapped against the huge metal rafts hung alongside" the transports.[26] At least the transports were new Navy ships in much better condition than those which had carried the First Division into its previous Pacific campaigns.[27]

About two hours after departing the Ulithi anchorage, Lieutenant Lynn heard the ship's loud gunnery exercises begin. Shortly afterward, a huge wave hit the ship, washing one of the ship's lieutenants overboard and injuring four other sailors. Sadly, the lieutenant who went overboard died. His body was recovered by the destroyer escort *Ulvert M. Moore* about thirty minutes after the incident. Lieutenant Lynn watched as the flag on the *Petrof Bay* was lowered to half-mast while the dead lieutenant was "buried at sea" from the *Ulvert M. Moore*. Heavy seas continued to buffet the *Petrof Bay* the next day as well.

On March 23, the destroyer USS *John D. Henley* (DD-553) came alongside with the mail, and the first U.S. Navy planes took off from the *Petrof Bay* flight deck for antisubmarine patrol. The very next day, March 24, a VC-93 plane crashed on the flight deck when the right-side landing gear folded, causing the plane to skid to a stop. Fortunately, no one was injured. A Japanese reconnaissance aircraft was spotted by a VC-93 plane the same morning. As the ship approached Okinawa, the number of combat air patrols and antisubmarine patrols taking off from the flight deck markedly increased. One can only imagine Lieutenant Lynn's thoughts at the time.

One pilot flying direct support patrols over Okinawa and the islands off its southwest coast was struck by antiaircraft fire on March 25, but the wounded pilot was able to land the plane back onto the *Petrof Bay*. Later the same day, general quarters was again sounded when enemy kamikaze planes were sighted. Lieutenant Lynn braced himself as the ship underwent a radical change in course and speed to avoid the planes, and the alert ended after an hour and a half. Other nearby escort carriers reported shooting down three planes in the kamikaze formation, and the escort carrier *Lunga Point* reported a VC-93 plane crash on its flight deck. (Two VMO-3 pilots and at least two Marine artillery spotters were quartered on the *Lunga Point* with two crated OY-1s.) Floating mines were sighted by the task force ships and sunk by gunfire. The action was definitely picking up.

The next day, March 26, Lieutenant Lynn watched the VC-93 pilots take off from the *Petrof Bay* to provide direct air support for the Allied landings on Kerama Retto, a group of islands west-southwest of Okinawa. This island group enclosed an ocean area Admiral Kelly Turner thought could be developed as a protected anchorage for both refueling and replenishing ammunition on naval ships near Okinawa. It could also provide a sheltered anchorage and runway space for the seaplanes needed for search and patrol missions, along with the seaplanes' tenders. Occupying these islands prior to the invasion of Okinawa itself was a bold move opposed by many planners, but the invasion and occupation by the U.S. Army's Seventy-Seventh Division went as planned, and the Kerama Retto "roadstead" area served the Navy well throughout the three-month Okinawa campaign.

The Kerama Retto occupation also eliminated the participation of 250 Japanese *maru-ni* motorboats in the battle for Okinawa. These small boats were discovered well hidden in camouflaged hangars and caves on the islands. Each one carried two 250-pound depth charges. They were designed to be driven close to a landing craft carrying American troops approaching the landing beaches. There the depth charges would be dropped, destroying the landing craft—and usually the *maru-ni* crew as well.

*Maru-ni* **suicide boats, the Japanese army version of the** *Shinyo* **suicide boat, Okinawa , June 1945** (U.S. Navy photograph)

On March 27, bogey alerts triggered three general quarters episodes on the *Petrof Bay*. Lieutenant Lynn was awakened by the first one at 3:40 a.m. Fortunately, no kamikazes approached the *Petrof Bay*. The Japanese were now sending out kamikazes periodically to attack the huge armada approaching Okinawa. Planes were also taking off from the *Petrof Bay* regularly as Lieutenant Lynn watched and waited for his role in the campaign to begin.

The first dead VC-93 crew member arrived back on board the *Petrof Bay* that same day. He was the turret gunner in a TBM that had received several antiaircraft hits over Okinawa while dropping propaganda leaflets. He was hit by shrapnel and died instantly. A VC-93 pilot of an FM-2 was able to survive by ditching his flak-damaged fighter in the ocean about three miles southeast of Okinawa after making a strafing run over the island. He was picked up by a nearby destroyer. Another FM-2 crash-landed on the *Petrof Bay*'s flight deck. Later in the afternoon, a brief burial-at-sea ceremony was held on the *Petrof Bay* for the crew member who had died in the morning. Lieutenant Lynn and the other Marine officers stood at attention as they watched the coffin slide into the sea.

Flight operations continued on March 28, and there were no resulting injuries or plane crashes. There was a fluke accident on board, though, when a ship's crewman accidentally hit the firing button on a set of .50-caliber machine guns being cleaned on the flight deck. At least one bullet went through the deck into the ship's mess hall on the deck below and wounded four crewmen. Lieutenant Lynn and his fellow Marine officers had to be wondering if there was any safe place on the ship.

Flight operations were limited on March 29 and 30 because of poor weather, but general quarters was sounded at least once on the twenty-ninth, and an airborne collision caused the first VC-93 pilot death on the thirtieth. The pilot of the other plane had to be extracted from his fighter but survived. On the last day before the land invasion of Okinawa began, March 31, an FM-2 crashed on the flight deck and slightly damaged the *Petrof Bay* itself.

Also on March 31, a Japanese plane dropped a bomb onto the flagship of Admiral Spruance, the cruiser USS *Indianapolis* (CA-35) off Okinawa's west coast. The ship had been raining eight-inch shells onto the landing beaches during the preinvasion bombardment. Nine *Indianapolis* crewmen were killed, and the ship slowly headed back to California for repairs. Admiral Spruance transferred his flag to the battleship USS *New Mexico* (BB-40) and carried on. (The *Indianapolis* would return to the western Pacific just a few months later, setting a speed record, to carry parts and enriched uranium to Tinian for the atomic bomb dubbed Little Boy, which would be dropped on the city of Hiroshima in August. The ship would be torpedoed four days after making the delivery and sink in less than twelve minutes after being hit. Tragically, out of a crew of 1,196, only 317 men survived.)

Lieutenant Lynn and the other men on the now damaged USS *Petrof Bay* watched the sun come out from behind the clouds during the late afternoon of March 31. The sea calmed as the sun sank lower in the sky. The sun set around 6:45 p.m., and the nearly full waning moon rose above the Pacific. After the day's flight operations ended, the *Petrof Bay* proceeded to its new operating area sixty miles east of Okinawa. The invading ground troops, including those in Lieutenant Lynn's First Battalion, Eleventh Marines, spent the evening close enough to the southwestern Okinawan beaches to hear the distant thunder of the ongoing naval bombardment and see the tracers and star shells leaving the battleships and destroyers nearer the shoreline. The intensive preinvasion bombardment had begun seven days earlier.

Like all the Marines anticipating L-Day, or Landing Day (or Love Day), on Easter morning, April 1, 1945, Lieutenant Lynn sharpened his knife yet again and cleaned his carbine carefully and repeatedly. He cleaned and loaded the Colt M1911 .45-caliber pistol he'd been issued to carry into battle. He checked his flying helmet and headphones. He studied the large plastic relief maps of the island and the officers' campaign book yet again. He reviewed the radio communication codes and procedures. He reviewed the anticipated artillery positions and each regiment's equipment. He packed and repacked his flight bag: field glasses, compass, artillery manuals, maps, ammunition, poncho, an extra canteen, first aid kit, pocket books, personal care kit, rations, hand grenades... He wrote letters to Necie and to his mother and dropped them off with the mail clerk on the ship.

Lieutenant Lynn didn't know for sure when he would be flying onto Okinawa, but he was as ready as he could be. He tried to get some sleep. He tried not to think about the horrors of Peleliu.

*March 31, 1945*
*Dear Necie,*

*This may be my last letter for a while. I'm still onboard ship but that will change soon, and I can't predict how soon I'll have the opportunity to write. One thing's for sure—I'll miss the Navy food. These guys really don't know how much better they have it than the Marines. Fresh vegetables ... ice cream ... I've been eating as much as I can because I know I'll be back to rations soon.*

*We've had good mail service, too. I received five of your letters in the last week, and they were all recently written. I really like hearing about your life in Washington. It's a great escape thinking about it.*

*Mother wrote, too. My brother Joe was wounded in France and is laid up in an English hospital. I guess it's not too serious, though. She didn't know if he'd go back to his Army unit or return to the States. It's awfully hard on her these days worrying about both of us in combat areas. Seeing what I've seen, I think it may be partly luck if you survive combat. I'm hoping Lady Luck is still with me...*

*Steve*

**WOUNDED IN FRANCE**

**Sgt. George W. Lynn**

Word has been received that Sgt. George W. Lynn has been wounded in France. He is in a hospital in England having been returned there by airplane. He was wounded in the right arm above the elbow.

Sgt. Lynn is the husband of Mrs. Jessie Lynn of Metropolis and the son of Mr. and Mrs. Stephen A. Lynn of Brookport. He received his basic training at Camp Blanding, Florida and his special training in weapon Infantryman at Camp Meade, Maryland.

Letters have been received from Sgt. Lynn since his return to England.

Local newspaper report of Steve's brother George Washington "Joe" Lynn's hospitalization in England
(Clipping in family collection)

# 16
## Vernice
## Arlington, Virginia, and Washington, DC
## November 1944–March 1945

> Washington's World War II Government Girls lived more boldly, bravely, publicly, and influentially than any fictional archetype.
>
> —Cindy Gueli,
> *Lipstick Brigade*

*November 1, 1944*
*Dear Steve,*

*I can only begin to imagine how different it is where you are than where I am right now. The trees are dropping their leaves, and it's getting colder. I wouldn't be surprised to wake up one morning and see frost on the roof of the house next door. My room is pretty warm though which is great because the drafty rooms at work are getting chilly. I think I'll try to get into town this Thursday night when the stores are open late to see if I can find a sweater I can pay for with the ration stamps I've saved up.*

*My exciting news is that I heard Bing Crosby sing at the Stage Door Canteen last night! One of the girls at work somehow found a way to get five of us in together to hear him. The place was jammed with people. It was almost impossible to move, but it was so exciting to be there, I didn't even mind. What a thrill! He's smooth as silk.*

*Not much to say about work except there's a lot of it. Last week, I worked 58 hours—almost beat my previous record...*

*Necie*


"Lipstick Brigade" ... "Government Girls" ... "g-girls" ... These terms heard by today's young women and certainly by women of the Gloria Steinem generation would sound cringeworthy, if not downright demeaning. But to the generation of women who flocked to Washington, DC, during World War II to do the work there weren't enough men to do—and work they could often do better than men—they were labels conveying patriotism and adventure.

Many of the nearly two hundred thousand young women who traveled to Washington to work for the government during

World War II had spent the previous ten years coping with Great Depression hardships. Some came from families whose farms and businesses had been lost. Others came from families whose very homes were taken away after mortgage payments couldn't be made. Except for a very few, most women who traveled to Washington understood economic hardship and frugality from firsthand experience.

Think about the fact, too, that Vernice Milleville and the other women who traveled to Washington after Pearl Harbor had rarely traveled far from their homes and family. From her central Illinois home in Champaign, Vernice had traveled only as far north as Milwaukee, Wisconsin, and only as far south as south-central Illinois, and those trips were taken with family members. Other women had never been outside their county. Their knowledge of the bigger world was based on what they had read, what they had heard on the radio, whom they had chanced to meet, or what they had studied in school. To get on a train alone and travel to Washington, DC, when the country was at war and the challenges ahead were unclear required special courage. It was a leap of faith in one's country and in one's self … and it was an adventure into an exciting world these women wanted to experience.

What did Vernice experience in the wartime Washington, DC, area after she settled into her new position at Arlington Hall Station in Arlington, Virginia, in 1944?

Working as many hours as she did—sometimes twelve hours a day—she often ate with coworkers and friends in the cafeteria on the Arlington Hall Station campus. Her personal food ration stamps were pooled with those of the other boarders to purchase shared food at the boardinghouse where she lived. It was probably the homeowner who waited in the long lines to purchase almost anything needed or desired in the crowded metropolitan area. Nearly everything was rationed, including meat, sugar, and clothing. To save a little money, Vernice often took a sandwich for lunch from "home" when she walked to work in the morning.

Many Government Girls formed close friendships and support groups. This seems to have been the rule rather than the exception for the female teams working at Arlington Hall, and Vernice was no exception. According to Betty Allan, who moved to Washington to work for the Signal Security Agency (SSA) after graduating from New York State Teachers' College, the women working at Arlington Hall developed a sense of belonging in a group doing important work. It kept them motivated and in good spirits.¹ Not being able to talk about their work with anyone else gave them a special identity within their own group and helped sustain a good attitude as they faced the day-to-day challenges of their work and their living conditions. In addition to encouragement, Vernice and her friends shared fashion tips, their limited clothes inventories, hairstyle ideas, and one another's company as they explored the Washington scene.

Work demands and material shortages didn't prevent Vernice and other Government Girls from having a good time in wartime Washington. Vernice used her camera frequently and kept some of the photos she took of friends she made, the men she knew, and the places she visited. They suggest she happily experienced the city described at the time as "the greatest goddam insane asylum of the universe."²

**Vernice, ca. 1944**
(Photograph in family collection)

When they could get a little time off work, Vernice and her SSA coworkers and friends—Peg, Libby, Betty Lou, Irene, Agnes, Bobbii, "Murphy," Mariana, Lili, and others—took buses across the Potomac and trolleys in Washington to explore the city and the surrounding area. Vernice later talked about visiting the city's monuments and other landmarks, and she kept her photos taken of Arlington National Cemetery, Mount Vernon and Washington's Tomb, the White House, and the Polish, Swiss, and Cuban embassies. Another photo in her collection catches her posing as she looks over the Potomac River.

The women also went to the flourishing motion picture theaters, cocktail lounges, and music clubs. Stores stayed open late on Thursday nights to accommodate the Lipstick Brigade. During the Christmas season, the stores were jammed with women who had saved their ration tickets to buy gifts for families they might not get to see over the holidays.

Washington, DC, overflowed with celebrities, international personalities, entertainers, and servicemen. When they could manage it, Vernice and her friends were in the crowds attending bond rallies and concerts hoping to see the Hollywood stars Hedy Lamarr, Frank Sinatra, James Cagney, Bing Crosby, Lucille Ball, Dick Powell, and comedians Abbott and Costello and the Marx Brothers. The Stage Door Canteen in Lafayette Square was a magnet for entertainers and their admirers. Describing Washington in 1945, Jesse Evans wrote:

> Its streets are a moving panorama of color, alive with the thousands of men and women in the uniform of our own country and those of our allies. It is now possible to see at midnight on its downtown thoroughfares more people than there were during the height of its pre-war days.[3]

Vernice felt comfortable in Washington. Unlike some Government Girls who quickly returned home after being overwhelmed by the city and their work schedules, she flourished. She met new people; she tried new things; she went out on the town. She met men and women from all over the country and the wider world.

Vernice had to be careful, though. She later told the story of having lunch with a Russian gentleman one day and being told the next morning by her SSA supervisor never to do it again because it was a security risk.[4] (It was very clear during the final years of the war that the Russians would not remain allies for long after the war ended.) When Vernice and her coworkers were out on the town, they had devised an agreed-upon "code" they would use when someone they met seemed too curious about their work. If one of the women said the code words, they would all leave together.

**Three of Vernice's SSA coworker-friends, 1944**
(Photographs in family collection)

**World War II–era "Be careful what you say *or write*" poster**
(Photograph from U.S. National Archives)

    Servicemen passed through the city constantly, either there on assignment or on leave before shipping out from nearby military installations. More than 365,000 servicemen stopped by United Service Organization clubs each month.[5] They and many Government Girls enjoyed the city's nightlife at the Capitol

Theatre, Lotus, Mayfair, Neptune Room, and Casino Royal. Photos taken by her friends capture Vernice happily sharing time with uniformed men she met—Bob, Johney, Jimmy, Rosey, Danny, Joe. Vernice sang along with everyone else, chatted with anybody and everybody around her, smoked cigarettes, drank, and danced. The photo of her nonuniformed, pipe-smoking friend Mel she later in her life notated with the phrase, "a long time ago."

**Vernice's friend Mel, 1945** (Photograph in family collection)

Area clubs, charities, churches, and relief agencies sponsored dances where Government Girls and servicemen could meet. A group called the Women's Battalion set up mixers and concerts at nearby military bases. Military bands played at the Sylvan Theater near the Washington Monument, and there were noontime concerts at the Treasury Building for those lucky enough to be able to get off work to hear them. There were even concerts on a floating barge in the Potomac River near the Lincoln Memorial featuring local musicians, the National Symphony Orchestra, big bands, and popular singer Frank Sinatra.

"Compared to today it was still a very puritan time," reminisced Joanne Lichty, a Treasury Department clerk.[6] Corinne Moyers, who worked at the Bureau of Yards and Docks, added, "I didn't even try to get involved with anybody because they were going to be here today and gone tomorrow."[7] With housing so limited and crowded, there was really nowhere for much sex, and the fact that there was not a significant increase in pregnancies in Washington, DC, during the war years tells the story in itself. Premarital sex was still taboo for most of the Government Girls working in town.

**Vernice (*far right*) and friends, early 1945**
(Photographs in family collection)

Many of the servicemen Vernice and the other women met asked the "girls" to write to them after they were shipped overseas. It wasn't uncommon for the Arlington Hall women to be pen pals with four, five, or even more men stationed overseas. It was fun, it was something to do, and it felt like they were helping the war effort by keeping up morale.[8] Sometimes both the men and the women would include small snapshots with their letters. Three photos Vernice kept are snapshots of servicemen smiling at her from foreign lands.

A November 1944 photo of a smiling naval officer named "Rosey" captures him standing among palm trees blowing in the wind along the seashore. Many days, more than one letter would be waiting for Necie in her boardinghouse mail basket.

**One of Vernice's pen pal snapshots, 1944**
(Photographs in family collection)

Vernice was still serious about Steve, though, and she often wore the U.S. Marine lapel pin he gave her in Champaign before he left for California and overseas. She later said when people saw it, she was given special treatment. Sometimes it even got her into the movies for free! Working where she did, she often knew where Steve was or quite a bit about where he was going before he did. Abiding by her secrecy oath, she never told anyone that part of the story when talking about "her" Marine.

As the steamy summer weather slowly gave way to cooler autumn weather in 1944, the code breakers working in Buildings A and B breathed a sigh of relief. By November, however, the weather started to turn cold, and the uninsulated buildings became chilly. In an era when women did not wear long pants, staying warm became the new challenge. Ice-cold Coca-Cola gave way to piping hot coffee, and it wasn't unusual as the winter weather intensified for the women to keep their coats on as they worked

**Several of Vernice's SSA coworker-friends, 1945**
(Photographs taken by Vernice in family collection)

In December 1944, Vernice moved to 2811 Twelfth Street South in Arlington. It was a bit farther away in the Columbia Heights neighborhood but near a bus line Vernice could take to work if she didn't want to walk. Built in 1940, the two-story red brick house on Twelfth Street had three bedrooms and four bathrooms---obviously built to accommodate boarders with some degree of privacy and comfort. (The house is still there, but the red brick has been painted grayish-blue, and a studio has been built in back.) Were the other boarders working for the SSA? Probably. Security was the number one priority. Vernice was even told to walk home by a different route every day so nobody would follow her.

**Vernice's SSA coworker-friend Betty Lou, ca. 1945**
(Photograph in family collection)

Vernice was able to get back to Illinois for a short visit in December 1944, but she couldn't tell anyone about her work. Nobody in Illinois really knew (or would ever know) what she was doing—some kind of low-level secretarial work, they supposed. Her family and hometown friends didn't know Vernice was secretly decoding Japanese army intercepts for the SSA at Arlington Hall Station. It was a pleasure, though, for Vernice to play with her niece, Margaret Ann, and her new baby nephew, Stephen Paul, children of her sister Norma Wilfong. When Norma was there to play the piano, her family spent time together in the evening singing late into the night. One time, they sang so late that a neighbor called the police, and they had to agree to quit by midnight. Her mother and father must have loved having them all there.

The number of coded intercepts flooding into Arlington Hall Station came in waves as military operations overseas ebbed and flowed. Thousands of Ultra and Purple messages were received every day, and it was nearly impossible to decode them all, even though that was the goal. When the traffic was exceptionally high, Vernice and the other Arlington Hall personnel worked very long hours. As American sailors, soldiers, and Marines fought their way through the Philippines and Iwo Jima in late 1944 and early 1945, they captured codebooks left behind by the Japanese. The codebooks would be sent immediately to Arlington Hall Station, where they were studied and incorporated into the decrypting work.

When Steve returned to Pavuvu from Peleliu, Vernice and the other women at Arlington Hall were already enmeshed in decoding radio intercepts concerning the Japanese preparations for the anticipated Okinawa operation. Vernice knew Steve would be fighting there. The work she was doing had to be done quickly and accurately. Steve's life and the lives of many others depended on it.

Apparently, Vernice did do her job quickly and well. Her first Report of Efficiency Rating for the period July through December 31, 1944, was "Very Good," with outstanding marks for skill in the application of techniques and procedures, accuracy of operations, ability to organize work, cooperativeness, and dependability. She was doing her part for the war effort working the required forty-eight hours a week plus an average of another eight hours a week overtime. She maintained the high quality of her work through the beginning of 1945, as indicated by her second Report of Efficiency Rating for the period January 1 through March 31, 1945. War Department payroll records indicate she was also contributing nearly 11 percent of her gross earnings for the purchase of War Savings Bonds.

There is no doubt that when time allowed, Vernice took the opportunity to experience the unique world of wartime Washington. However, while Steve was training on Pavuvu and Guadalcanal for the largest battle of the Pacific war, Vernice was spending most of her time following events in the Pacific and fighting the war in Washington as a Government Girl just like Wonder Woman in the Lipstick Brigade.

*February 1, 1945*
*Dear Stevie,*

*We had a big snowfall today! I walked home with Lib and Bobbii and we threw snowballs at each other. The snow-covered trees are beautiful. Even though it was cold, we walked home slowly taking it all in. People say it melts more quickly around here than it does in Illinois so I wanted to see it all before it's gone.*

*I got your letter about your Christmas dinner and your training regimen. It sounds like you have so much to learn before you head out again. It must be really nice to be meeting up again with guys you met in training back in the States, though. Like old times ... in a way.*

*Lots of work here, too, but I had the chance to see the movie "Arsenic and Old Lace" starring Cary Grant last week. Really funny even though the idea of two old ladies killing old men and burying them in the basement doesn't seem like it should be. Jean Adair and Josephine Hull played the sisters just as they did in the Broadway play. Can't wait for the day when we can go to the movies together, Stevie.*

*Take care of yourself. I'm already looking forward to your next letter ...*

*Necie*

# 17
## Steve
## Okinawa
## April–June 1945

> There are few great men. There are only great challenges,
> which ordinary men are forced by circumstances to meet.
> —Fleet Admiral William Halsey, U.S. Navy

> If there was any group of indispensable officers in IIIAC
> [Third Amphibious Corps] Artillery on Okinawa, it was our
> air spotters ... the courage and daring of our AOSs [aerial
> observers] and the VMO [Marine observation squadron] pilots
> was an outstanding feature of the campaign.
> —Lt. Col. Frederick P. Henderson, USMC, G-3, III AC Artillery

Operation Iceberg was a huge and complicated campaign. The main amphibious landings onto the island of Okinawa itself began on Easter Sunday, April 1, 1945. While units of the Second Marine Division feinted a mock invasion onto beaches on the eastern side of the island, the infantry regiments of the First and Sixth Marine Divisions and two divisions of the U.S. Army's Twenty-Fourth Corps, the Ninety-Sixth and the Seventh, landed on the Hagushi beaches on the western side of the island. The U.S. Army's Seventy-Seventh Division was still finishing up the Kerama Retto operation west of the island, and the Twenty-Seventh Division was being held in reserve aboard ships offshore. Including rear echelon support troops, the Tenth Army numbered over 548,000 American troops and was led by Lieutenant General Simon Bolivar Buckner Jr.[1] The nearly 183,000 amphibious infantry ground units would bear the brunt of fighting the 110,000 well-led, well-positioned troops of the Imperial Japanese Army's Thirty-Second Army led by Lieutenant General Mitsuru Ushijima. Knowing how tough the fighting had been in the previous campaigns of Peleliu, Saipan, Iwo Jima, and the Philippines, everyone in the U.S. forces anticipated that the landings on Okinawa, only 375 miles south of the Japanese home islands, would be horrific.

It didn't turn out that way. What the Americans didn't know was that General Ushijima and his fellow combat commanders, General Isamu Cho and Colonel Hiromichi Yahara, had made the tactical decision to cede the western beaches and two airfields closest to the beaches to the invading American forces. The

Japanese chose instead to force a costly battle of attrition (a *jikusen*) by developing and then defending elaborate coral and concrete defensive positions within the limestone walls of the ridges running east and west on the southern third of the island. Their goal was to hold each defensive line as long as possible and then retreat to the next defensive line. They knew they couldn't win in the end, but they would make the Americans pay as high a price as possible and buy time for the home islands to maximize their defenses. They hoped the high cost in American lives on Okinawa would force a negotiated end to the war, thus avoiding an invasion of Japan itself.

**Location of Okinawa, 1945**
(Map first printed in *War in the Western Pacific* by Eric Hammel, reproduced by permission)

The role of the fighter and bomber pilots aboard the escort carrier USS *Petrof Bay* (CVE-80) was to support the landings of the Third Amphibious Corps (the U.S. Marine Corps components of the Tenth Army under the command of Major General Roy Geiger) on the western beaches of the island. The flying and landing conditions were excellent on Okinawa's D-Day, also known as L-

Day---: partly cloudy skies, calm seas, negligible surf on the landing beaches, moderate offshore winds, temperatures in the mid-70s°F. First Lieutenant Stephen A. Lynn Jr. watched as the planes catapulted off the flight deck beginning early in the morning, and he listened to the scuttlebutt passed among the sailors as the day progressed. It had all gone surprisingly well. "Where are the Japanese?" they wondered. By late evening, sixty thousand U.S. Marines and U.S. Army soldiers were on Okinawa, and two of the island's airfields, Yontan and Kadena, had been taken. All divisional artillery landed early, and by nightfall, direct support artillery battalions were in position.[2] The infantry units of the First Marine Division had crossed nearly all the way to the east side of the island by the end of the day.

Okinawa, April 1945
(First printed in *War in the Western Pacific* by Eric Hammel, reproduced by permission)

By the end of the first day, too, the weather turned very cool—especially cool for men who had recently spent so much time in the tropics. The temperature would not rise above 60°F for the next few days, and the men were issued new wool and gabardine field jackets to warm up. It was quite a testimony to the stellar supply logistics on the first day after the landing. Many of the men appreciated the change from the tropical heat, insects, and disease they had been dealing with for months or years in the South Pacific.

The Japanese had left local Okinawans pressed into service to defend the Yontan Airfield, where Lieutenant Lynn would land, and the Kadena airfield only three miles away, but the Okinawans offered only light resistance. They quickly abandoned the airfields, leaving them ripe for easy taking by units of the Sixth Marine Division and the Seventh Army Division, respectively. By the end of that first day, bulldozers were clearing destroyed Japanese planes, supplies, and fake dummy soldiers, tanks, and airplanes made of sticks and cloth from the landing strips. The enemy antiaircraft emplacements at Yontan even contained fake guns.

**Fake Japanese plane at Yontan Airfield, April 1, 1945**
(U.S. Marine Corps photograph #116373, U.S. National Archives #127-GR-103)

The VMO-3 squadron's executive officer, Lieutenant Robert Jackson, and the unit's aviation ground officer, Lieutenant S. L. Fraser, landed on Yellow Beach One with the invading Marines at about 11:00 a.m.[3] As soon as Yontan was nearly secured by Sixth Division Marines, both officers went to the airfield to reconnoiter. Then, Lieutenant Jackson left Yontan to make contact with the First Marine Division headquarters while Lieutenant Fraser began the process of preparing the squadron area and landing strip. The only undemolished buildings on the strip were used to begin operations. The stage was set for Lieutenant Lynn's participation in the battle.

The sun rose at 6:15 a.m. on April 2, and again the weather was perfect for flight operations. Early in the morning, aviation machinist mates on board the *Petrof Bay* began to assemble the two small Stinson OY-1 Sentinel "Grasshopper" aircraft on the carrier's hangar deck under the watchful and inspecting eyes of Lieutenant Lynn, his friend and fellow observer First Lieutenant Charles Aldrich, and the two VMO-6 pilots, First Lieutenant Thomas Alderson and Second Lieutenant Lester E. Bartels.[4] As the Grasshoppers were being assembled and the four Marine Corps officers waited and watched, seven Wildcat fighters and six Grumman TBF Avenger torpedo bombers were launched from the flight deck to support the troops on Okinawa.

From Okinawa itself, Lieutenant Jackson returned early in the morning to the USS *Carroll* (APA-28), where the rest of the VMO-3 squadron gear was being unloaded and the ground crew was getting ready to depart for the beaches. In the meantime, Lieutenant Fraser secured a bulldozer from the beach and leveled one short taxi strip on Yontan Airfield. The enlisted men of the VMO-6 ground crew disembarked from the USS *Caswell* (AKA-72) and arrived at Yontan midday to begin setting up for air operations and digging in shelters. They were joined by the ground crew of VMO-3 early the next day, April 3.

While the Yontan airstrip was being cleared and leveled on April 2, the other four Marine artillery spotters on board the *Petrof Bay* were transferred by destroyer escort to two other escort carriers nearby. Two of them were transferred to the USS *Sargent Bay* (CVE-83). Aboard the ship, they joined two VMO-2 pilots, Lieutenants Richard Case and George Armstrong, who were closely watching the assembly of their VMO-3 OY-1s on the *Sargent Bay*'s hangar deck. The four of them flew off the *Sargent Bay* to Yontan Field around 2:00 p.m. and were there to greet Lieutenant Lynn later in the day. Because of the unavailability of adequate radio equipment, Lieutenant Case landed on the wrong airstrip and ground-looped the plane into a bomb crater. The OY-1 was rendered unrepairable and had to be "struck" from further operations. Fortunately, neither he nor the artillery observer was injured in the mishap. In the official VMO-2 war diary, Lieutenant Frank Milliken is credited with flying the first OY-1 onto the Yontan airfield from the escort carrier USS *Natoma Bay* (CVW-62) just a bit earlier than Lieutenants Case and Armstrong, but there seems to be some debate about who really landed first.⁵

**OY-1 Grasshopper flying off one of the escort carriers, April 2, 1945**
(U.S. Marine Corps photograph, U.S. National Archives)

At about 3:30 p.m. on April 2, the two OY-1 Grasshoppers took off from the *Petrof Bay*. The first to take off was piloted by Lieutenant Alderson, with Lieutenant Aldrich sitting in the backseat. The second Grasshopper was piloted by Lieutenant Bartels, with Lieutenant Lynn in the backseat. It was the first flying the two VMO-6 pilots had done since leaving the United States a few months earlier. The unit history reported, "Happily, the OY's short take-off characteristics and the CVE's ability to provide optimum launch conditions made for an uneventful operation."⁶ Riding along with "rusty" pilots they hadn't flown with before, Lieutenants Lynn and Aldrich were pretty happy about the "uneventful operation," too.

The two remaining spotters on the *Petrof Bay* were transferred to the USS *Tulagi* (CVE-72) via the destroyer USS *Evans* (DD 552). One of them flew off the *Tulagi* with another VMO-6 pilot, Lieutenant James Calhoun, at 3:24 p.m. the same day. The remaining Marine artillery spotter was transferred yet again from the *Tulagi* via the destroyer USS *Boyd* (DD-554) to a third escort carrier in the area. He would land at Yontan Airfield the next day.

Some of the OY-1 Grasshopper pilots on Okinawa (*from left*): 2nd Lt. Donald H. Rusling, Capt. Donald R. Garrett, 2nd Lt. Lester E. Bartels (who flew Lt. Lynn onto Yontan Airfield on April 2, 1945), and 2nd Lt. Glenn R. Hunter, May 6, 1945
(U.S. Marine Corps photograph #121039, U.S. National Archives #127-GR-95)

When they arrived at Yontan Airfield, Lieutenant Lynn and the other Marine officers and enlisted men of the observation squadrons found the field littered with wrecked Japanese aircraft. Most airfield buildings had also been demolished by the prelanding American air bombardments. Bombers and fighters from the escort carriers had destroyed all the Japanese planes there and at the Kadena Airfield during daylight hours on March 28, but the Japanese flew about thirty more planes onto Yontan during that same night. Noticed by an alert pilot from the USS *Makin Island* (CVE-93) the next morning, the newly arrived enemy planes were destroyed that afternoon. The escort carrier pilots also destroyed a large active underground installation just north of the field itself.

**First group of Grasshoppers to land at Yontan Airfield, April 2, 1945
(Lt. Lynn landed in one of these planes)** (U.S. Marine Corps photograph #117769,
U.S. National Archives #127-GW-529)

After he landed, Lieutenant Lynn undoubtedly heard the story of the Japanese pilot who landed his plane at Yontan not knowing the airfield was held by the Americans. The Japanese pilot's amazement was short-lived. Lieutenant Lynn might have heard, too, that two hours after he and Lieutenant Bartels took off from the *Petrof Bay*, an American FM-2 Wildcat crashed into the second barrier on the flight deck of the ship, totaling the plane.[7] Accompanied by two destroyers, the *Petrof Bay* left in the evening for anchorage at Kerama Retto. The ship needed repair, but the crew was nervous about heading to Kerama Retto. Because the anchorage had become the target area of several random attacks from Japanese suicide planes, it had become known as "kamikaze corner." The *Petrof Bay* would be awarded five battle stars for its service in the Pacific.

All remaining pilot/observer teams for both observation squadrons arrived on April 3, and artillery spotting operations began on April 4. Again, one of the VMO-3 aircraft taxied into a bomb crater after a radio miscommunication, but the damage to the plane was minor.

Radio shortages and malfunctions continued to dog the squadrons throughout April. The high humidity fouled the components of the RCA radio transmitters and receivers. They were eventually replaced by SCR-610 (Signal Corps Radio) units, which seemed to hold up better in the wet environmental conditions.

The VMO-3 and VMO-6 ground crews worked diligently with Army and Marine engineers and the Navy's Seabees throughout the next few days to make the Yontan and Kadena airfields serviceable for larger aircraft. They stopped only during enemy bombing and strafing runs. They also dodged the "friendly" antiaircraft fire from ships offshore, which killed and injured several soldiers and Marines on the two fields. Amid the organized mayhem, the VMO pilots, Lieutenant Lynn, and the other observers continued to take off and land in their small OY-1s.

Both fields were ready for fighters to land by the end of the day April 4 and for medium bombers by April 8. As the kamikaze attacks intensified over the fleet supporting the ground troops with naval gunfire, the island-based aviation became essential. The Marine F4U Corsairs flew onto the fields from the escort carriers offshore and immediately began Combat Air Patrols (CAP) over the fleet. Lieutenant Lynn and the observation squadron pilots now shared the runways with the faster and larger fighter aircraft.

**F4U Corsair at Yontan, April 6, 1945**
(U.S. Marine Corps photograph)

The official War Diaries of Marine Observation Three (VMO-3) written by Captain Wallace J. Slappey Jr. provide the most detail about the activities of the joint pilot/aerial observer teams during the Okinawa campaign. Beginning April 4, full squadron operations began. Lieutenant Laurence Stien took the unit's first plane up to do artillery spotting and immediately received small arms fire as it successfully called artillery fire onto an enemy troop concentration on a bridge. The second plane up also received fire that tore the vertical and horizontal stabilizer. Another plane was damaged when it received a rifle ball in the engine. In fact, only one plane that first day did not receive enemy fire. That plane was flying a reconnaissance mission over the Motobu Peninsula to the north, where Sixth Marine Division infantry troops were going to be heading next.

To add to the day's excitement, a TBF crashed on takeoff from the Yontan Airfield, and the VMO-3 ambulance and crash truck serviced the accident. An F4U fighter plane heading onto the field from the escort carrier *Bunker Hill* crashed upon landing. Again, the VMO-3 ambulance and crash truck serviced the accident, and the squadron's corpsman, B. J. Dugas, probably saved the life of the pilot.

The VMO squadrons were hybrids in the sense that operationally they were attached to the artillery units of the Third Amphibious Corps and the First and Sixth Marine Divisions, but administratively they had to live and work within the realm of the Marine Air Wing based at Yontan Airfield. Unfortunately, the specific needs of the VMO squadrons were not adequately taken into consideration by either entity. For example, there was no specific plan in effect for the automatic provision of aircraft supplies and spares. Since they were the only aviation units flying OY-1s, parts were hard to come by. The VMO mechanics often had to rely on scavenged parts from stricken U.S. planes and on parts from the Japanese planes that littered the site to repair the damage to the OY-1s caused by enemy ground fire.

Additionally, no "messing equipment" or personnel had been provided for the observation squadrons. They were too far from the Marine division units to which they were attached to travel there for meals without impairing squadron efficiency, and the air wing units at Yontan were reluctant to feed the officers and enlisted men of the observation squadrons because of their own shortages. By the end of April, the VMOs had, with "considerable difficulty," borrowed some mess equipment of their own. However, as Captain Donald Garrett reported in the April war diary of VMO-6, "The squadron was forced to use enlisted men who have work necessary to the maintenance of aircraft for cooking and mess duty to the detriment of our aircraft and flight operations."

By April 5, the VMO-3 and VMO-6 squadrons were collectively providing artillery spotting for fifteen artillery battalions rather than the four battalions each was organized to serve. VMO-3 was operationally attached to the First Marine Division's four artillery battalions (the Eleventh Marines); VMO-6 to the Sixth Marine Division's four artillery battalions (the Fifteenth Marines). Now they were also flying for all the artillery units of the Third Amphibious Corps, which included six Marine Corps battalions and one Army battalion. The observation squadron that had been scheduled to spot for the Third Amphibious Corps artillery, VMO-7, did not arrive from the United States for the beginning of the campaign, and it didn't become fully operational until June 1. Army artillery units had their own small cadre of pilots and observers flying in Piper L-4 aircraft. In the large, complex Operation Iceberg, these two small squadrons of Marine OY-1 pilots and their accompanying aerial observers had a lot of weight to carry for the Third Amphibious Corps. In one postoperational analysis, the inadequate number of aerial observation planes was noted:

> Although both pilots and observers were experienced and turned in excellent jobs in spite of heavy antiaircraft fire, there simply were not enough planes to do the work properly. It was generally impossible to keep one plane on station with one on call at Yontan Field, whereas ideally two or even three planes should have been on station during the daylight hours.[8]

There would be very little rest for Lieutenant Lynn and his fellow aerial observers or for the pilots of VMO-3 and VMO-6 for the duration of the three-month campaign. As noted earlier, Lieutenant Lynn knew many of the other observers personally. He had attended Field Artillery Class (FAC) in Quantico with at least six of them: Clarence J. Echterling (attached to the Sixth 155 mm Howitzer Battalion), Jim Frink (Fifteenth Marines, Sixth Marine Division), Bill Lynch (Ninth 155 mm Gun Battalion), Gene McDonald (Fourth Battalion, Eleventh Marines), Allen Scher (Fifteenth Marines, Sixth Marine Division), and, of course, Charlie Aldrich (Fourth Battalion, Eleventh Marines). One of Lieutenant Lynn's FAC classmates would lose his life fighting for the island.

All in all, there were thirty-three battalions of American corps and divisional artillery (including both Army and Marine units), or 396 pieces ranging from 8-inch to 75 mm howitzers, on Okinawa.[9] It was the responsibility of the aerial pilots and spotters to fly low over enemy positions seeking targets for the artillery to fire upon. With so many Army and Marine Corps artillery units on the island, and with additional fire coming from naval gunships as well as Marine and U.S. Navy warplanes, coordination was complicated and critical. Lieutenant Lynn and the other aerial spotters called in target coordinates to the Target Information Centers (TICs) maintained near the fire direction center of each corps and artillery headquarters.[10] On a daily basis, they were assigned specific TICs with which to communicate. After calling in the target coordinates, the pilot would fly their OY-1 to a higher elevation to avoid being hit by the gun barrages and to reduce the effects of bombardment concussion on their small planes. After the artillery fired onto the targets, the pilot/observer teams would return to low altitude over the target to evaluate the effectiveness of the barrage. They then reported their observations back to the TIC.

On April 6, four days after Lieutenant Lynn landed on Yontan, the Japanese launched *kikusui* 1, a large raid of 355 kamikazes targeting both the fighter planes on the carrier decks of Task Force 58 and the Yontan and Kadena airfields. The kamikazes were challenged by American fighters in the air, but their attack still lasted for five hours. Five American ships were sunk, including two ammunition ships supplying ordnance for the Tenth Army. Eighteen other ships—including destroyers, destroyer-escorts, and mine vessels—were also damaged. The Japanese lost 135 planes. On the same day, the mighty Japanese battleship *Yamato* began its suicide mission, sailing toward Okinawa accompanied by a light cruiser and eight destroyers. The *Yamato* had been provided with only enough fuel for a one-way trip to the battle zone, where it was expected to cause major damage to the American fleet.[11]

Lieutenant Lynn experienced three air raids on Yontan Airfield that morning. During one of them, one enlisted man in the ground crew of VMO-6, Private Richard J. O'Donnell, received shrapnel wounds and died two hours later. Nevertheless, VMO flights went out for artillery spotting, message drops, scouting, and photographic intelligence. There were also two crashes on the airstrip that day, both serviced by the VMO-3 ambulance and crash truck. That night, a bomb dropped during an air raid exploded at the entrance of a shelter containing a number of personnel from the various units on the base. The VMO-3 squadron corpsman, the only corpsman at Yontan at that time, again rendered efficient medical aid to the wounded and probably saved several lives.

Because the First Marine Division infantry units were encountering little resistance in their sector, the Eleventh Marines and Third Amphibious Corps Artillery units were directed to the southern front to provide artillery support for the Army divisions encountering stiffening enemy resistance there. All VMO-3 artillery spotting flights flying over the southern front that day received small arms fire, but the damage was negligible.

**Third Amphibious Corps 150 mm howitzer battalion,
one of the first Marine artillery units directed to the southern front**
(U.S. Marine Corps photograph, U.S. National Archives #127-GW)

The good news Lieutenant Lynn and all the other servicemen on Okinawa heard late in the day on April 7 was that the *Yamato* and five of its escort ships had been blown out of the water by scores of planes from the U.S. Fast Carrier Task Force. The remaining four Japanese ships sailed back to Japan. This feat was accomplished because of the radio intercept decoding work done by Vernice Milleville and her coworkers at Arlington Hall Station.

By April 8, the Sixth Marine Division infantry units had moved through the north-central part of the island fairly rapidly but were starting to encounter stiffening resistance in the increasingly rugged terrain of the Motobu Peninsula at the island's north end. VMO-6 pilots and accompanying observers were supporting the Sixth Marine Division infantry. VMO-6 pilot Lieutenant Emanuel Moyses and his accompanying observer, Lieutenant John Robert Parsons of the Fifteenth Marines, were shot down by enemy machine gun fire while directing artillery fire. They died on impact. (Lieutenant Parsons, who was from Elmhurst, Illinois, was buried in the Rock Island National Cemetery in Rock Island, Illinois, by his parents. Lieutenant Moyses is buried at the National Memorial Cemetery of the Pacific in Honolulu, Hawaii. Both men received the Purple Heart posthumously.)

On the same day, the first four-engine transports were able to land on the Yontan airfield to begin evacuating the growing number of wounded soldiers and Marines resulting from the intensifying combat on the island.

On April 9, the Japanese tried something new to disrupt the highly effective aerial spotters. They used bells, whistles, and garbled "verbiage" to disrupt the spotters' radio communications. New radio frequencies had to be set up for air-to-ground communication, but the observation flights continued in short order.

Sadly, on April 10, a second VMO-6 pilot and another observer were lost when a sudden rainstorm moved in from the ocean, restricting visibility as they were calling in artillery fire over the Motobu Peninsula. During his last radio communication, Lieutenant Charles Hanmer reported he was lost, running out of fuel, and going down at sea. A radio bearing of Hanmer's position was taken by the ground station at Kadena Airfield, and Air-Sea Rescue started an immediate search. No trace of Lieutenant Hanmer or the observer, Lieutenant James L. Frink of the Fifteenth Marines, was found. Lieutenant Frink had been one of the six graduates of Lieutenant Lynn's FAC who went directly to Aerial Observers School. It was an especially personal loss for Steve ... and he knew it could have been him instead. (Both men received a

Purple Heart posthumously and are commemorated at the Honolulu Memorial at the National Memorial Cemetery of the Pacific in Honolulu, Hawaii.)

Over the course of this first week on station, Lieutenant Lynn and his pilots dodged Marine Corsairs landing at Yontan and Kadena airfields. These fighter aircraft were ground-based rather than carrier-based and were deeply and rightfully feared by the Japanese. Before dawn on April 12, Lieutenant Lynn experienced the bombing of the airfields by Japanese aircraft targeting the Corsairs. This bombing attack was the precursor for *kikusui* 2, a raid on the fleet by 185 kamikazes flying out of Kyushu and Formosa. *Kikusui* 3–10 took place periodically throughout the rest of the battle with generally decreasing numbers of kamikazes. By the time the last *kikusui* occurred June 21–22, there were only 45 planes in the raid.

Yontan Airfield looking northwest on April 10, 1945, taken from OY-1 Grasshopper
(U.S. Marine Corps photograph, U.S. National Archives #127-GW-637-118302)

The continuing daily entries in the VMO-3 war diary record one artillery spotting mission after another. Flying at low altitude, Lieutenant Lynn's plane sometimes received heavy to medium caliber antiaircraft fire over enemy strongholds such as the Yonabaru airstrip and the city of Naha, both of which were still held by the Japanese. Other times the diary records spotting missions in areas under fire from U.S. naval gunships offshore. Artillery fire was directed onto caves, enemy troop concentrations, radio stations, artillery emplacements, vehicle collection points, mortar positions, antiaircraft emplacements, supply warehouses, munition dumps, fuel dumps, enemy airstrips, and observation towers. Additionally, the pilot/observer teams carried out photographic and reconnaissance missions.

The planes themselves soon passed the standard maximum length of service, and the excessive wear and tear as well as damage from enemy fire kept planes grounded in spite of the mechanics' best efforts. Shortages of planes for called missions became problematic for the artillery battalions dependent on them for accurate targeting.

It became clear by April 12 that American advances on the ground were nearly at a halt. American forces had run into a Japanese defensive "wall" that came to be called the Machinato Line. It ran the entire width of Okinawa. Behind it was the inner defensive ring around the ancient Okinawan capital of Shuri, capped by the Shuri Castle, which came to be known as the Shuri Line. The bulk of the Japanese Thirty-Second Army was dug in along these two lines and ready to "defend to the death" every yard of ground in their approach. U.S. Army casualties were staggering.

Japanese defensive lines on Okinawa
(U.S. Marine Corps photograph, U.S. National Archives #127-GW-557)

As the fighting on the island was intensifying, the American forces on Okinawa learned on Friday, April 13, that

President Franklin D. Roosevelt had died. He was the only president many of these young men had ever known, and the grief was real. Some men wept; others prayed. In rear areas and on naval ships, brief memorial services were held, but on the front lines, the only thing to be done was to console each other and "move out." One senior officer of the First Marine Division said later:

> It was amazing and very striking how the men reacted. We held services, but services did not seem enough. The men were peculiarly sober and quiet all that day and the next. Plainly each of them was carrying an intimate sorrow of the deepest kind, for they paid it their highest tribute, the tribute of being unwilling to talk about it, of leaving how they felt unsaid.[12]

On the same day, an effective Japanese artillery barrage on American artillery positions inflicted heavy casualties, including two battery commanders and the executive officer of a third battery. The barrage also destroyed the battalion ammunition dump and two 105 mm howitzers. It was up to the aerial spotters to find the large well-placed Japanese guns and call in fire to destroy them. Sometimes the guns were hidden in well-camouflaged caves behind steel doors. The doors could be opened, the guns rolled out and fired, and the doors closed again before the fire coordinates could be called in.

Small well-concealed groups of Japanese soldiers were inflicting high numbers of officer casualties throughout the American positions generally. They targeted any individual carrying either a map or the handgun an officer was issued. After the initial easy walk onto the beach, the American ground casualties were mounting, and infantry units had to find their own leadership sometimes among the enlisted men themselves. Enemy nighttime infiltration and guerilla tactics were commonplace and lethal.

Japanese Type 89 150 mm gun inside its protected cave on the Motobu Peninsula of Okinawa, ca. 1945
(U.S. Marine Corps photograph #122207, U.S. National Archives #127-GW)

The VMO-3 squadron personnel worked through their grief over President Roosevelt's death by starting to set up their own squadron mess. They'd had enough of trying to beg for food from the other aviation units on base or traveling several miles to regimental headquarters just to get a meal. They installed a generator and strung wire they were able to scrounge. The next day, they picked up a field stove from somewhere. That same night, one of the VMO-3 planes was struck by an enemy plane strafing the airfield, but it was repaired the next day by ground mechanics taking a break from their mess construction.

While flying a supply flight with ground crewman Corporal Bill Little, one of the VMO-3 pilots, Lieutenant Robert Severson, crashed his OY-1. Both the pilot and the noncommissioned officer (NCO) suffered severe shock and abrasions. Lieutenant Severson also had a puncture wound in his hand and a severe concussion. Both were hospitalized at the Sixty-Ninth Field Hospital. Lieutenant Severson died the next day, but Corporal Little survived. The OY-1 was demolished and partially burned. (Lieutenant Severson received the Purple Heart posthumously, and his remains were returned to his family in Minnesota for burial.)

After Lieutenant Severson's death, the VMO-3 squadron found small consolation in the fact that on April 15, their squadron mess hall finally became operational.

And on it relentlessly continued for Lieutenant Lynn and his fellow Marine observers for the rest of the month—flying low-altitude observation behind enemy lines; receiving enemy antiaircraft fire, small arms fire, machine gun fire, "friendly" naval gunfire; calling in fire on enemy command posts, radar installations, truck concentrations, troop concentrations, rocket launching positions, more caves, camouflaged buildings and artillery emplacements; registering artillery batteries as they moved forward to support the ground troops; photographing island landmarks for intelligence; limping back to base with damaged aircraft for the mechanics to patch together for the next day's missions.

Very occasionally, inclement weather would halt operations for part of a day. Torrential rains and strong winds on April 10, for example, grounded the small OY-1s. The flak-shredded tents Lieutenant Lynn and the other observers, pilots, and ground crew "lived in" offered little protection from the downpours.[13]

By the middle of April, Lieutenant Lynn and the other Third Amphibious Corps observers were bivouacked at Kadena Airfield.[14] This meant that the pilots of VMO-3 and VMO-6 had to take off from Yontan Airfield and fly to Kadena Airfield to pick up the aerial (artillery) observers. Lieutenant Lynn and the other observers probably didn't mind the better food at Kadena, though. Apparently, the mess tent the artillery observers could use at the airfield had a super cook, much better than the VMO-3 mechanics back at Yontan. He could somehow perform magic with the issued rations.

Throughout the month of April, both Yontan and Kadena experienced regular nighttime air raids and artillery fire. On a sign hammered onto the door of one of the buildings at Yontan Airfield, someone painted, "Welcome to Yontan. Every Night a Fourth of July." Antiaircraft defense battalions were set up around both fields, but the fields were fired upon repeatedly by a huge Japanese artillery piece (or pieces) that came to be known as "Kadena Pete."

**Antiaircraft fire a nightly event over Yontan and Kadena airfields, 1945**
(U.S. Marine Corps photograph, U.S. National Archives #127-GW)

Kadena Airfield was heavily bombed early on April 15 by planes that preceded another wave of kamikazes, and the artillery fire from Kadena Pete persisted throughout the night and intermittently through the next day, killing one soldier and wounding three others in the bivouac area.[15] Lieutenant Lynn spent his sleepless, nonflying hours hunkered down in Kadena's bomb shelters.

One of Lieutenant Lynn's fellow aerial observers, Lieutenant John May, was critically injured on April 17 while flying with Lieutenant Jeremiah Riordan. Pilot Riordan made an emergency landing at an Army airstrip south of Yontan so Lieutenant May could be treated immediately. Lieutenant May would recover and spend more time with Lieutenant Lynn at Air Observer School in Hawaii after the battle for Okinawa ended in July.

At 8:45 a.m. on April 19, VMO-3 pilot Lieutenant Harold Lief Saastad and Lieutenant Lynn's fellow observer, Lieutenant Harold J. Prewitt from the Third 155mm Howitzer Battalion, left Kadena Airfield for an observation flight. Radio contact was lost at

9:00 a.m., and Lieutenants Saastad and Prewitt were listed as Missing in Action. It's possible the aircraft exploded in midair after being hit by a U.S. naval gun barrage. Both men were declared killed in action later in the summer. (On September 2, 1945, the Yontan Airfield was dedicated by Eleventh Marine Regiment Chaplain Hardman and renamed Saastad Field. Both men received the Purple Heart posthumously and are commemorated at the Honolulu Memorial in the National Memorial Cemetery of the Pacific in Honolulu, Hawaii.)

Photo of VMO-3 pilots 2nd Lt. Harold Saastad (left) and 2nd Lt. Harold Fincel taken at Yontan on April 8, 1945—eleven days before Lt. Saastad was reported missing in action.
(U.S. Marine Corps photograph #117740, U.S. National Archives #127-GW-528)

In their April monthly reports, the commanding officers of both VMO-3 and VMO-6 urged the Third Amphibious Corps Artillery command to improve its air liaison communications. Too many of the VMO flights were being ordered into areas where naval gun barrages and air strikes were in progress.

As they mourned the loss of Lieutenant Saastad and Lieutenant Prewitt, the VMO-3 pilot/observer teams were involved in calling in target coordinates for the massive artillery barrage that took place in preparation for a major American ground offensive designed to crack the Shuri Line. Supported by six hundred land-based and carrier aircraft, twenty-seven battalions of artillery (324 pieces) joined by six battleships, six cruisers, and six destroyers offshore fired steadily into the enemy's lines while the infantry waited to push forward to attack the hardened enemy position on Kakazu Ridge.[16] Nineteen thousand shells were expended in this one barrage within forty minutes.[17] It covered the five-mile front with a density greater than one weapon to every thirty yards.[18] Nevertheless, the bombardment failed to dent the Japanese defenses deep in the limestone caves, and the subsequent infantry attack by elements of three U.S. Army divisions failed to achieve a single breakthrough.

By April 20, the worst fighting on the northern end of the island was over, but the gruesome close-in fighting for the southern ten miles of the island continued. The Japanese had spent months fortifying their positions around Shuri Castle and had abundant supplies and ammunition. Their interconnecting tunnels and caves as well as secured outposts in Okinawan tombs and concrete pillboxes created innumerable ambush points as well as nearly impenetrable firing positions. It was truly brutal for the attacking Americans.

On April 27, the VMO-3 ground crew mechanics assembled a functional aircraft using a cannibalized plane and parts from a Japanese aircraft. It wasn't used for observation flights but came in handy for short hops between Yontan and nearby destinations.

The nightly enemy bombings and strafing of the two airfields became more than aggravating on April 28 when eighteen bombs were dropped on Yontan, and both airfields were subjected to intermittent strafing from midnight until 4:00 a.m. The next night, Kadena Pete dropped twenty-eight artillery shells onto Kadena Airfield at 12:15 a.m. Amazingly little damage was done, but neither Lieutenant Lynn nor anyone else got much sleep.

On May 1, sporadic showers accompanied the cloudier and cooler weather typical of Okinawa's rainy season. The First Marine Division was moved south to begin relieving the depleted Twenty-Seventh Division of the Tenth Army and help break the Shuri Line where even sixteen-inch naval shells bounced off the concrete and coral defenses of the Japanese.

Marine Corps General Pedro del Valle assumed command of the former Army zone at two o'clock that afternoon. The VMO observation flights flew almost exclusively over the southern part of the island around Naha and the Shuri defensive zone during late April, May, and June. They and the rest of the Eleventh Marines had been supporting the Army division slugging its way south. Now it would be their own First Marine Division infantry the VMO-3 and Eleventh Marine artillery observers would be supporting as well as the Sixth Marine Division and the two Army divisions that would continue the fight.

First Division Marines moving south, May 1, 1945
(U.S. Marine Corps photograph, U.S. National Archives #127-GR-106)

The First Marine Division's artillery regiment, the Eleventh Marines, supported the Division's infantry regiments as they moved south, but additional artillery units were always available on call. They included the artillery of the Third Amphibious Corps and the U.S. Army's Twenty-Fourth Corps. The Sixth Marine Division's artillery regiment, the Fifteenth Marines, and the U.S. Army's Ninety-Sixth Infantry Division artillery were on call on each flank. Lieutenant Lynn and the other aerial artillery observers communicated with them all through the TICs. Forward ground observers communicated with the TICs by radio and through the many miles of wire laid down by the Marine wiremen on their teams, but more often than not, ground conditions dictated the use of aerial spotting instead.

Historians Benis Frank and Henry Shaw Jr. describe what the Tenth Army soldiers and Marines were up against as they faced the formidable Japanese strongholds to the south:

> The nature of the Shuri defenses demanded the fullest employment possible of all available weapons. Artillery especially was needed to reduce prepared positions and denude them of their skillfully prepared camouflage, to seal off the firing ports, and to collapse the labyrinth of interconnecting tunnels that housed and protected the defending troops. Since their operations were not subject in the same degree to the restrictions of inclement weather and enemy air attacks, as were air and naval gunfire, corps and divisional artillery, of necessity, served as the support workhorses for [ground] assaults.[19]

It was up to the low-flying VMO observation teams to find the camouflaged caves, tunnels, and firing positions for the artillery to hit.

By the end of the battle, the Tenth Army artillery units would fire 2,046,930 rounds down range, all in addition to 707,500 rockets, mortars, and five-inch or larger shells from naval gunfire ships offshore. Half the artillery rounds would be 105 mm shells from howitzers and the M7 self-propelled guns. Compared to the bigger guns, the old, expeditionary 75 mm pack howitzers of the First Battalion of the Eleventh Marines (1/11) were the "Tiny Tims" of the battlefield. Their versatility and relative mobility, however, proved to be assets in the long haul. Colonel Wilburt Brown, the Eleventh Marines' commander, augmented the 75 mm pack howitzer battalion of the regiment with LVT-As, which fired similar ammunition. According to Brown, "75mm ammo was plentiful, as contrasted with the heavier calibers, so 1/11 (Reinforced) was used to fire interdiction, harassing, and 'appeasement' missions across the front."[20]

By targeting fire onto regrouping enemy forces, the artillerymen were highly effective in suppressing Japanese attempts to retake positions already won by the Marine and Army infantrymen. Additionally, they played a key role in "counterbattery" fire. The Japanese had about four hundred pieces of artillery including 70 mm guns, 75 mm and 150 mm howitzers, and five-inch coast defense guns.²¹ They were carefully camouflaged and well defended, but when their positions could be spotted, it was up to the artillerymen to silence them. No other Tenth Army units remained continuously in line on Okinawa as long as the Marine and Army divisional artillery units.

**Marines cleaning a 75 mm pack howitzer on Okinawa, May 1945**
(U.S. Marine Corps photograph, U.S. National Archives #127-GW-637)

Even with the extensive artillery support, the ground troops took heavy casualties as they moved south through May and June. As the cold rain poured down, American troops struggled forward in the mud against heavy machine gun fire, grenades, and mutually supporting small arms positions from enemy-held ridge positions. Japanese artillery bombarded American infantry positions until the heavily camouflaged Japanese firing positions could be destroyed. Hand-to-hand fighting filled the nighttime hours as Japanese soldiers used the darkness to infiltrate American positions. American Marine flamethrower and demolition teams had to systematically burn out and seal, or "cure," the enemy cave installations and Okinawan burial vaults converted to Japanese defensive positions. General Hodge's dire prediction at the beginning of the April 19 attack, that "it is going to be really tough ... I see no way to get [the Japanese] out except blasting them out yard by yard," was being all too grimly borne out.²²

The Japanese tried to attack the American flank positions using landing barges, small craft, and Okinawans' canoes. Staring out over the sea at night watching for Japanese attackers occupied the shoreline-positioned Marines and soldiers in their foxholes even as they listened for enemy infiltrators sneaking up on them from behind. Sometimes Japanese artillery barrages continued through the night. They were answered in turn by American artillery and naval gunfire. As the night sky lit up with the tracings of the weapons fire, the noise was continuous and loud. In the words of one Marine, "the normal battlefield sounds became an almost unbearable cacophony" both day and night.[23]

**Marine Pfc. Lucien Vanasse and Doberman pinscher war dog King standing sentry, watching for Japanese attackers along the Okinawa shoreline, May 1945**
(U.S. Marine Corps photograph #118951, U.S. National Archives #127-GR-16-107)

Very slowly, though, the two Marine divisions (on the right) and the two Army divisions (on the left) were working together to push the Japanese back. Between April 8 and May 31, the U.S. Tenth Army gained an average of 133 yards a day.[24] Tragically, some days the troops would have to retake the same ground, enduring yet more casualties.

Starting late in the day on May 7, torrential rains began to fall on the island. More than fifteen inches of rain poured down over the course of the next seventeen days. Equipment and tools rusted. Ammunition stuck together because of mold. Foxholes filled with water. Feet began to rot. Everything, including food and letters from home, was soaked and covered in mud. What primitive roads there were became impassable, making delivery of ammunition, food, and clean water a major logistical challenge. Even the tanks became bogged down in the quagmire, and the airfields turned to mush.

**American tank buried in Okinawan mud, May 1945**
(U.S. Marine Corps photograph, U.S. National Archives #127-GR-16-106)

Trying to survive this morass and under constant Japanese attack, frontline Marines and soldiers on Okinawa could hardly be blamed for not getting too excited when they heard the news that Germany surrendered to Allied forces on May 8. Europe seemed as far away as the moon. In his book *The Ultimate Battle,* Bill Sloan described the reaction of the combat troops on Okinawa this way:

> For American ground troops at Okinawa, it was unquestionably the worst of times. Mourning, misery, and terror were the order of each day. May 1945 would rank among the deadliest months in the history of the U.S. military, and the higher the casualty count soared, the more the reports of peace in Europe resembled a taunting fantasy.[25]

Thanksgiving services were held aboard many of the ships off Okinawa, but the ground troops on the island itself were just trying to survive another day. No one on the island, though, was able to ignore the three volley "Time on Target" barrage fired simultaneously at noon by naval gunfire and every single one of the American artillery batteries upon Japanese positions to commemorate the occasion. In the words of one observer, "It made one hell of a big noise."[26]

**U.S. Army soldiers on Okinawa listening to the news about Germany's surrender, May 1945**
(Photograph from U.S. National Archives)

In spite of the rain, Lieutenant Lynn, the other spotters, and the Marine observation squadron pilots continued to fly aerial observation missions. The weather had to be really bad for the small OY-1s to stay on the ground. On May 2, Lieutenant Laurence Stien of VMO-3 took Captain John F. Rogers, the chief aerial observer for the Third Amphibious Corps Artillery (and Lieutenant Lynn's superior officer), up in the air to determine the possibility of any observation flights[27] He had to be personally convinced that the weather prevented the flights. May 8, 21, 22, and 30 were the only days in May when the OY-1s were unable to fly at all because of the weather. On the eighth, the VMO-3 personnel used the down time to build a shelter that could be used for periodic checks and maintenance of the aircraft during inclement weather. They also heard the unit would now be spotting for the Seventh Battalion of the Third Amphibious Corps Artillery, which was being moved south in addition to all the other artillery battalions they were already serving. On May 21 and 22, flights were attempted but returned to base because of poor visibility over the target areas.

The aerial artillery observer flights on Okinawa had begun on April 4 and would end on June 21. Out of those seventy-eight possible days, the turbulent and rainy weather that characterized much of the campaign prevented flying the OY-1s only nine days. On other days, the planes were not all available because they were so often damaged by ground fire, and they were being overused and abused far beyond their factory specifications.

Lieutenant Lynn flew fifty-six flights across the enemy lines during those sixty-nine flight days. The flights averaged about two-and-a-half hours in length and were usually flown at altitudes lower than five hundred feet. He and the other spotters and the pilots flying the unarmored planes were often under fire from enemy ground fire and antiaircraft fire and sometimes in the trajectory of artillery fire and naval gunfire from U.S. forces as well.

In Major General del Valle's words, the Marine First Division and the two Army divisions of the Twenty-Fourth Corps continued "processing" their way down the island. It was cold, wet, gruesome work. Lieutenant Lynn saw it all through his field glasses as he was flown at low altitude over the terrain looking for Japanese artillery, mortar emplacements, and troop positions where fire could be called in. The American Marines and soldiers would move forward through the mud during the day, and the Japanese would counterattack at night.

Marine tankmen Pvt. Byron Barber and Pfc. Melvin Johnson wearing sandbags in the Okinawan mud, May 1945
(U.S. Marine Corps photograph, U.S. National Archives #127-GR-16-106-12294))

For several days in May, Lieutenant Lynn could see from his plane seat groups of exhausted troops from the rear slogging through the mud on foot to carry ammunition, food, medicine, clean water, and other supplies to the frontline troops. The frontline units wouldn't be fully resupplied again by road until the beginning of June. When weather allowed, Marine air units began dropping supplies by parachute to targets the ground troops marked with colored smoke. Between May 22 and June 5, Marine air crews dropped 135 tons of supplies in 1,350 parachute loads.[28]

Often Lieutenant Lynn and the other pilot/observer teams would work in close coordination with tank and infantry units grinding their way down the island. Flying very low across the enemy lines, they would act as scouts locating Japanese machine gun, mortar, and artillery positions ahead of the ground troops. They would forewarn the oncoming ground Marines by radio. Working in tight coordination, the tank/infantry teams could then plan countermeasures against the enemy positions. Consequently, the Marines on the ground came to love the small OY-1 planes overhead and took to calling the planes "Piperschmitts" or "Messercubs."

While working one of these ground support scouting missions on May 9, an Army spotting plane was shot down in enemy territory just beyond the front lines. Both the pilot and observer had to be rescued by a Marine rifle team.[29] The plane was one of the artillery spotter Piper Cub L-4s operating in support of the Army's 361st Field Artillery Battalion.

**Piper Cub spotter plane shot down on May 9, 1945**
(U.S. National Archives #127-GW-638)

The tank/infantry teams on Okinawa are given a great deal of credit for the eventual victory of American forces over the Japanese defenders in the Shuri defense zone. In their book *Okinawa: The Last Battle*, authors Appleman, Burns, Gugeler, and Stevens summarize their importance this way:

> The American answer to the enemy's strong and integrated defenses was the tank-infantry team, including the newly developed armored flame thrower, and supported by artillery; each team generally worked in close coordination with assaults of adjacent small units. Although rockets, napalm, mortars, smoke, aerial bombing, strafing, naval bombardment, and all the others in the array of American weapons were also important, the tank-infantry team supported by 105's and 155's was the chief instrument in the slow approach on Shuri. A captured Japanese commander of a 47-mm. antitank battalion stated that in view of the success of this combination he did not see why any defense line, however well protected, could not be penetrated.[30]

**Marine tank/infantry team moving forward on Okinawa, ca. May 1945**
(U.S. Marine Corps photograph, U.S. National Archives #127-GR-15-100-121525)

The Seventh Marines of the First Marine Division were relieved on May 19. In ten days, they had suffered 1,249 casualties (158 killed, 820 wounded, 6 missing, and 265 "non-battle"). The number of hospital corpsmen casualties was so high that substitutes had to be rapidly trained. Officers were targeted so often that the command of any given rifle company shifted rapidly to NCOs or sometimes a low-ranking Private First Class.

The official war diary of VMO-3 continues to recount the specific missions of the squadron through the month of May—which pilots flew them, what they accomplished, and the damage the planes sustained. Multiple missions were flown every day for artillery spotting, artillery registration, photographic intelligence, infantry support, personnel transport, general reconnaissance, and so on. Occasionally throughout the month, the Japanese would transmit radio countermeasures that disrupted the VMO target transmissions, and the OY-1s would have to return to base to adopt new radio frequencies.

The VMO-6 pilot who had flown Lieutenant Lynn off of the USS *Petrof Bay*, Lieutenant Lester Bartels, had a harrowing experience on May 21.[31] He was flying an observation mission over enemy lines when he encountered engine trouble and started back to base. On the way, his engine failed completely, and he was forced to make a water landing offshore. He and the aerial observer were only slightly injured and were picked up by a nearby ship. The plane was recovered, too, but it was completely beyond repair.

Two days later, another VMO-6 pilot, Lieutenant James Morris, also experienced an engine failure while he and an observer were on a mission. They, too, went down at sea several hundred yards offshore. Suffering slight lacerations, they were both picked up by an amphibious tractor. Now having lost two planes in just three days, all the planes in the squadron were grounded while squadron maintenance personnel figured out the problem. It turned out that lint from the chamois cloths used to filter fuel during refueling operations had been clogging the aircraft carburetors. They all had to be thoroughly cleaned before the squadrons' five remaining planes could be put back into service. In the meantime, the VMO-3 squadron picked up the slack and started observing for the Fifteenth Marines' four artillery battalions as well as the other eleven artillery battalions they were already serving. VMO-3 was now the only observation squadron flying.

In late May, the Japanese line started to buckle and withdraw, but the Japanese were not done yet. In fact, the Yontan and Kadena airfields on Okinawa were the targets of a daring Japanese *giretsu*, a suicidal commando attack that began with both airfields being bombed around eight o'clock the evening of May 24. The entire event stretched into the morning hours of the twenty-fifth. After the initial bombing, twelve Japanese twin-engine bombers known as "Sallys" flew into the area around 10:30 p.m. with the planes of *kikusui* 7 and tried to land on the two airfields. The bombers carried a total of 120 commandos armed with demolition charges, grenades, and light arms they hoped to use to cripple American air operations. Heavy American antiaircraft fire broke up the attack, shooting down eleven of the planes, which still tried to crash land into aircraft or ground facilities as they fell to the ground.

One bomber, however, did skid successfully onto one of Yontan's runways, and an estimated dozen Japanese commandos jumped out of the plane before it came to a complete stop. They threw heat grenades and phosphorous bombs at the parked planes near the runway and sprayed the area with small arms fire. Confusion among the surprised Americans followed, and soon American rifle and machine gun fire from ground personnel and pilots was being sprayed everywhere as well. When it was all over, two Marines were killed and eighteen others were wounded. Nine U.S. planes were blown up, and twenty-nine others were damaged. Two fuel dumps containing seventy thousand gallons of aviation gasoline were destroyed as well.[32] No Japanese prisoners were taken, but sixty-nine Japanese bodies were counted. The last Japanese commando was killed at about 1:00 p.m. the next day about a quarter of a mile from the airfield when he tried to crawl across a road into the underbrush.[33]

One of the airplanes used in the *giretsu* attack at Yontan airfield, May 24, 1945
(U.S. Marine Corps photograph, U.S. National Archives #127-GW-638)

The number of Marine fatalities could have been higher. Nearly twenty Marines had run into a bomb shelter during the initial bombing without their carbines, M1s, or any other weapons. If they had been seen by one of the marauding Japanese commandos, they could all have been easily killed with one grenade. As it was, they were "rescued" by three armed Marines who ran down the field and shot the Japanese commando unknowingly approaching the bomb shelter.[34]

Meanwhile, the approximately 445 remaining Japanese aircraft of *kikusui 7*, of which nearly one-third were kamikazes, struck the American fleet and the airfield on the American-held nearby island of Ie Shima. They concentrated on the early-warning radar picket ships encircling the island and the fleet. Even though Marine and Army pilots shot down the majority of the Japanese planes, twelve more American ships were sunk or damaged.

The *kikusui* raids continued through the end of May and into June, killing sailors and damaging ships. The last mass *kikusui* attack began on May 27 and lasted until the evening of the twenty-eighth. The alert lasted for more than nine hours as 292 Japanese aircraft flew over and into the fleet and ground targets. One third of the planes were kamikazes. The very last kamikaze attack occurred on June 21–22, 1945, the last official day of the battle. Most of the kamikaze planes in the *kikusui* were destroyed by American

CAP fighters before they could hit any targets, but by the end of the battle for Okinawa, the Japanese planes sank 36 ships and crafts, damaged another 371, and caused over nine thousand U.S. Navy casualties.[35]

**OY-1 flying over Marines at the Okinawan city of Naha in late May 1945**
(U.S. Marine Corps photograph, U.S. National Archives #127-GW)

Finally, on May 29, a unit of the First Marine Division took Shuri Castle, the ancient stone fortress which had been the center of the Japanese defense on Okinawa. The same First Division's American flag that had flown at Cape Goucester and Peleliu was raised over Shuri Castle on May 30.

**Marines' American flag raised over Shuri Castle, May 30, 1945**
(U.S. Marine Corps photograph, U.S. National Archives #127-GW)

The battle wasn't over because the majority of the remaining Japanese troops had escaped to the south, but the Americans were now able to see the light at the end of the tunnel. Three more weeks of tough fighting lay ahead of them. Because the maintenance issues of the VMO-6 planes had been resolved, the VMO-3 squadron was relieved from flying for the Fifteenth Marines (Sixth Marine Division artillery) on the same day.

When VMO-7 became operational on June 1, the VMO-3 squadron was relieved of duty with the III Amphibious Corps Artillery battalions. Now the squadron was able to concentrate its efforts on the needs of the First Marine Division's infantry squads as they continued the relentlessly violent slog south. Colonel "Big Foot" Brown of the Eleventh Marines (First Division artillery) was continuing to develop the fine-tuned coordination between artillery, tanks, and infantry, building on tactical lessons learned on Peleliu. The tactic included Lieutenant Lynn and the other aerial observers overhead:

> Working with Lt. Col "Jeb" Stuart of the 1st Tank Battalion, we developed a new method of protecting tanks and reducing vulnerability to the infantry in the assault. We'd place an artillery observer in one of the tanks with a radio to one of the 155mm howitzer battalions. *We'd also use an aerial observer overhead.* We used 75mm, both packs and LVT-As, which had airburst capabilities. If any Jap [suicider] showed anywhere we opened fire with air bursts and kept a pattern of shell fragments pattering down around the tanks.[36]

The Marines also perfected the integration of the Army's 4.2-inch mortars that Lieutenant Lynn and other artillery officers had first trained with back on Pavuvu and Guadalcanal before the campaign began.

On June 2, two aircraft, three VMO-3 pilots, two mechanics, and three artillery aerial observers—perhaps Lieutenant Lynn among them—supported the Second Marine Division's invasion of Iheya Jima. Iheya Jima is an island north of Okinawa where radar and fighter direction centers were to be placed. They returned to the squadron shortly after the June 3 operation.[37]

As the violent ground battle continued on Okinawa itself, Marine infantry units under constant fire had to be relieved by other units as combat fatigue, casualties, and exhaustion took their agonizing toll. According to Frank and Shaw, on June 13, "one Japanese sharpshooter alone killed and wounded twenty-two Marines before the sniper was finally located and eliminated."[38]

The last opposed amphibious assault of World War II occurred on June 4 when units of the Sixth Marine Division stormed the beach to take the Oroku Peninsula. During the ten-day battle, the division suffered 1,608 casualties. The shore-to-shore operation across the Naha harbor was designed to flank enemy forces on the peninsula. As the assault ended and Japanese soldiers fled, they were sealed off by First Marine Division troops, and they began to surrender. By the end of June, 10,755 Japanese soldiers had been captured; many of them surrendered after this assault.

Numerous daily artillery spotting, scouting, registration, and photo reconnaissance missions continued to fill the days of VMO-3, VMO-6, and VMO-7 through June 21.[39] The observation squadron pilots would pick up Lieutenant Lynn and the other aerial observers at the Kadena Airfield or at the Itoman strip (the last four days of the operation). Then they would scour the southern end of the island for targets in support of the infantry on the ground. Poor visibility over the target areas on June 4 and 5 canceled afternoon flights. A typhoon passing through the area damaged thirty-six naval vessels offshore.

On June 6, the VMO-3 plane carrying pilot First Lieutenant Donald Manley and Lieutenant Lynn's good friend, artillery observer First Lieutenant Gene McDonald, received a Japanese antiaircraft burst when they were flying over enemy lines above southern Okinawa. The rudder and elevator controls were damaged, the instrument board was shot up, and much of the fabric on the fuselage was torn away. They returned to the Yontan Airfield with great difficulty. Lieutenant Manley was wounded in the neck, but Lieutenant McDonald was unharmed. The plane was a total loss. Lieutenant Manley was back in the pilot's seat by June 9, making a photo intelligence flight over the southern end of the island where there was still heavy enemy resistance.

VMO-3 OY-1 flown by Lt. Manley hit over southern Okinawa on June 6, 1945
(U.S. Marine Corps photograph, U.S. National Archives #127-GW-638-125637)

Artillery observer 1st Lt. Gene McDonald and OY-1 pilot 1st Lt. Donald Manley beside their plane, June 10, 1945
(U.S. Marine Corps photograph, U.S. National Archives #127-GW-638-126596)

First Division Marine casualties continued to mount as the Japanese fought tenaciously to hang on to every last foot of ground at the southern end of Okinawa. In response, VMO-7 pilots began making medical evacuation flights on June 11 from a narrow road running between the two towns of Naha and Itoman. On both sides of the narrow Itoman landing strip were two-foot drops into soft rice paddies. It didn't always go smoothly. Captain William Seward wrote in the VMO-7 official squadron war diary about the Japanese artillery trying to target their position on the very first day of evacuations; they were only eight hundred yards behind the front line.

A few days later, one of the planes nosed over after taxiing in the soft sand of the airstrip, and the propeller broke. Another time, one of the planes taxied through a foxhole and into a stone wall. The pilots of the damaged planes then had to be transported out of the area by tractor, amtrack, or truck under sniper fire.

During the twelve-day period from June 11 to June 22, VMO-7 flew a total of 369 evacuation flights in addition to 243 artillery spotting and 17 photo-reconnaissance missions.

**VMO-7 "Grasshopper" on Itoman landing strip awaiting a wounded Marine for evacuation, June 13, 1945**
(U.S. Marine Corps photograph, U.S. National Archives #127-GW-529-124807)

Soon, the pilots and planes of VMO-6 joined the VMO-7 pilots making medical evacuation flights. Critical First Marine Division casualties were flown to hospitals twelve miles in the rear in about eight minutes rather than transported over barely existing roads in ground transport vehicles. Many of these evacuation flights took place in the dark.

Between June 11 and 22, the two squadrons together flew 641 critical Marine casualties off of the narrow airstrip and consequently saved many lives. Even though VMO-6 was down to only three operable planes by mid-June, it managed to evacuate 94 wounded Marines from the southern reaches of Okinawa on June 1 and 18 alone while still maintaining other normal combat support flights. For these medical evacuations and others totaling 195 seriously wounded men, VMO-6 received a Meritorious Unit Commendation from the Commanding General of the Third Amphibious Corps, Major General Roy Geiger.

VMO-7 OY-1 piloted by First Lieutenant Jack McClain taxiing on the Itoman airstrip to receive another wounded Marine; two other OY-1s can be seen in the background flying wounded Marines to the hospital twelve miles north, June 19, 1945
(U.S. Marine Corps photograph #125956, U.S. National Archives #127-GW-529)

Captain Slappey noted in the VMO-3 June war diary that Lieutenants Boesch and Fincel both flew artillery spotting missions on June 15 calling in fire on a ridge extending along the southern tip of the island believed to be the "ridge with the last organized position of the enemy on the island." Scouting, photo intelligence flights, and artillery spotting flights directing fire onto that same ridge and other enemy targets continued through the nineteenth.

Finally, on June 20, artillery fire could no longer be called in because American ground troops were too close to the last available targets. The pilot/observer teams continued to fly scouting missions, though, and still received concentrated small arms fire which did considerable damage to one of the VMO-3 OY-1s.

The headquarters of General Ushijima and his chief of staff, Lieutenant General Cho, was overrun by American Marines on June 21. U.S. Marine Corps Major General Geiger, who had taken over command of the U.S. Tenth Army after General Buckner was killed by shrapnel two days earlier, declared organized resistance on the island of Okinawa to be at an end at 1:05 p.m. that day. VMO-3's Lieutenant Manley flew a staff photographer down to the southern end of the island to photograph the enemy troops making suicide leaps from the cliffs. The squadron also received nine new OY-1s for their use that day. The unit was ready to fight on but wouldn't need to.

OY-1 photo of southern tip of Okinawa taken in June 1945
(U.S. Marine Corps photograph, U.S. National Archives #127-GW-569)

General Ushijima and Lieutenant General Cho committed ceremonial suicide, *seppuku*, before they could be captured, and they were buried under U.S. military auspices on June 27 near the cave where they died. Upon orders from General Cho, Colonel Yahara tried to escape American forces so that the Japanese side of the story could be told back in Japan. Disguised as an elderly schoolteacher, he was picked up with a large group of refugees and later identified as a Japanese soldier by a suspicious Okinawan. Having spent time in the United States before the war, Colonel Yahara spoke excellent English, and he decided to cooperate with his American interrogators after the war ended. His recounting of the preparation for the battle and the battle itself has been invaluable in understanding the history of the Okinawa campaign. Upon returning to Japan, Colonel Yahara wrote a captivating account of the campaign entitled *The Battle for Okinawa*.

Among other important pieces of information Colonel Yahara shared with his interrogators was that the small planes of the observation squadrons

> were a constant threat to the Japanese. They learned quickly that the presence of an observation plane overhead usually presaged enemy fire. And, although they appeared to present fine targets, observation planes were tantalizingly hard to hit with small arms. Observation planes were, therefore, treated with great respect, all movement being kept to an absolute minimum while these planes were overhead.

Colonel Yahara also reported that Japanese countermeasures against the American tank/infantry teams were ineffective in part because "of the undesirability of firing (artillery and mortars) during the daytime when *under air observation*."[40]

The coordinated "mop-up" of the island officially lasted until June 30. The mop-up involved several brief and bloody firefights with Japanese individuals and groups determined to inflict every American casualty they could to protect the Japanese home islands. VMO-3 pilots continued to fly "flutter hops" dropping leaflets announcing Japan's surrender near suspected Japanese hideouts in the hills as late as August 29. Additional prisoners were also taken; by the end of November, a total of 16,346

Japanese troops had been captured.[41] Even so, a low-level guerilla war against U.S. occupation forces was conducted by Japanese renegade soldiers and Okinawan rebels well into 1947.

Although Operation Iceberg was a devastating defeat for the Japanese military, General Ushijima had succeeded in accomplishing his given mission—inflicting painful losses upon the American military forces and buying time for Japan to work on its homeland defense. Colonel Yahara suggested in his accounting of the battle that the Japanese on Okinawa could have been even more effective in inflicting American casualties and delaying the end of the battle if General Cho's May 4 major counteroffensive had not taken place. He was convinced that if they had not lost so many of their best soldiers and used up so much of their ammunition in that twenty-four-hour fight, they could have continued to fight their battle of attrition for another month.[42] It would have been worse, too, for the Americans if nearly a third of the Japanese combat forces had not been transferred away from Okinawa in December 1944 to bolster the defenses of Formosa, which the Japanese feared would be the next American target.[43] (Back at Arlington Hall Station, Vernice had seen the radio intercepts conveying the news of this troop transfer well before the battle began.)

By the end of the battle for Okinawa, American casualties (dead and wounded) totaled more than sixty-two thousand from all services.[44] Thousands of the wounded died within weeks or months from their injuries. The U.S. Navy losses at Okinawa exceeded those of any other single World War II engagement.[45] Nearly ten thousand American sailors were killed, wounded, or reported missing during the battle.

More than twenty-six thousand American servicemen were treated for neuropsychiatric disorders, or "combat fatigue," the highest number of any World War II battle.[46] The length and close combat of the battle as well as the intense and nearly constant artillery and mortar fire took a heavy toll on the mental stamina of soldiers and Marines. About half the cases were treated with rest away from the front lines in divisional installations on the island itself. Many of these men could return to their units within a few weeks. The more seriously traumatized servicemen were treated in field hospitals; many of these men could only be reassigned to noncombat duties after treatment. About 20 percent of the more serious cases had to be evacuated to hospitals offshore. It is difficult if not impossible to know how many servicemen died during combat because they lost the mental ability to make sound judgments during the battle itself. The majority of the combat troops who fought on Okinawa carried psychological scars with them for the rest of their lives. Lieutenant Lynn was one of them.

Japanese casualties are not accurately known, but Japan stated that it lost 77,166 soldiers on the island itself. The American forces recorded the burial of 107,539 Japanese bodies, but some of them may have been Okinawans rather than Japanese. An estimated 23,764 more Japanese were sealed in caves or buried by the Japanese.[47] Another 10,755 Japanese soldiers were captured by June 21; some of them surrendered. Another 5,591 soldiers surrendered or were captured during the mop-up phase after June 21.[48]

Tragically, there may have been as many as 100,000 deaths of indigenous Okinawans—about one-third of the civilians living on Okinawa in 1945.[49] Many were the male citizens over age eighteen, and both male and many female students younger than eighteen who were drafted by the Japanese to fight on their behalf. Some of the Okinawans killed themselves because they believed the Japanese propaganda describing the horrors that would be inflicted upon them by the American invaders. The Japanese killed some non-Japanese-speaking Okinawans as spies and evicted other civilians from protective caves when they needed the space for Japanese troops.[50] Many civilians were caught in the crossfire as the two raging armies fought for every foot of ground in the countryside, villages, and cities of Okinawa.

With Okinawa declared "secure," Lieutenant Lynn and the other artillery observers assigned to the Third Amphibious Corps returned to their home units. By June 22, Lieutenant Lynn and the other Eleventh Marine aerial artillery observers were back with their artillery battalions in camp on northern Okinawa's Motobu Peninsula. Many of the observers didn't stay long enough to get comfortable. On June 28, Lieutenant Lynn and several other artillery officers received orders to proceed the next day by government air transport to Pearl Harbor, Hawaii, where they were to report to the Fleet Marine Force "for temporary duty in connection with tactical and gunnery air observer training."

Lieutenant Lynn's battalion commanding officer, Lieutenant Colonel R. W. Wallace, noted in Lieutenant Lynn's officer fitness report for the period April 1 through June 30 that he would "particularly desire to have [Lieutenant Lynn] under his command," and he rated him outstanding in "physical stamina and endurance under hardship, adversity, or discouragement" as well as "loyalty." He was also rated very highly in "the ability to think and act promptly and effectively in an unexpected emergency or under great strain." Interestingly, Lieutenant Lynn's fitness report indicated that he was "recommended for and *desires* a regular commission" rather than staying in the reserves. In the meantime, however, Lieutenant Lynn (and all the other fighting Marines of the First Division) needed a break. Pearl Harbor sounded just fine to him.

Later that year, Lieutenant Lynn and five fellow Eleventh Marine aerial artillery observers (Robert E. McClean, Charles J. Aldrich, Clarence E. Emery, Francis W. McCalpin, and Gene E. McDonald) learned they would be awarded the Distinguished Flying Cross for "extraordinary achievement while participating in aerial flights while serving as an air observer for a Marine artillery regiment on Okinawa Shima, Ryuku Islands, from 1 April to 21 June, 1945." A total of only seven Distinguished Flying Crosses were awarded to Marines in the First Division during the entire war. Lieutenant Lynn's Distinguished Flying Cross citation reads as follows:

> **For extraordinary achievement while participating in aerial flights while serving as an air observer for a Marine artillery regiment on OKINAWA SHIMA, RYUKU ISLANDS, from 1 April to 21 June, 1945. First Lieutenant LYNN made fifty-six flights over enemy lines totaling one hundred and thirty-one hours. In order to more effectively search out enemy targets and maintain observation despite low ceiling flight conditions, he frequently flew at altitudes of less than five hundred feet in an unarmored plane. Seldom flying above two thousand feet, he performed his missions while flying within the trajectory of friendly artillery fire and while**

subjected to repeated enemy small arms and antiaircraft fire. Constantly searching for enemy targets and making precision artillery adjustments thereon, he was instrumental in destroying a considerable quantity of enemy materiel. His actions throughout were in keeping with the highest traditions of the United States Naval Service.

Roy S. Geiger, Lt Gen USMC

Distinguished Flying Cross Medal
(Wikipedia photograph in the public domain)

After June 21, the activities of the VMO-3, VMO-6, and VMO-7 squadrons also wound down but did continue during the mop-up phase. (The VMO-2 pilots had returned to Guam in mid-April and had stayed "on operational standby status" there until June 3.) By the end of the Okinawa campaign, the four VMO squadrons' pilots had flown 3,486 missions for artillery spotting, message pickup and drops, wire laying, aerial photography, personnel ferrying, evacuation of wounded men, and general utility. Ten planes were lost, and five officers and two enlisted men were killed.[51] Their contribution was important and substantial. In the opinion of artillery commanders, the role of the aerial observers/spotters and the pilots who flew them over the Okinawan terrain to find targets was absolutely critical in defeating the enemy. As Lieutenant Colonel Frederick R-P. Henderson of the Third Amphibious Corps Artillery later wrote:

> The nature of the terrain in southern Okinawa seriously limited ground observation—especially while we were fighting our way uphill on the Shuri massif. Without our AOs [aerial observers], III AC would have been blind. The courage and daring of our AOs and VMO pilots was an outstanding feature of the campaign. I think that VMO pilots are the unsung heroes of Marine Aviation. ... When they wanted to really investigate something ... they would go right down on the deck. Often they would fly past cave openings at the same level so they could look in and see if there was a gun there.[52]

As usual, Captain Wallace J. Slappey recorded the most detail of his unit's postbattle activities in his official VMO-3 war diary. On June 22, VMO-3 immediately began reconditioning its aircraft and bringing up the rear echelon equipment put ashore fifty miles north of Yontan Airfield. Captain Slappey noted with aggravation that some of the men's personal effects had been lost in transit and much of the rest of it had been "badly damaged by wetting and subsequent rotting." Much of the aviation gear was totally destroyed as well, and the rear echelon vehicles were in particular disrepair. One can understand how he might have been chagrined to learn all this after what he and his squadron had been through. By the next day, he had his squadron personnel assembling two new aircraft and overhauling the rear echelon vehicles that were "in particular disrepair." In fact, throughout that last week of June, Captain Slappey kept his men busy assembling more new aircraft and repairing a generator, a decontaminator, and other equipment. The officers kept busy supervising the enlisted men and looking for a possible site for a new camp. Four pilots flew observation flights for the invasion of the nearby island Kumi Shima, which turned out to pose no enemy opposition.

On June 30, dashing their fervent hope they would go to Hawaii to rehabilitate and reorganize before their next campaign to invade the home islands of Japan, the news came down that the First Marine Division would be settling in to rest and regroup on the Motobu Peninsula of Okinawa. The VMO-3 squadron was assigned a camp site with the First Division's Eleventh Marines. "The countryside was clean, open, pine-wooded, and really attractive," Lieutenant Christopher Donner later recalled, but it wasn't Hawaii.[53]

Captain Slappey was relieved of command of VMO-3 on July 1, 1945, by Captain Peter Fritz, USMCR, and he headed back to the States for reassignment. Captain Slappey was awarded the Bronze Star for meritorious achievement and service in the Okinawa Campaign. He stayed in the Marine Corps and later fought in Korea. He retired with the rank of lieutenant colonel and died at the age of seventy-five in Los Angeles, California.

The VMO-3 squadron was awarded a Presidential Unit Citation "for extraordinary heroism in action against enemy Japanese forces during the invasion of Okinawa, April 2 to June 21, 1945." Two of the squadron's pilots, First Lieutenant Robert C. Jackson and Second Lieutenant Herbert C. Fincel, were awarded the Silver Star for "gallantry in action against an enemy of the United States."

In keeping with his customarily concise fashion, Captain Donald R. Garrett's VMO-6 war diary notes for the last week of June 1945 are cursory. He recorded only that the unit flew 429 hours during the month of June. From Gary Parker and Frank Bartha's *A History of Marine Observation Squadron Six*, it's clear the time was used in part to begin packing up the squadron's equipment and crating its aircraft because on July 6, all the squadron personnel and its equipment were boarded onto the USS *Bollinger* (APA-234). On July 8, they departed for Guam where they arrived on July 14.[54] (All the Sixth Marine Division eventually returned to Guam to rest and regroup.) The majority of the original officers and men, including Captain Garrett, were relieved in early September and returned home for reassignment. As noted earlier, the VMO-6 squadron received a Meritorious Unit Commendation from the commanding general of the Third Amphibious Corps, Major General Roy Geiger. It was also awarded a Presidential Unit Citation "for extraordinary heroism in action against enemy Japanese forces during the invasion of Okinawa, April 2 to June 21, 1945."

**Captain Donald Garrett, VMO-6, with observer flying over Okinawa, May 1945**
(U.S. Marine Corps photograph, U.S. National Archives #127-GW-529-121235)

VMO-7, which became operational on Okinawa on June 1, continued to evacuate wounded Marines from the Itoman airstrip in southern Okinawa. Its pilots flew six evacuation flights on June 22 alone. Captain William A. Seward, VMO-7's commanding officer, wrote in his official war diary that the strip was renamed Youngren Strip in memory of the Marine whose life a Marine Corps doctor attempted to save by building the strip earlier in the month. By mid-June, the strip had been lengthened by bulldozers.

On June 22, too, Captain Seward noted, too, that the engineering chief of the squadron, Master Technical Sergeant Maurice McTyre, landed on the strip with a new propeller and tire for a plane damaged earlier in the week so the plane could be flown out.

**Wounded Marine being carried to VMO-7 OY-1 for evacuation, June 19, 1945. Hit by a sniper, this evacuated Marine was on the hospital operating table in 16 minutes.**
(U.S. Marine Corps photograph #125962, U.S. National Archives #127-GW-529)

Through mid-November, VMO-7 continued to serve the needs of the Third Amphibious Corps by ferrying officers around the island and flying photography and familiarization flights. By late July, the squadron personnel were satisfactorily camped at the squadron rest camp at the Nago Air Strip on Okinawa. Captain Seward noted:

> Here living conditions were much better [than at the Chatan Cub Field]. There are organized sports and a nice beach for the men to go swimming on. A security guard was kept to protect the personnel and the planes from Japanese stragglers in the hills.[55]

The short-lived VMO-7 squadron which had saved so many First Division Marines' lives during June 1945 was deactivated on November 16, 1945.

The First Marine Division, Reinforced, was awarded the Presidential Unit Citation "for extraordinary heroism in action against enemy Japanese forces during the invasion and capture of Okinawa Shima, Ryuku Islands, from April 1 to June 21, 1945."

**THE SECRETARY OF THE NAVY**
WASHINGTON

The President of the United States takes pleasure in presenting the PRESIDENTIAL UNIT CITATION to the

FIRST MARINE DIVISION, REINFORCED,

consisting of: The FIRST Marine Division; Fourth Marine War Dog Platoon; Fourth Provisional Rocket Detachment; Fourth Joint Assault Signal Company; Third Amphibian Truck Company; Third Provisional Armored Amphibian Battalion; First Amphibian Tractor Battalion; Eighth Amphibian Tractor Battalion; Detachment, First Platoon, First Bomb Disposal Company; Second Platoon, First Bomb Disposal Company (less First Section); Battery "B", 88th Independent Chemical Mortar Battalion, U.S. Army; Company "B" (less First Platoon), 713th Armored Flame Thrower Battalion, U.S. Army,

for service as set forth in the following

CITATION:

"For extraordinary heroism in action against enemy Japanese forces during the invasion and capture of Okinawa Shima, Ryukyu Islands, from April 1 to June 21, 1945. Securing its assigned area in the north of Okinawa by a series of lightning advances against stiffening resistance, the FIRST Marine Division, Reinforced, turned southward to drive steadily forward through a formidable system of natural and man-made defenses protecting the main enemy bastion at Shuri Castle. Laying bitter siege to the enemy until the defending garrison was reduced and the elaborate fortifications at Shuri destroyed, these intrepid Marines continued to wage fierce battle as they advanced relentlessly, cutting off the Japanese on Oroku Peninsula and smashing through a series of heavily fortified, mutually supporting ridges extending to the southernmost tip of the island to split the remaining hostile force into two pockets where they annihilated the trapped and savagely resisting enemy. By their valor and tenacity, the officers and men of the FIRST Marine Division, Reinforced, contributed materially to the conquest of Okinawa, and their gallantry in overcoming a fanatic enemy in the face of extraordinary danger and difficulty adds new luster to Marine Corps History and to the traditions of the United States Naval Service."

For the President,

Secretary of the Navy

**First Marine Division Presidential Unit Citation for heroism in the Battle for Okinawa**
(From Steve Lynn's personal papers in family collection)

*June 28, 1945*

*Dear Necie,*

*I'm headed to Hawaii. A few of us have orders to report for more training there. I feel like the action during the last ten weeks has given me all the training I'll ever need and more than I wanted, but I'm not complaining. After having been away from "civilization" for so long, I'll gladly go along with the Corps on these orders.*

*It's been over a week since I flew an observation flight, but I still feel like the air is rushing past my head, and small arms fire is flying through the fuselage around me. It's going to take me some time to relax, but I'm ready to try. I wouldn't mind some decent food and some sleep, too.*

*Thanks for all the letters. You'll never know how much they meant to me during this fight. Maybe I'll be able to find a way to actually call you on the telephone when I get to Hawaii. I'll sure try...*

*Steve*

# 18
# Vernice
## Arlington, Virginia, and Washington, DC
## April–June 1945

> Perhaps not since the dawn of history has the passing of a great man been mourned contemporaneously by so many different nations, so many different religions and races, spread over the earth.
> –State Department veteran Joseph Davies, referring to Franklin D. Roosevelt

> The gravest question mark in every American heart is about [Harry S.] Truman. Can he swing the job?
> –Michigan senator Arthur Vandenberg

*April 20, 1945*
*Dear Steve,*

*The funeral procession for President Roosevelt was so incredibly sad. Everyone stood along the streets shoulder to shoulder and several people deep. Everyone, man or woman, was weeping. It seemed like we had all lost a dear family member. Seven white horses pulled the casket draped by an American flag. Except for the sound of crying, everyone was silent as it was pulled down Constitution Avenue.*

*Everyone was unsure, too, about Harry Truman taking over, but since he gave his speech in the House Chamber on April 16th, people have become a little less worried. At work, we all crowded around the radio to listen. He seems like a good man—down to earth and smart. I think he might be okay.*

*Since it's been in the newspapers already, I guess it's all right to write that I know you're fighting on Okinawa. There hasn't been too much specific news reported about the battle yet. I think about you there constantly. Please take care of yourself....*

*Necie*

On April 12, 1945, U.S. President Franklin Delano Roosevelt died, and Washington wept. Vernice Milleville attended the funeral procession alongside her coworkers and stood among the crying masses. FDR was the only president she had really ever known. He had led the nation through the Great Depression and World War II ... and the war wasn't over yet. In fact, the nation was enduring the war's bloodiest months, both in Europe and in the Pacific. How would Harry Truman manage the tasks at hand?

Anxiety and uncertainty rivaled the nation's grief. Washington was subdued. Vernice and her SSA coworkers at Arlington Hall Station did not lose their focus, though. There was work to be done.

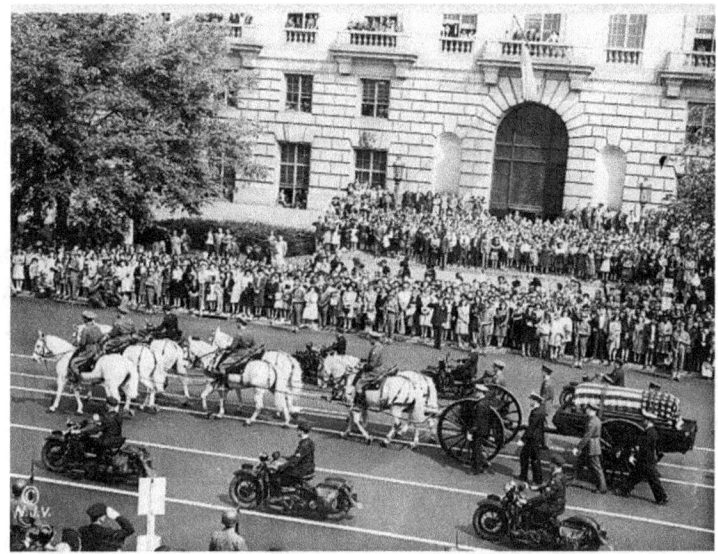

**President Franklin D. Roosevelt's funeral cortege, April 14, 1945**
(Library of Congress photograph)

On April 20, 1945, while Lieutenant Steve Lynn was flying his small unarmored plane over enemy lines on Okinawa, the U.S. Army Signal Corps' commanding officer, W. Preston Corderman, presented Vernice with an "emblem" recognizing six consecutive months of "faithful service" to the War Department. By this time, observes military historian John Ray Skates, "the interception, decryption, and distribution of ULTRA intelligence [German and Japanese military codes] had become well organized and organizationally integrated."[1]

At the same time, too, Generals George C. Marshall and Douglas MacArthur and Admiral Chester Nimitz were working out the details for Operation Downfall, the planned invasion of the Japanese home islands. Operation Downfall had two phases: Operation Olympic and Operation Coronet. Operation Olympic focused on occupying Kyushu, Japan's southernmost home island. The landings were scheduled to begin on November 1, 1945.

Olympic would be a massive amphibious operation much larger than the D-Day invasion of Normandy. Involving 650,000 troops, nearly twenty-five hundred ships, and five thousand planes, it would be the largest amphibious operation in the war. In a nutshell, the equivalent of fourteen American divisions would land on three separate beaches on Kyushu's southern end.

After the area was secured, southern Kyushu would become a huge Allied naval and air base, which would be used to further increase the pressure on the Japanese to surrender. If they still did not choose to surrender, the allied base would be the staging area for Operation Downfall's second phase, Operation Coronet.

Operation Coronet would be an even larger American invasion of the Kanto (Tokyo) Plain on Honshu, the main Japanese home island. Attacking Japan's industrial, political, and cultural core, twenty-five divisions of Allied troops would assault the beaches of Yokosuku Naval Base at the mouth of Tokyo Bay and drive across the Kanto Plain to the city of Tokyo itself. Operation Coronet was tentatively scheduled for March 1, 1946. The First Marine Division would be a lead component in the attack.

Very few Allied military planners had any idea that during the summer of 1945, a deadly new weapon would be tested, capable perhaps of ending the war without Operation Downfall.

Vernice and the other code breakers at Arlington Hall Station provided essential intelligence for planning Operation Downfall. Radio interceptions flooded into Arlington Hall, and Vernice worked long hours every week analyzing the Ultra Japanese army air coded intercepts.

It was clear from Ultra intelligence reports that until mid-1944, the Japanese Imperial General Staff had paid little attention to home island defense. They were busy elsewhere, and they just didn't think a home island invasion would ever occur. By mid-April 1945, however, the Philippines were nearly lost, and Okinawa was embattled. Ultra decryptions indicated that Japanese planners were now shifting their attention to *Ketsu-Go*, the decisive operation to defend the homeland. Allied military planners needed to know and understand what this shift in Japanese attention meant for planning the Operation Downfall details.

The code breakers at Arlington Hall and in MacArthur's Australian Central Bureau were under the gun. Their work was critical for planning operations that could end the war and save

American lives—perhaps Steve's life. These men and women were funneling the information from thousands of decrypted messages to the intelligence officers who then wrote intelligence analyses for the military planners working under the direction of Generals Marshall and MacArthur. They were also providing Magic, the diplomatic and political eavesdropping that kept Allied leaders in the loop on internal Japanese deliberations.

For example, the planners needed to know about and understand the implications of Japanese efforts to strengthen and reposition their troops in southern Kyushu. Additionally, they needed complete and accurate information on the number of suicide planes the Japanese would have available to fly into the ships of the American fleet. Where were they? How much fuel was available? They needed to know the numbers and locations of Japanese suicide boats (*shinyo*), small submarines (*koryu* and *kairyu*), suicide rocket planes (*ohka*), and manned torpedoes (*kaiten*). Where were the remaining nineteen Japanese destroyers, and how would they be used? They needed to know if the Japanese were going to revert to their earlier banzai war strategy, attempting to stop the invasion in the sea and on the beach, or if they were going to continue the "war of attrition" defensive strategy they had used on Peleliu, Iwo Jima, and Okinawa.

In addition to the military intelligence provided through Ultra, Allied civilian and military leaders needed to understand what Magic intelligence was revealing about the political atmosphere within the Japanese government. Were the militants still holding sway? Was there serious diplomatic discussion going on with the Swiss or the Russians to negotiate a surrender? If there was, did the Japanese military support the negotiating efforts? Few SSA decoders at Arlington Hall knew if President Truman would know what to do with the information, but it was their job to provide it.

The reaction in Washington, DC, to the German surrender on May 7, 1945, had been wildly different from the reaction of the troops mired in Okinawa's violence. V-E Day (for Victory in Europe) was declared in America on Tuesday, May 8, 1945. The crowds in Washington danced and sang, and the nighttime lights were turned on again for the first time since December 1941. The Washington Monument and the Jefferson and Lincoln Memorials were illuminated. Horns honked. Drinks flowed.

Vernice shared in the elation but with a bit of reservation. The "boys" in Europe were going to start coming home or be transferred to the Pacific theater where the killing war was still raging. Steve and his fellow Marines, soldiers, and sailors were still painfully pushing the Japanese toward Okinawa's southern end, and the Japanese were turning their attention to defending their home islands.

Vernice knew, too, that political and social pressure to quickly end the war was growing on the home front. President Truman's advisors predicted that the American people had enough patience for only one more year of war after the Germans surrendered. Additionally, President Truman was aghast at the Okinawa casualty rate, and he and the military planners spent long hours searching for a way to end the war and prevent more bloodshed. Truman and his military planners needed to find a way to end the Pacific war as soon as possible.

Both President Truman and the British prime minister Winston Churchill understood and shared the public sentiment to end the war quickly, but they had both fought in World War I. Consequently, they adamantly insisted that World War II should not end the same way the Great War had—with an armistice or negotiated "peace" setting the stage for yet another war a generation later. In their view, Japan needed to be unarguably defeated; it needed to surrender unconditionally. The question was how to make that happen as soon as possible.

Vernice may have been one of the nearly one million people who lined Washington's streets when General Dwight D. Eisenhower returned to Washington, DC, from Europe on June 18, 1945. As the supreme commander who had orchestrated the Allied victory in Europe, Eisenhower spoke in the House of Representatives chamber before the members of Congress, the Joint Chiefs of Staff, the Supreme Court justices, and other government luminaries. In an effort to give General Eisenhower the day's entire attention, President Truman stayed away and listened to the address on the radio in the White House. That night Truman hosted Eisenhower at the White House for a "stag party" with about one hundred other guests and was quoted as saying about the presidency, "I'd turn it over to him now if I could."[2]

A few days later, the Arlington Hall code breakers were reminded that the Pacific war was still going on and that secrecy was still as important as it had ever been. They each had to sign the "restricted" certificate Vernice signed on June 22, 1945, stating the following:

> I have been informed and understand that the termination of the war in Europe does not affect the necessity for continuing to maintain secrecy concerning the classified activities and operations of the Signal Security Agency, and that existing security standards must be maintained for the remainder of the war and after the war is terminated.

On the same day, victory in the Battle of Okinawa was declared. Churchill summed up the battle this way:

> The strength of will-power, devotion, and technical resources applied by the United States to this task, joined with the death-struggle of the enemy, of whom 90,000 are reported to be killed, places this battle among the most intense and famous in military history.[3]

Finally, by the end of June, Vernice knew that Steve had survived Okinawa and was being sent to Pearl Harbor for rest and additional training. At Arlington Hall Station, Vernice and the other Government Girls continued to work long hours diligently sorting through the thousands of intelligence nuggets tumbling across their desks regarding Japanese capabilities and intentions. They continued to fight the war by providing as much information as they could for the planners and decision makers trying to finally end it.

Vernice's reported efficiency ratings remained "Very Good" to "Excellent" through these months. She was doing her part. She would pull her weight until the war was truly and completely over.

*June 26, 1945*

*Dear Stevie,*

*The victory in Okinawa was just announced on the radio! Everyone is relieved, but more details have come out about the casualty rate, and everyone is shocked and stunned.*

*The last letter I got from you is dated June 12th so I'm anxious to hear from you. I'll be running home nearly every day now hoping to get another letter letting me know you're okay.*

*It's time for this war to end!!!*

*Necie*

# 19
# Steve
# Oahu, Hawaii
# July 1945

> One truism about the stress of continuous combat is that *every* soldier, no matter how well trained or how experienced, has a breaking point. "There is no such thing as 'getting used to combat,'" wrote a group of psychiatrists in a 1946 report titled "Combat Exhaustion." "Each moment of combat imposes a strain so great that (all) men will break down in direct relation to the intensity and duration of their exposure."
> —Duane Schultz, "The Breaking Point: Combat Stress in WW II"

At 8:00 a.m. on June 28, 1945, Lieutenant Steve Lynn received his orders. He and twelve other artillery officers were to leave the First Marine Division encampment on Okinawa's Motobu Peninsula the next day at 8:00 a.m. to fly to Pearl Harbor in Hawaii for tactical and gunnery air observer training. He had already been an aerial observer in two brutal Pacific campaigns and probably wondered why he needed to go to school to learn how to do the job, but he didn't mind the transfer to Pearl Harbor, where he could sleep in a real bed.

He'd spent the last fourteen months away from the United States sailing aboard a crowded troop transport ship, training in an abandoned coconut plantation and the jungles of Guadalcanal, living in a tent, showering in the rain, sleeping on a field cot or on the ground, eating mostly canned and dried food, sailing aboard a fighting escort carrier, and, of course, flying at low altitude across enemy lines in a small unarmored plane dodging ground fire, antiaircraft fire, naval gunfire, and artillery shells. The rest of the time during the battles he had been taking shelter from the incessant bombing, enemy artillery, mortar fire, "friendly" fire, and kamikaze attacks on the Yontan and Kadena airfields, where he had bivouacked in shrapnel-shredded tents, bomb shelters, or foxholes in the pouring rain.

Lieutenant Lynn had seen many fellow Marines die and many more wounded. Friends had succumbed to combat fatigue, battle wounds, and disease. He had seen small children and other civilians suffering indescribable hardship, anguish, and death. He had seen Japanese soldiers carry out suicidal actions he found incomprehensible. He had gone days on end without sleep.

Lieutenant Lynn had seen, heard, felt, and smelled hell, and he was exhausted and jumpy. He was somewhere on the spectrum from mild to extreme combat fatigue, as were all the surviving First Division combat Marines by the end of the battle for Okinawa.

In the First Division final report on the Okinawa campaign sent to Admiral Chester Nimitz and the Marine Corps commandant (among others), real concern was expressed about what could become a serious morale problem for the division if more men could not be rotated for at least some time away from Okinawa. A thirty-month limit away from the States was the standing rule, but it wasn't always possible to send the men home as promised. There just weren't enough trained Marines to replace everyone, especially those with specific essential specialties. The commanding general of the First Division, Major General Pedro del Valle, wrote to the Marine Corps commandant on July 10, 1945:

> After Okinawa, there will once again exist the problem of necessary officer and enlisted rotation. Present survey indicates there may remain 205 officers of various ranks having twenty-four or more months overseas as of 30 June, 1945. Over half of these will have over thirty months. There will be approximately 3,200 enlisted [men] with two years or more in the field, of which nearly 800 will have thirty months. As the fall of 1945 approaches, the situation will become more acute from the morale viewpoint, inasmuch as the personnel entering the two-year category will have spent their entire tour in coconut grove or jungle with not a single opportunity for leave or liberty.[1]

Within a ten-month period, the Peleliu and Okinawa campaigns had placed an incredible strain on the First Division Marines. In addition to suffering very high losses during the battles, the division had not been anywhere close to "civilization" where the men could relax and enjoy a rejuvenating leave. Now they were encamped on Okinawa's Motobu Peninsula having to build their own encampment yet again and preparing for the invasion of Japan's home islands. At the same time, the division was absorbing thousands of greenhorn replacements coming into the division's ranks from the United States. Adding to the growing sense of isolation for the Old Breed veterans was the fact that none of the greenhorns could really begin to comprehend what the veteran Marines had endured.

Sending Lieutenant Lynn and the other artillery officers to Pearl Harbor for air observer training reflected three realities. First, aerial observers (AOs) were now deemed essential not only for an amphibious landing but also for a prolonged ground engagement, as the invasion of Japan's home islands would certainly be. Quoting Paul Reese in the article "New Views on Aerial Observers" in the February 1945 issue of the *Marine Corps Gazette*, "the AO is the 'eyes' for the amphibious operation."[2]

Second, the role of aerial observers was evolving. Initially, the Marine AO's job was to identify targets for artillery and naval gunfire and report the effects of those firings, but the job was expanding to include other tactical and strategic tasks involving intelligence. Observers were being asked to call in the positions, activities, and strength of both friendly and enemy troops; ground survey and mapping information; the condition of landing beaches and the flow of traffic on them; weather; hydrographic conditions; enemy logistics and capabilities, and many other details. As noted by Thomas A. Watson and F. W. McCalpin in their article "Aerial Spotters" in the October 1944 *Marine Corps Gazette*:

> Started as a medium to reduce the percentage of unobserved fire and so increase the effectiveness of artillery support, it [aerial observation] has come to be a valuable, many-purpose tool. ... Possibly the greatest single assistance rendered by the Aerial OP [observer and pilot team], in addition to its fire direction duties, is its work in conjunction with the Two section [intelligence].[3]

Consequently, it was felt that even experienced aerial observers like Lieutenant Lynn could benefit from additional training beyond that of an artillery spotter—a skill he had learned only informally at Pavuvu prior to the battle for Peleliu.

Third, Lieutenant Lynn and the other artillery officers leaving Okinawa to fly to Pearl Harbor on June 29 needed a mental and physical break. They would be critically important in training the new artillerymen replacing both the casualties lost to the Eleventh Marines on Okinawa and those men who would be rotated back to the States, having served overseas for twenty-four months or more. If the officers of the Eleventh Marines and the rest of the First Marine Division were not mentally and physically fit, it was highly unlikely the division could reorganize efficiently and rapidly enough to be maximally effective in the upcoming anticipated invasion of Japan. Whenever possible during this period, every effort was made to send the division's officers who had fought at both Peleliu and Okinawa away for a thirty-day leave in Australia, New Zealand, or Hawaii. The hope was that they would return to the division refreshed enough to effectively train and lead the men in their units. Sending Lieutenant Lynn to Air Observers' Training Center at Pearl Harbor was an efficient way to get him off Okinawa for a while.

The thirteen artillery officers from the First Division were ordered to fly with priority status to report for duty at Fleet Marine Force Headquarters at Pearl Harbor. From Okinawa, Lieutenant Lynn and his fellow officers first flew eight hours to Guam and then waited five days for a six-hour flight to Kwajalien in the Marshall Islands. They landed around 5:00 p.m. on the Fourth of July. An hour later, they boarded a third flight, which carried them across the International Date Line to land on Johnston Island, a U.S.-administered atoll southwest of the Hawaiian Islands, in the middle of the night. Five hours after that, they boarded the last flight in their journey and landed at Pearl Harbor around 2:00 p.m. on what was still July 4, 1945.

It was a great way to celebrate Independence Day! They were to report to the commanding officer of the Air Observers' Training Center for training on July 16, but first they learned they would be bivouacked at the Royal Hawaiian Hotel on Waikiki Beach until July 15 "awaiting assignment." With a per diem of $7.00 a day (about $102.00 in 2021 dollars) and a bed with clean sheets in a room overlooking a safe beach, life suddenly became much better. The deep pink Royal Hawaiian Hotel was (and still is) at the epicenter of Waikiki Beach in Honolulu. All Marines, sailors, and soldiers congregating on the beach used it as a landmark. Sunbathers, swimmers, and surfers enjoyed the beach outside the hotel's back doors, which open onto a wide veranda, swimming pool, and the famous beach.

When Lieutenant Lynn arrived, Waikiki Beach had a high barbed wire fence strung along its length. Lines of razor wire were pulled taut along the top of the fence leaning out toward the ocean. To swim or surf farther out in the water, people had to pass through gates. While the threat of a Japanese invasion was by this time negligible, the war wasn't over yet. In fact, most military planners anticipated another two years of fighting.

Lieutenant Lynn could see Diamond Head from the hotel's veranda. The famous volcanic cone east of Waikiki Beach looks out over the beach and the rest of Honolulu. In 1945, it was the location for several military defensive pillboxes and observation lookouts.

It must have seemed like a dream for Lieutenant Lynn to be able to pull back the sheets on a real bed with a real pillow and just lie down in it. To drink a beer (or two), to play basketball or baseball in a nearby park, to read during his occasional times alone in his room, to swim, to watch and flirt with the American women on the beach or in town, to eat real food that wasn't C or K rations, to shop for a few souvenirs to send home to Necie and his mother and sisters, to buy liquor and beer at the large Marine Officers' Club, to ogle at the graceful Hawaiian luau dancers on the beach every night—and all without the threat of Japanese artillery fire or *giretsu* attacks or the anticipation of having to climb into a small unarmored plane to fly over enemy positions the next morning—was a balm to his frayed nerves.

Sleeping was problematic, though. Still jumpy from combat, it was hard to even fall asleep at first. After a few days, it got easier to fall asleep, but then the dreams would start ... dreams that would continue off and on for the rest of his long life. Faces of the dead and wounded, sounds of bombardment and diving kamikazes, the stench of Peleliu, the ground shaking from mortar and artillery explosions, the taste of fear, the images of blood and mutilated bodies, remembered conversations with Marines who wouldn't make it back home, the feelings of kickback and vibration from the weapons he fired—all awakened him with his heart pounding and his body covered in sweat. He didn't talk about the dreams, and he hoped he didn't scream or cry or do anything else in his sleep that would let his roommates know he was having them. The men weren't supposed to admit that the combat experiences they had survived bothered them in any way, but Lieutenant Lynn started to rethink his "desire for a regular commission" if he survived the war.

On July 16, Lieutenant Lynn and the twelve other First Marine Division artillery officers joined forty-six additional Marines from other units at the Air Observers' Training Center. The relaxing and partying continued during the evenings. On July 30, fellow trainees Bill Lynch, Frank McCalpin, Harry Murray, Chuck Robertson, and Leslie Wondrash extended their nighttime activities through the next day and were missing from class until late on the thirty-first. Lieutenant Lynn apparently followed the rules closely enough to make it to class on time.

While Lieutenant Lynn and the other Marines were "studying," President Truman was working with America's allies to write what became known as the Potsdam Declaration. Issued on July 26, it called for the unconditional and immediate surrender of the Japanese armed forces. The declaration warned the Japanese that the alternative to surrendering would be "prompt and utter destruction." Driven by the hardline militaristic forces still holding sway, the Japanese government rejected the ultimatum:

> The Japanese government "does not consider [the Potsdam Declaration] of great importance," Prime Minister Kantaro Suzuki said in a press conference. "We must *mokusatsui* [ignore] it." Another report from a Japanese news agency quoted the Japanese reaction to the ultimatum, saying Japan would "prosecute the war of Great East Asia to the bitter end."[4]

The Japanese rejection of the Potsdam Declaration was underscored the next day, July 29, by swarms of kamikazes attacking American ships off Okinawa's coastline, damaging several and sinking the destroyer USS *Callaghan*.

Hearing the news reports on the radio, Lieutenant Lynn and his fellow Marines could only speculate about how soon they'd be making their way west again to rejoin the First Marine Division as it prepared for the war's final battles. They all tried to live in the moment and enjoy Hawaii's delights, but Lieutenant Lynn's bad dreams didn't go away.

*July 8, 1945*
*Dear Necie,*
   *This is more like it! As a tropical Pacific island, Oahu beats Pavuvu, Guadalcanal, and Peleliu hands-down! The weather is beautiful, and the Royal Hawaiian Hotel where we're staying on Waikiki Beach is really nice. It's the nicest place I've ever been. The food is good—lots of fresh meat and fruit grown right here on the islands.*

*The people are nice, too. Except for some of the shore-based Navy jerks, everyone treats us well. It's so great to see people whose faces aren't scrunched up with fatigue and stress.*

*We're enjoying it while we can because it looks like we'll be heading back to the division sooner than later. Damn Japanese! Why can't they just call it quits?*

*Keep the letters coming, Necie. They mean as much as ever to me...*

*Steve*

## 20
## Vernice
## Arlington, Virginia
## July–August 1945

> We shall probably have to kill at least 5 to 10 million Japanese [and] this might cost us between 1.7 and 4 million casualties including [between] 400,000 and 800,000 killed.
> William B. Shockley, U.S. Department of War
> "Proposal for Increasing the Scope of Casualty Studies,"
> July 21, 1945

> Until the Japanese leaders realize that the invasion cannot be repelled, there is little likelihood that they will accept any peace terms satisfactory to the Allies.
> Naval Intelligence analysis in Magic Diplomatic Summary based on Ultra intercepts, July 27, 1945

*July 25, 1945*
*Dear Steve,*

*The amount of work to be done here is still staggering even though the war in Europe is over. We're still working lots of overtime. I'm saving the money I'm making knowing I won't always get as many hours as I am now. Sure is exhausting, though.*

*Hawaii sounds really nice, and you deserve the time there after all you've been through. Enjoy every moment.*

*President Truman continues to win people over here in Washington and around the country. He seems to be able to talk to people even better than Roosevelt, and his strong push for the new United Nations seems to be popular. The press likes him because he actually answers their questions.*

*Aloha, Stevie...*

*Necie*

Knowing that Steve was in Hawaii training for participation in Operation Downfall, Vernice was undoubtedly troubled as she read the translated intercepts coming through Arlington Hall. All she could do, though, was do her job as quickly and as accurately as she could, and she could not talk to anyone about it. Her competence and diligence were recognized, however, and in early July 1945 she was awarded a pay increase from $1,800 to $2,100 a year. In early August, it was raised again to $2,166 per year (about $31,700 in 2021 dollars).

During summer 1945, the military intelligence officers and planners who read the decrypted Ultra (Japanese military) and Magic (Japanese diplomatic) messages did so with growing concern. It appeared that the Japanese were predicting Operation Olympic with startling accuracy and were mounting their defenses accordingly. Ultra intercepts were tracking a huge Japanese force buildup on the southern third of Kyushu, the southernmost of Japan's four main islands.

When the planning for Operation Downfall began in April 1945, there had been about 27,500 Japanese combat troops (the equivalent of about 1.5 American divisions) and another 28,000 ground, support, and service troops in southern Kyushu. American intelligence officers then predicted that by the November 1 Operation Olympic landing date, there could realistically be about 65,000 Japanese combat troops in the area and perhaps 2,500 aircraft.[1] This was a manageable number given the massive size of the American invasion force.

During May, June, and July, Ultra decryptions began to paint a much different landscape. They identified the units moving into the area and then their geographic assignments on the island. By mid-June, Kyushu held five Japanese divisions, two brigades, and two unidentified units of troops. Another division appeared to be on the way.[2] By the end of July, Kyushu held seven divisions, four brigades, and the two unidentified units. By early August, the intercepts decrypted by Vernice and the other cryptographers in Arlington Hall Station's Building B indicated that the number of Japanese troops had grown in a matter of weeks from 80,000 to 206,000, and it was still on the uptick. Ultra intercepts suggested there were another 225,000 Japanese troops already gathered on the northern two-thirds of Kyushu whose movement south would be possible unless their travel could be prohibited by American air strikes.[3] Magic intelligence suggested that 2,110,000 Japanese troops might be on Kyushu to defend the island by the planned November invasion date.[4] Planners now had to contend with the fact that when the invasion took place, there might be more than thirty-two times the number of Japanese defenders originally predicted.

Additionally, a second Japanese army headquarters had been added to direct the defense forces in the area, and the combat units were being positioned exactly to defend the three Operation Olympic assault beaches.[5]

Ultra decryptions provided insight into Japanese defensive tactics as well. A decoded radio intercept provided the verbatim set of instructions from the Japanese General Staff in Tokyo to all Japanese field commanders in southern Kyushu:

> The air and sea forces must make every effort to annihilate the Allies at sea. If the Allies are so bold as to risk a landing on Japan proper, a full-scale offensive will be launched against him with the intention of utterly destroying his forces ... on the beaches.[6]

Every Japanese effort would be made to keep American forces from establishing a beachhead, and any Americans reaching the beach would be countered vigorously by Japanese forces awaiting them. The confused fighting on the beach would discourage American naval gunfire and air strikes because the strikes could hit American troops as well as Japanese forces.

Additionally, Japanese forces would be positioned in defensive positions away from the beaches similar to those encountered on Peleliu and Okinawa, "an all-around defense-in-depth."

In early July, Ultra decryptions also indicated there was a concerted effort on the part of the Japanese to move their estimated 2,700 remaining suicide aircraft to southern Kyushu. (Postwar discovery indicated there were many thousands more than the number Ultra indicated.) Additionally, the Japanese had discovered that their 5,400 wood-and-fabric training biplanes couldn't be detected by American radar, which made them an ideal addition to the kamikaze force. The kamikaze pilots were being trained to concentrate their attacks on American troop transports at sea before the troops hit the beaches. Both Japanese and American planners anticipated that the kamikazes would be Japan's most destructive weapon. When Captain Inoguchi Rikiei, Tenth Air Fleet, Imperial Japanese Navy, was interrogated in 1947, he stated:

> Inasmuch as the *Kamikaze* attacks were the last means of any favorable results in the war and the only chance for breaking down American resistance a little, we did not care how many planes were lost. Poor planes and poor pilots were used, and there was no ceiling on the number of either available for use. ... If enough damage could be done to

American ships and enough American casualties resulted, perhaps there would be a "new deal" later in which some form of *victory might be salvaged* from the war."[7]

There was also a growing threat from an increasing number of Japanese suicide boats, midget subs, and manned torpedoes (*kaiten*). "The Japanese are planning in great detail for the preparation and equipping of surface suicide attack bases" was the warning written in an Ultra summary the first week of August.[8] Ultra intercepts could sometimes provide the exact unit locations and even individual boat numbers in this growing suicide fleet.

Apart from the suicide planes and boats, Ultra decryptions indicated that the 5,600 remaining conventional combat aircraft in the Japanese air force would not be a serious threat, especially following the preinvasion Allied bombardment of airfields. (Postwar discovery indicated that the number was closer to 12,700 total aircraft and 18,600 pilots available, and that the Japanese had secretly built up an impressive aviation fuel reserve obtained from the Philippines in March 1945 just prior to the islands' loss to the Americans.)[9]

On a more reassuring note, Ultra intercepts suggested that the few remaining Japanese navy destroyers had only enough fuel for one suicide mission each. The intelligence analysis noted it was unlikely the Japanese would use chemical or bacterial warfare in their home islands defense. The approximately sixty remaining Japanese submarines, however, would be a "considerable threat."[10]

Ominously, Olympic planners were notified in the "G-2 Estimate of Enemy Situation on Kyushu, U.S. Sixth Army, August 1, 1945" that the Japanese planned to use a number of *new* weapons in their home island defense.[11] Rockets, guided missiles, antiaircraft artillery, improvised land mines and booby traps, antitank weapons, and new tanks had been developed and deployed using German designs and technical assistance.

At home, the Japanese government was organizing civilian militias under the slogan "The Glorious Death of the 100 Million." Every civilian fighter was to try to kill at least one "barbarian" before he or she died in their country's defense.[12]

The concern about the Japanese buildup on southern Kyushu became so great in early August that the Joint War Plans Committee recommended that the Joint Staff Planners "prepare plans for operations against ... alternative objectives."[13] On August

6, General George C. Marshall and General Douglas MacArthur shared communications to consider alternative objectives but decided to recommend proceeding with Operation Olympic as planned.

U.S. President Harry S. Truman fervently hoped an imminent event most military planners did not know about would force a Japanese surrender before the massive assault had to take place. He dreaded the anticipated casualty rates exceeding those on Peleliu, Iwo Jima, and Okinawa. As British troops redeployed to assist their American allies in the Pacific, British Prime Minister Winston Churchill, too, was deeply worried that an invasion of Japan itself would cost another half million British lives.[14]

Considering alternatives to Operation Olympic became a moot point within the week. On August 6, the same day Generals Marshall and MacArthur considered the Joint War Plans Committee recommendation, an American B-29 bomber dropped the first atomic bomb over Hiroshima. It was followed by a second bomb over Nagasaki on August 9. Vernice listened to the radio with her coworkers at Arlington Hall as President Truman's statement about the bomb was read:

> It was "a harnessing of the basic power of the universe. ... We are now prepared to obliterate more rapidly and completely every productive enterprise the Japanese have above ground in any city. We shall destroy their docks, their factories, and their communications. Let there be no mistake; we shall completely destroy Japan's power to make war. ... If they do not now accept our terms, they may expect a rain of ruin from the air, the likes of which has never been seen on this earth."[15]

On August 10, a noncoded Japanese radio transmission was received stating the Japanese would surrender if the emperor could remain the "Sovereign Ruler." The Anglo-American Allied leadership had generally agreed this was the best outcome because only Emperor Hirohito could credibly order the surrender of *all* Japanese forces throughout eastern Asia and on the bypassed islands in the Pacific Ocean. Only he could be the stabilizing backbone for rebuilding a peaceful, democratic postwar Japan. (Some of the embittered American public did not agree and wanted the emperor tried as a war criminal.) On August 11, the Allies accepted the Japanese terms with the stipulation that the emperor would be subject to Allied authority. Then there was silence.

Two long days of worry followed with no word from the Japanese. Both Magic and Ultra intercepts indicated that militarists within the Japanese inner circle were resisting surrender and urging combat on the home islands, which they believed would finally "win" the war for Japan. The Japanese had not lost a war since imperial rule had been restored in 1868, and surrender was a hard and bitter pill for the militarists to swallow.

By Monday morning, August 13, President Truman and his advisors—including Secretary of War Henry Stimson and General Marshall—had lost patience. With President Truman's permission, General Marshall ordered a resumption of the B-29 incendiary bombing of Japanese cities. Additionally, General Marshall began preparing a plan to present to Secretary Stimson and President Truman to use chemical weapons (phosgene and cyanogen chloride gasses) and tactical (rather than strategic) nuclear weapons to "soften" the invasion beachhead defenses on southern Kyushu ahead of American landings.[16] He was searching for ways to reduce the number of anticipated casualties in Operation Olympic, and knowledge about lingering radiation effects was minimal at the time. General Marshall was assured the same morning that eight (and possibly nine) more nuclear bombs could be ready by November 1, the target date for the amphibious landing phase of Operation Olympic.[17]

Early on August 14, 1945, Arlington Hall Station translators of decoded Magic messages learned two hours before the Swiss minister presented Japan's surrender to the U.S. secretary of state in Washington that the war had finally ended. The word spread quickly around the station. Because it was not public knowledge, Vernice and everyone else at Arlington Hall were called together, asked to raise their right hand, and take a vow of silence.[18]

The Japanese announced their surrender through a special radio broadcast, and President Truman made the formal announcement to the American people that evening. At the same time, he announced that General MacArthur would play the role of supreme allied commander over Japan. About seventy-five thousand people spontaneously assembled outside the White House gates, shouting, "We want Harry! We want Harry!" He and his wife, Bess, walked outside to greet them.[19]

The war was finally over. It was none too soon because the preliminary preinvasion components of Operation Olympic were scheduled to begin in just a few short weeks.

As archival material has been declassified over recent decades and more information has been made available to historians and other interested readers, it is staggering to imagine how close America, its Allies, and Japan came to a more horrific tragedy in 1945. Many Americans have heard about the potentially enormous number of American casualties that would have resulted from the invasion of the Japanese home islands. Some Americans may have taken the next step to ponder the even greater number of Japanese casualties. Historian John Ray Skates wrote in 1994:

> Considering the continuing high casualties of the incendiary (bombing) raids, the imminent sealing of the naval blockade, the growing food shortages in the cities, and the promise of high Japanese casualties in the invasion, it can be argued that the early end of the war saved far more Japanese lives than American.[20]

What is unclear is whether many Americans or Japanese alive today understand the scope and intensity of what both the Japanese and the Americans were planning in their final decisive battles to end World War II. As General MacArthur's intelligence chief, Charles Willoughby, succinctly put it, it would have been "a hard and bitter struggle with no quarter asked or given."[21]

Reading and proofreading the Magic and Ultra intercepts about the growing enemy opposition on Kyushu, Vernice could imagine the incredible cost in American lives if the Operation Downfall invasions had to take place. Consequently, she never doubted that the dropping of the atomic bombs in 1945 was the right decision. President Truman was one of her lifetime heroes because he made that decision.

On August 15, 1945, V-J Day was declared. The Allies had defeated Japan. Washington, DC, went crazy! Vernice was there during what the *Times Herald* writer Roland Nicholson described as "the wildest, noisiest, most joyous and most colorful night this capital has ever known."[22] Church bells rang. Strangers hugged and kissed each other. People linked arms and sang their way through the streets. Musicians spontaneously formed celebratory parades. City offices, restaurants, and stores closed so workers could rejoice. President Truman declared a two-day holiday for all government workers, and Vernice and the other code breakers at Arlington Hall Station flowed into Washington's streets with everyone else. Cars gathered at the White House to continuously honk their horns. The city's streets were deeply covered with ticker tape and confetti.

There was a "spectacular fireworks" display over the city that night.[23] For a war-weary world, it was a glorious day!

The war was over, but there was still unfinished work to do both in Washington and in the Pacific. On August 16, Vernice was notified that she was being promoted to cryptographic clerk (CAF-4), an "executive position" within the General Cryptographic Branch, B-III, of the Signal Service Agency (soon to be renamed the Army Security Agency, the ASA). Her pay would be raised to $2,469.24 per year (about $36,135 in 2021 dollars), and she would be responsible for both reading and writing encoded messages as well as summarizing them for their intended recipients. She would also be supervising the cryptographic aides in her unit. During the war, the B-III Branch had produced intelligence from foreign communications other than those of the Japanese military. Now the entire ASA (officially formed from the SSA on September 6, 1945) was being consolidated and reorganized, and new intelligence objectives were being defined by world events.

Vernice was being encouraged to stay at Arlington Hall Station while the majority of women working there were being asked to leave. On August 18, the commanding officer of the SSA, Brigadier General W. Preston Corderman, gathered the cryptographic staff employees together to thank everyone for the great job they had done and let them know it was time to go home. In the agency's view, "it was their patriotic duty to get off the government payroll."[24] Vernice, on the other hand, was being given the opportunity to help transform the cryptographic services as America entered the Cold War period. The U.S. Army and Navy code-breaking units would eventually merge to form the National Security Agency, the NSA, and she could be a part of it if she chose to.

Steve wasn't done, either, but he didn't have any choices to make. He was a U.S. Marine, and the U.S. Marine Corps told him he was going to north China with his artillery battalion.

*August 16, 1945*
*Dear Stevie,*

*Can you believe it?! The war is finally over! It's hard to think about anything else...*

*Necie*

## 21
## Steve
## Oahu, Hawaii
## August 1945

> I stood there on the lip of the pulsating volcano, and I know I was terrified at what might happen and damned relieved when the invasion became unnecessary. I accept the military estimates that at least 1 million lives were saved, and mine could have been one of them.
> –James Michener, American writer and Pacific war veteran

> Thank God the war is over and I don't have to get shot at anymore. I can go home.
> –Theodore "Dutch" Van Kirk, navigator on the *Enola Gay*, after seeing the explosion over Hiroshima

After the Japanese ignored the dire Potsdam Declaration warning, Lieutenant Steve Lynn heard the news on the radio about the five-ton atomic bomb, dubbed Little Boy, that the United States dropped over Hiroshima, Japan, on August 6, 1945. Even for an artilleryman, it was impossible to fathom the strength of such a weapon or to begin to understand its significance. How could a single blast essentially wipe four square miles of a city off the face of the earth?

All Marines listened, too, as the radio announcers shared the news of the Soviet Union's declaration of war on Japan on August 8. Reportedly, nearly a million Red Army soldiers crossed the border into Japanese-held Manchuria that same day. Americans generally rejoiced, hoping the additional pressure on the Japanese would speed up a decision to surrender. Others who understood the Russians' long-term intentions knew that with the Manchurian invasion, Soviet Premier Joseph Stalin's quest to take advantage of the power vacuum in China, Korea, and even Japan had begun.[1] On the same day, American B-29s continued conventional bombing runs over Japan as well as missions dropping leaflets over civilian population centers asking Japanese citizens to "petition the Emperor to end the war."[2] Yet the war continued.

On August 9, Lieutenant Lynn listened with his fellow Marine officers to the announcement that the United States had dropped a second atomic bomb, called Fat Boy, over Nagasaki. Would Japan surrender now? Or would Lieutenant Lynn and the rest of the First Marine Division still have to face the formidable Japanese on their own land? It was hard for any Marine in the division to think about anything else.

Five days later, everyone on Hawaii heard the news that the Japanese had announced their surrender to the Allies. Finally, everyone everywhere could begin to believe the war was truly over. Impromptu parades in Honolulu and celebrations on Waikiki Beach broke out immediately as President Truman's announcement was broadcast over the loudspeakers originally set up to warn of Japanese air raids. People ran out into the streets and hugged strangers. Men and women alike jumped on cars and trucks and drove through town dragging cans and beating containers like drums. Impromptu military bands marched through the streets. Civilians tore down camouflage nets and hauled away the barbed wire coils along the beaches.[3]

Back on Okinawa, rear echelon troops and new replacements on the island celebrated exuberantly with gunfire and shouts of "We'll go home!" Many veteran combat Marines, however, were more subdued. Private First Class E. B. Sledge reported that the veteran infantrymen of the First Marine Division:

> ...received the news with quiet disbelief coupled with an indescribable sense of relief. We thought the Japanese would never surrender. Many refused to believe it. Sitting in stunned silence, we remembered our dead. So many dead. So many maimed. So many bright futures consigned to the ashes of the past. So many dreams lost in the madness that had engulfed us. Except for a few widely scattered shouts of joy, the survivors of the abyss sat hollow-eyed and silent, trying to comprehend a world without war.[4]

Lieutenant Lynn and his fellow Marines in class at the Air Observers' Training Center had trouble believing it, too. Some officers sat quietly; some whooped and hollered. Most ended the day trying to guess what they would be doing next and wondering whether the nightmares that haunted their sleeping hours would now end.

It didn't take long to find out what was coming next. Two weeks later, on August 28, Lieutenant Lynn received modified orders to leave Hawaii and "report to the Commanding Officer of Fleet Marine Force, Pacific, for first available Government surface transportation to such place as the 1st Marine Division may then be."

The class at the Air Observers' Training Center ended abruptly, and Lieutenant Lynn prepared to rejoin the First Battalion, Eleventh Marines, which was headed for north China. One item he had to check off his preparation list was getting a new set of inoculations for cholera and other diseases he might be exposed to in chaotic postwar China.[5]

When Japanese representatives signed the instrument of surrender on the American battleship USS *Missouri* (BB-63) on September 2, 1945, World War II officially ended. On the same day, Lieutenant Lynn reported on board the USS *Guilford* (APA-112) at Pearl Harbor. The Bayfield class attack transport ship headed out to sea that afternoon, bound for the Fleet Marine Force Transient Center on Guam. From there Lieutenant Lynn would travel on to Okinawa to rejoin his artillery battalion and the rest of the First Marine Division.

**USS *Guilford* (APA-112) at anchor, 1945**
(U.S. Navy photograph)

Many soldiers, sailors, and Marines were gleefully heading east back to the United States. In fact, the USS *Guilford* itself would make two round trips during late 1945 from San Diego to Guam, Saipan, Okinawa, and Japan transporting more than five thousand troops home in Operation Magic Carpet. Lieutenant Lynn and many of the other First Division Marine veterans, however, were headed to north China as the lead combat element of the Third Amphibious Corps.

*August 29, 1945*

*Dear Necie,*

*Anything you want me to buy for you in China? Yup ... China. The Division is being sent there to protect and repatriate Japanese military and civilian personnel. One day we're supposed to kill them. A few weeks later, we're supposed to protect them. The world sure is a crazy place.*

*Well, at least I'll get to see some of the guys in my old battalion again before we all split up to finally go home. In the meantime, keep the letters coming ...*

*Steve*

## 22
## Vernice
## Arlington, Virginia, and Washington, DC
## September–December 1945

> I wonder if I should have a change ... something new, something better, perhaps. A life has to move or it stagnates. Even this life, I think. It is no good telling yourself that one day you will wish you had never made that change; it is no good anticipating regrets.
> —Beryl Markham, *West With the Night*

*September 15, 1945*
*Dear Stevie,*

*Washington is changing quickly. So many of my friends are leaving. Those of us who are still here have plenty of work to do mostly because there are so few of us compared to before. There's no overtime work anymore so it's a good thing I got a pay raise to make up for the loss of paid hours. I'm not complaining, though. I'm flattered that I've been asked to stay when so many others have been asked to leave.*

*My roommate at the boarding house left for home two days ago so at least for the time being I have the room to myself. I'm really missing her. I haven't had a room to myself since I've been here, and it seems strange. We had a party to send her off. She's getting married next month to her high school sweetheart who survived the fighting in France. Sounds like Carolene and Ray will be getting married early next year, too...*

*Necie*

When the Japanese formally surrendered on board the USS *Missouri* on September 2, 1945, the work of the Military Cryptographic Branch (soon to be renamed the General Cryptographic Branch) at Arlington Hall did not end. There were still Japanese troops, civilians, and ships scattered throughout Asia that needed to be accounted for and monitored. In addition, there were many other pots being stirred throughout the world—the Chinese civil war between the Nationalists and the Communists, the developing turmoil on the Korean peninsula, the Russian occupation and expansion into eastern Europe and possibly China and Korea. Chaos was pretty much pandemic.

As an emerging world power, the United States needed to know what was happening everywhere, and the cryptographic unit's workload at Arlington Hall Station continued to be wide-ranging and challenging. The total intercept traffic had fallen by nearly 80 percent since its high in July 1945.[1] However, 351 code systems (down from 426) and the intercepted traffic of 65 governments using 25 different languages were being read at the Station.[2]

Immediately after the war ended, the work on Russian codes at Arlington Hall expanded significantly. The Russian work (later code-named Venona) had begun in early 1943 as a very small, very secret "Special Problem" in the General Cryptographic Branch, B-III. Intriguingly, a then-secret SSA report written in July 1945 contains the following statement:

> Personnel for this section usually are recruited from small towns, and from persons who have a religious background. People who are graduates of large universities and who majored in economics are not accepted, without further check on their loyalty.[3]

After V-J Day, key personnel were shifted from German and Japanese code sections to the newly created Far East Traffic section which studied and decrypted Chinese and Russian intercepts. The majority of the ASA's retained civilians were absorbed into this unit.[4] By 1946, the code breakers in the Far East Traffic section would make significant progress toward understanding the underlying structure of both the Russian diplomatic codes and the KGB spy agency codebooks.

Vernice, however, was transferred to section B-III-A-1, the French subsection of the Romance Languages Section. The mission of the Romance Languages Section was the "research, development, and exploitation of two hundred diplomatic and miscellaneous systems from twenty-four governments using seven different languages."[5] It was divided into seven subsections: French, Portuguese and Brazilian, South American, Spanish, Italian, Romanian, and Swiss. Because of her previous training in French, Vernice was a good fit for the French subsection. She slid right into her new position in wing 8 on the second floor of Building A.

At the same time, nearly all Americans were woefully war-weary and wanted to get back to "normal." They politically clamored for the soldiers, sailors, and Marines to be returned home—not later but *immediately*. The politicians listened to their constituents and relentlessly pushed the military to return veterans from around the world to the United States as quickly as possible. Military and diplomatic officials argued it was being done too quickly, and situations in many parts of the world could be more humanely stabilized if troop withdrawals were done less precipitously. Nevertheless, the Magic Carpet operation was bringing the troops home in droves, and the social ramifications were dramatic.

What did the war's end and the troops' return mean for Vernice and the other Government Girls in the Lipstick Brigade?

On V-J Day, there were 160,000 female employees in Washington, making up 60 percent of the work force. Seventy-five percent of those women hoped to stay.[6] Initially, many agencies continued to hire Government Girls to bridge the transition to a postwar organization, and some Government Girls transferred to permanent agencies as war agencies downsized and closed. Within a year after V-J Day, however, the ratio of women employed in the District of Columbia fell from six out of every ten to four out of ten.[7] Social pressure waves were beginning to swamp the Lipstick Brigade.

Male veterans returning home needed jobs and were often given priority for new or vacated positions, and the social pressure on women to quit their work in Washington and resume their "proper place" in the home was intensifying as well. Just as the propaganda machine urged the Rosie Riveters, the Wendy Welders, and the Wonder Women to help fight the war in the early1940s, it now worked overtime to persuade women it was time to return to their traditional child-rearing and homemaking roles.

It is clear from her official personnel file that Vernice was being encouraged to stay in the ASA. Shortly after V-J Day, she had been promoted to the executive position of cryptographic clerk in the General Cryptographic Branch, B-III, of the SSA. The position carried with it a great deal of responsibility and a sizable wage increase. Vernice had proven herself reliable and competent, and her efficiency ratings continued to be stellar throughout this entire period. As the SSA transitioned into the "new" ASA, Vernice continued to work diligently.

As she watched her wartime friends leave town to marry and return to their prewar homes, what were her thoughts? Washington, DC, settled down a bit as the collective war mentality transitioned into one of peace and "normalcy," but there was still so much to do and think about in the city. There were still so many interesting people to meet and places to go.

Work was both demanding and self-affirming, and she had her own income to spend the way she wished. She had a unique and independent identity apart from her family and the central Illinois culture in which she had grown up.

**A photograph of Vernice in Washington sent to her by a friend, Joe, October 1945**

(Photograph in family collection)

**One of Vernice's friends in Washington, November 1945** (Photograph in family collection)

It was all up in the air when her sister Anita visited her in Washington in December 1945. Vernice gave Anita a grand tour of the city, and they stayed up late into the night catching up.

At least for the time being, Vernice decided to continue working hard at the ASA and enjoy the Washington scene. In November, she was awarded a certificate to "acknowledge with appreciation [her] loyalty and devotion to duty ... while serving with the Military Intelligence Division, War Department." It was signed by Major General Clayton Bissell, the assistant chief of staff for Intelligence.

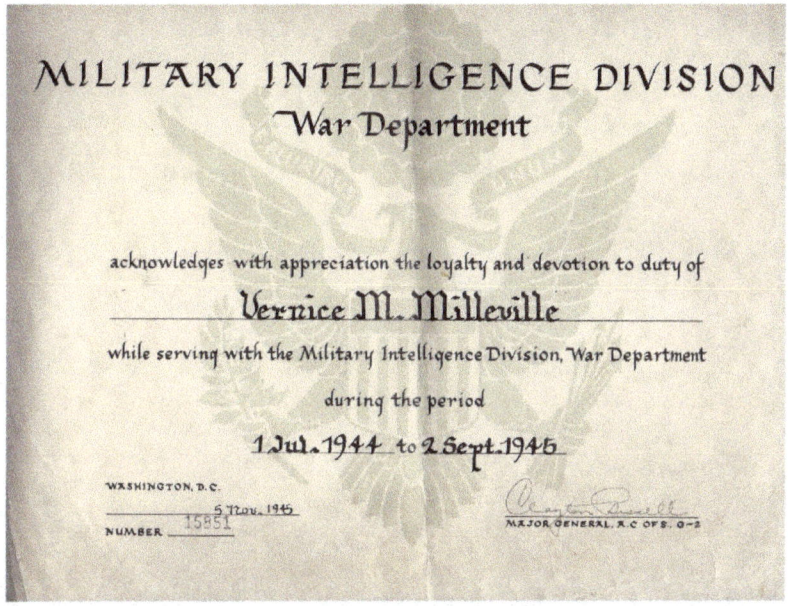

**Vernice's certificate of recognition, November 5, 1945**
(Document in family collection)

There was no way for Vernice to know how events would play out in the new year, 1946. There was no way for her to know her life's emotional framework would be forever changed in the year ahead.

*December 16, 1945*
*Dear Stevie,*

*Having to work no overtime hours has its advantages! Now I have time to see more of the sights around town. Last night after work, I was able to see the new Susanna Foster movie, "That Night With You." Franchot Tone, Louise Albritton and David Bruce starred in it, too. Susanna Foster plays the role of a singer who lies about being the daughter of a famous producer so she can get a chance at a big singing role in a movie. It was pretty funny at times but definitely not as good as the other movies she's been in. She has a beautiful voice, and she was wonderful playing Christine in "The Phantom of the Opera" a couple of years ago, but this movie didn't hold a candle to that one.*

  *Tell me how it's going in China. I love hearing about what it's like there. Any word when you'll get to leave for the States? Missing you...*

*Necie*

## 23
## Steve
## Tientsin, North China, and Home
## September–December, 1945

> Due to the uncertainties of China's civil war, all who left felt like escapees from the unknown. To have survived the Pacific War was prodigious luck, not to be stretched thin in chaotic China of 1945.
>
> —E. B. Sledge, *China Marine*

*September 26, 1945*
*Dear Necie,*

*Made it back to my unit on Okinawa just in time to get on the ship bound for China with my battalion. The ship I was on from Guam to Okinawa was a real dump—an old freighter that was noisy and dirty. Sure made me sorry I had to leave Hawaii. Now we're on a newer transport that's more comfortable but still not luxury cruising.*

*We're all curious about China. We've been told my battalion will be bivouacked in the old French quarters near Tientsin with the First Marines but no one is too sure what condition the quarters are in. Most of the older China Marines have returned to the States so there's not too much information yet on how things are really going to work. The other officers and I have been getting some briefings on the political situation there. It sounds chaotic. We'll see.*

*We all wish we were heading back to the States instead of to China, but the Marine Corps has other ideas...*

*Steve*


Lieutenant Steve Lynn and the other First Marine Division officers traveling from Pearl Harbor to Guam on the USS *Guilford* disembarked at Guam on September 13, 1945. The ship then headed farther north to drop off troops at Iwo Jima and Japan. Three days later, Lieutenant Lynn boarded the USS *Howell Lykes*, an old freighter used as a troopship and manned by merchant marines. The ship had been bombed and damaged during the battle for the Philippines in November 1944 but was back in service to transport troops during the postwar period. The *Howell Lykes* left Guam at 4:00 p.m. on the sixteenth with Lieutenant Lynn on board; it arrived at Okinawa at about 4:00 p.m. on September 24.

On Okinawa, Lieutenant Lynn rejoined the First Battalion, Eleventh Marines encamped on the Motobu Peninsula. He was just in time. Two days later, the Eleventh Marines left Okinawa for North China as participants in Operation Beleaguer. At least initially, the goal of Operation Beleaguer was to assist the Chinese government with the repatriation of nearly seven hundred thousand Japanese and Koreans remaining in China when the war ended.

Lieutenant Lynn traveled to China on the USS *Collingsworth* (APA-146). In early October, the ship arrived off the Taku Bar where the Hai River empties into the Gulf of Chihli (or Bo Hai). Landing craft carried Lieutenant Lynn and the other Marines across the bar to the docks of the small town of Taku (now Dagu). Trucks took them about seven miles farther to Tangku (or Tanggu), the railhead for Tientsin (today better known as Tianjin), thirty-six miles inland. A steam locomotive belching black smoke pulled the train filled with Marines on into Tientsin.

**Location of Tientsin (Tianjin) municipality in north China**
(Map reproduced by permission from Wikimedia Commons,
https://commons.wikimedia.org/w/index.php?curid=16493865)

By 1900, Tientsin had become an important commercial city in North China. Located at the head of the Grand Canal flowing into the Yellow Sea, it was a major international trading city with an expanding railway network. It had been occupied by Japanese forces since July 30, 1937, and now those occupying Japanese troops as well as the Japanese civilians moved into the area to manage the city's commercial interests had to be safely disarmed and repatriated to Japan. Koreans, many of whom had been drafted as laborers by the occupying Japanese, also had to be repatriated to their homeland. The Chinese Nationalist government was technically responsible for the repatriation process. The Marines' Third Amphibious Corps and the U.S. Navy's Seventh Fleet were there to provide support and assistance.

The U.S. Marines had a long history in China, going back to the Boxer Rebellion in 1900 when hundreds of Europeans, Western missionaries, and Chinese Christian converts had been besieged in the English Legation of Peking. Several battalions of Marines had joined other foreign troops to break the siege in heavy fighting. After the Boxer Rebellion ended, the Marines were stationed in the country to protect American lives and property off and on until late 1941. Seasoned "China Marines" were highly respected in the Marine Corps and provided important experience and perspective in training young Marines at the beginning of World War II.

All Marines in prewar China except for the embassy guard staff were withdrawn in November 1941. The remaining forty-eight Marines in Tientsin did not get out in time. Their compound was surrounded by the Japanese on the morning of December 8, 1941, two days before their scheduled evacuation. They, along with 156 naval support personnel, spent the rest of the war in Japanese slave labor camps.[1]

During October 1945, the First Marine Division's three infantry regiments–the First Marines, the Fifth Marines, and the Seventh Marines–were stationed in Tientsin, Peiping (now Beijing), and Chinwangtao (now Qinhuangdao), respectively. Each battalion of the division's artillery regiment, the Eleventh Marines, was attached to an infantry regiment. Lieutenant Lynn's First Battalion was stationed in Tientsin with the First Marines. The Marines stationed in Tientsin and Peiping were assigned comfortable billeting in steam-heated buildings. Many of the Seventh Marines and their associated artillerymen in Chinwangtao farther north where the Great Wall of China meets the sea lived in pup tents and faced not only colder temperatures but also more aggressive antagonists. Elements of the Sixth Marine Division were posted at Tsingtao farther south.

As they proudly marched in formation from the train terminal in Tientsin to their barracks in the old French arsenal east of the city near the airfield, the Marines of the First Marines and Lieutenant Lynn's First Battalion, Eleventh Marines were greeted enthusiastically by the Chinese. Photos taken at the time show large crowds of awed and grateful Chinese citizens waving American flags and smiling as the Marines marched by in close order. They shouted, "Ding hao [very good]!" so loudly that the sound became deafening. They tried to break into the Marines' marching ranks to shake hands, and they gestured and yelled from the windows overlooking the streets. The Marines themselves were slightly stunned but touchingly gratified. It was the only heartfelt welcome or thank-you they would experience as a unit.

LEATHERNECKS OCCUPY TIENTSIN 1 OCT. 1945 AMID JOYOUS CHINESE. Marine Corps Photo 26-18

**Marines entering Tientsin, October 1, 1945**
(U.S. Marine Corps photograph)

To support the Chinese Nationalists, the Marines initially managed the bivouacking and repatriation of the Japanese soldiers and civilians in the Tientsin area. They were also sent out to protect the rail and communication lines between the coalfields of Chinwangtao to the north and Peiping to the west. They guarded the coal shipments on the railroad because the coal was desperately needed by the utilities in Tientsin, Peiping, and Shanghai during the cold fall and winter months. The Chinese Communists continually tried to disrupt the coal train deliveries to sow political discontent. Other armed groups attacked the railways for the food and coal they carried. It was wintertime, and people were trying to survive (and, in some cases, take advantage of the postwar chaos).

Officially, the Marines were to take no part in the resuming power struggle between the Nationalists and the Communists after the war ended; they were just there to get the Japanese and Koreans repatriated. It soon became clear, however, that in spite of their best intentions, the Marines were caught in the middle of a civil war between the Nationalist forces led by Chiang Kai-shek (Jiang Jie-shi) and the Communist forces led by Mao Tse-tung (Mao Zedong). Adding to the chaos were the armed Japanese-trained and Japanese-equipped puppet government soldiers and the Chinese warlord-led bandits. Marines were involved in three firefights along the railroad rights-of-way within just the first month after their arrival.

The first clash occurred during the first week after the First Marines arrived in Tientsin. Engineers and a First Marines rifle platoon were trying to clear roadblocks some twenty miles outside Tientsin when they were fired on by approximately fifty Chinese Communists. Three Marines were wounded, but no one was killed. The Marines withdrew to Tientsin. The next day, a First Marine rifle company and a tank platoon returned to remove the roadblocks under the cover of carrier-based aircraft. The pattern of using supporting arms to accomplish most tasks was set then and there. Before Operation Beleaguer ended in May 1949, however, thirty-four Marines would be killed and forty-two more would be wounded. Fourteen Marine aircraft would be lost as well.

Upon their arrival in north China, the Marines had thought the Japanese soldiers and civilians would be their most dangerous challenge. In fact, most Japanese were respectful, disciplined, and compliant. They held the U.S. Marines in high esteem for their fighting ability and for defeating their best soldiers. According to Private First Class E. B. Sledge, who later wrote the book *China Marine*, all Japanese soldiers saluted all Marines regardless of rank.[2]

In some situations, the Japanese troops were armed by the Marines and served as allies trying to maintain order. During what became known as the Lang Fang incident, for example, the Marines armed Japanese troops with firearms and two tanks and sent them out to guard a railroad station against "puppet soldiers" overnight. The small group of U.S. Marines waited within a nearby walled village.³

The Japanese were grateful to the U.S. Marines for treating them with respect, legitimacy, and courtesy. On more than one occasion, American Marines protected Japanese civilians from Chinese mobs eager for payback for the atrocities the Chinese had endured during Japanese occupation. The Japanese were so impressed by the Marines' conduct, in fact, that Japanese Major General Eiji Nagano wrote in a December 1945 letter to U.S. Marine Corps Major General Lemuel C. Shepherd:

> Exemplary conduct and actions on the part of your soldiers inspired our minds with respect and wonder ... [and] every Japanese ... feels grateful to you for your fair and square dealings. This is the last thing that we expected of your Marines of the Okinawa Battle fame.⁴

U.S. Marine Pfc. John Casinelli helping a Japanese family leave Tientsin, China, 1945
(U.S. Marine Corps photograph, U.S. National Archives(#127-GW-187-226644))

After settling into the French arsenal in Tientsin, Lieutenant Lynn was not alone among the Marines in taking advantage of one of the time-honored benefits of serving in China: hiring servants, or "houseboys." After what seemed like a long time in the Marine Corps taking care of his own uniform and eating C rations, Steve delighted in having someone else wash his clothes, shine his boots, run errands, find decent food to eat, and then cook it, too. The houseboys hired by the Marines—including the enlisted men—appreciated the American currency they were paid and were usually hardworking and well liked. Sometimes they learned enough English, and the Marines learned enough Chinese, to allow solid friendships to form. Sledge wrote, "He [his houseboy, Hao] and I both had tears in our eyes when I left Peiping to return home."[5]

Steve later told occasional stories about the houseboy working for him and some of the other officers. Apparently, their houseboy became a pretty good poker player ... good enough to occasionally beat the Marines "at their own game."

Lieutenant Lynn sought out non-Marine food because the Marines were still issued only K and C rations. Sometimes he found good food in Tientsin's restaurants. Sometimes he and the other officers gave their houseboy money to scrounge fresh food including eggs and meat. Lieutenant Lynn said he and the other Marines were, like Private Sledge, "out of our heads" for fresh food after nearly two years or more with very little fresh meat or vegetables.

Of course, Lieutenant Lynn had spent some time eating "real food" during his brief stay in Hawaii after the battle for Okinawa, but he apparently hadn't had his fill. After buying and cooking the food for Lieutenant Lynn and the others, their houseboy cleaned everything up, including their mess kits.

Almost immediately upon arriving in north China in October, the Marines felt the weather turning cooler. The climate is similar to that of the north-central United States. By November, it was downright cold. Lieutenant Lynn and the others were issued their winter-service green uniforms and green wool overseas caps as well as thick Marine-green wool, double-breasted overcoats. All Marines were responsible for the perfect tailoring of their own personal uniforms. The houseboys stepped up for this important task as well. If they couldn't do the tailoring themselves, they knew skillful local tailors who could handle the job. It had to be done right because a Marine's uniform had to fit perfectly for inspection if he wanted to go on liberty and avoid being assigned extra duty.

Lieutenant Lynn may have also taken advantage of the guided tours arranged by the Marine Corps to visit Peiping, about seventy miles from Tientsin. There he would have seen the ancient palaces and temples of the capital city.

Leaving the French arsenal to go on leave in Tientsin (or Peiping) was not something a Marine could do inconspicuously. Their green wool uniforms and their (mostly) Caucasian identity just would not allow Marines to blend into the Chinese throngs, especially since many Chinese were thin and sickly after years of war and deprivation. Marines walking through town often found themselves with a trail of Chinese walking behind them. Some Chinese folks simply wanted to shake the Marines' hands in gratitude. Some were beggars who quickly learned how generous many Marines were. Some were children wanting to watch how the Marines walked and what they did and maybe get a piece of chocolate. Some wanted to sell services or products. Lieutenant Lynn even had a man try to sell him his daughter. The rampant poverty in postwar China took many forms.

There were so many new sights to see. Coolies (unskilled laborers) picking up dung for fuel, Gobi Desert camels carrying large loads through the street, rickshaw drivers transporting people around town, Chinese money changers trying to exchange various types of Chinese currency for American dollars, shopkeepers selling ancient Chinese porcelain and arms, Chinese stilt dancers celebrating a national holiday … it was a far different world from the one Lieutenant Lynn had experienced growing up in southern Illinois.

**U.S. Marines watching a camel caravan heading for the Gobi Desert in Mongolia, 1945**
(U.S. Marine Corps photograph, U.S. National Archives (#127-GW-89-226472))

In spite of the novelty, every single Marine in China really just wanted to go home. The idea that they had survived the brutal Pacific island battles but might be shot by Chinese bandits haunted them. The "points system," or Advanced Service Rating (ASR) score was always on their minds. It was a system initially set up by the U.S. Army to determine which soldiers would be eligible to go home when the European war ended and which soldiers would be sent to the Pacific to fight the Japanese. The Marine Corps adopted the same system to determine the order in which Marines would return home after Japan surrendered.

Initially, the target ASR score needed to go home, was eighty-five. One point was awarded for each month of service since September 16, 1940. Another point was added for each month overseas. Five points were awarded for each award received (Distinguished Service Cross, Silver Star, Legion of Merit, Distinguished Flying Cross, Bronze Star, Air Medal, Purple Heart, Soldier's Medal) and each campaign star worn on theater ribbons. Twelve points were awarded for each child the soldier or Marine had in his immediate family under the age of eighteen, up to a limit of three.

The ASR system sometimes seemed to reward the rear echelon troops (supply troops, administrative aides, etc.) over combat troops. Many of the rear echelon troops had been overseas for two or three years and participated in several campaigns behind the scenes, which gave them a fair number of points, but a combat infantryman often didn't survive that long without being wounded. Even among the highly disciplined Marines, this weakness in the system caused consternation and discontent as the months dragged on after the Japanese surrender—and as the Marine infantrymen who had survived Peleliu and Okinawa continued to dodge the bullets flying around postwar China. Because the social and political pressure both at home and within the military ranks themselves to get American troops home as soon as possible was so great, the ASR score was lowered to seventy-five after Japan surrendered. Later in 1945, the ASR score was dropped even lower.

Operation Magic Carpet, the name given to the massive logistical effort to "get the boys home," became a frenzied attempt to satisfy the insatiable American clamor to demobilize. Military leaders at the time continued to warn the policy makers that the rapid demobilization was seriously weakening the military forces left in destabilized areas such as north China, Korea, and parts of Europe. General George C. Marshall even remarked, "It was not a demobilization; it was a rout."[6] Historians since that time have argued that in Asia, "the American public paid with the Korean War for its misplaced sentimentality."[7] Certainly, in north China, the number of Marines available to carry out the assigned mission began to dwindle almost immediately after their arrival.

Lieutenant Lynn felt comfortable enough in the steam-heated French arsenal billet and confident enough that he would leave for home within a reasonable period that only a week after he arrived in China, he turned in much of his field equipment (782 gear) to the regimental quartermaster for credit: a pistol belt with a magazine pocket, a can for processed meat with its cover, a canteen with its cover, a dispatch and map case, a lensatic compass in its leather case, a metal cup, an electric flashlight, field glasses, a steel helmet, his fighting and utility knife in its scabbard, an M3-10-6 gas mask, a first aid packet, a poncho, a first aid pouch, his bedding roll, and his clothing roll. Not knowing for sure how long he would still be there or what he would need to travel home, he kept his two-part M-1941 olive drab haversack (no. 34676), his .45-caliber pistol with its lanyard, holster, suspenders, pistol belt, and ammunition magazines; his haversack knife, fork, and spoon; his officer's whistle, and his .30-caliber carbine with its sling, oiler, magazine carrier, and cleaning brush and thong.

He also kept his pair of flying goggles, his summer flight helmet, and his pair of earphones. He was still the designated battalion aerial observer, and the VMO-3 squadron was stationed at the nearby airfield. Although many of the VMO-3 pilots and ground personnel Lieutenant Lynn knew from Okinawa traveled to Tientsin at the same time he did, almost all of them were detached and headed back to the United States very soon afterward. Observation "cover flights" were flown by the pilots of the squadron over railroad and communication lines, but no artillery spotting flights were needed throughout October, and Lieutenant Lynn turned in his flight equipment to the quartermaster for credit on November 5. His days as an aerial observer were over.

**Marine flying helmet**
(Displayed in Flying Leathernecks Aviation Museum; photograph by M. Vieregg)

As more and more individual Marines were sent home from Tientsin, the remaining Marines had to assume increasing responsibility. There were a few new Marines filtering in to replace the detached veterans, but they were straight out of boot camp or officers' training and knew very little about what they were supposed to be doing. On November 1, Lieutenant Lynn stepped up to become the battery commanding officer, replacing the former commander who headed back to the States. By December 1, he had also been delegated the responsibilities of battalion chemical officer and battalion intelligence officer. The ranks of experienced Marine officers were becoming thinner and thinner.

When not on duty, Lieutenant Lynn passed the time reading Armed Service Edition books and listening to the Marine-operated radio station, XONE-Peking. The *Hit the Deck* show was broadcast in the morning; *Jive for Gyrenes* in the afternoon. Mail was delivered every day to Tientsin, too—a welcome diversion.

At the U.S. Marine Corps 170th birthday celebration on November 10, the official cake cutting in Tientsin was done with a captured Japanese saber. In the Third Amphibious Corps Officers' Club, Red Cross workers danced along with the drinking celebrants.

Finally, on December 18, Lieutenant Lynn received the orders he had been waiting for:

> Effective 19 December, 1945, you will stand detached from the First Marine Division, Fleet Marine Force, and such duties as may have been assigned you, and will report when directed to the Commanding Officer of an orally designated vessel for government surface transportation to the United States.

First Lieutenant Jack E. Dearmore, Lt. Lynn's lifelong friend, received the same orders on the same day.

In Lieutenant Lynn's final officer fitness report dated December 23, 1945, the commanding officer of the First Battalion, Eleventh Marines, Lieutenant Colonel R. W. Wallace, rated Lieutenant Lynn's performance as "very good" to "excellent" in all categories. He also noted that Lieutenant Lynn had changed his mind since his last fitness report in June and no longer desired a regular officer's commission in the United States Marine Corps. He, like so many World War II combat veterans, had seen and done enough ... more than enough. He just wanted to get back to the country he'd fought for and begin his civilian life anew.

Lieutenant Lynn took the early morning train from Tientsin to Taku with five other Marine Corps officers and boarded the USS *Adair* (AP-91) on December 21, 1945. After transporting replacements from the States to the Transient Center on Guam, the ship had picked up and transported Third Marine Division replacements for the First Marine Division units in Tientsin, Peiping, and Chinwangtao. It set sail the same day Lieutenant Lynn embarked. He and the other Marines on board hoped the ship would take the direct northern route home after picking up some more Marines in Japan. Instead, the *Adair* headed for Shanghai and then Guam, where it picked up even more Marines, sailors, and soldiers. The trip home from north China took more than three weeks. This would be the *Adair*'s fourth and last trip in Operation Magic Carpet. All in all, it carried over seven thousand troops back home.

December 1945 was the peak month for Operation Magic Carpet in the Pacific. During that one month, 695,486 people of all categories — Army, Navy, Marine Corps, and civilians — were returned to the United States from the Pacific. They were transported by 369 U.S. Navy vessels as well as ships of the War Shipping Administration.[8] The size of the Marine Corps in August 1945 was 485,000 men and women. By 1946, the strength of the

Marine Corps had fallen to 155,679 men and women, and it would continue to be reduced into 1950.[9]

Along with Lieutenant Lynn on the USS *Adair* were fellow aerial observers Frank "Bill" McCalpin and Gene McDonald. They had been through a lot together. Lieutenants McDonald and Lynn had been in the same Field Artillery Class back at Quantico, and all three had flown as artillery spotters over Peleliu and Okinawa. Now they celebrated Christmas and the New Year on the ship as it churned through the waves across the Pacific. As officers aboard ship, they had to stand three types of watch: mine watch (on the bow of the ship), troop officer of the day, and troop liaison officer (up on the bridge).[10] When they weren't on watch, though, they had plenty of free time to think, read, talk, and play cards.

How much time did they spend leaning against the rail smoking a cigarette and looking out over the ocean horizon trying to put the last three years' experiences in perspective? How much time did they spend talking about other fellow Marines who had been injured or killed or were still waiting in China for transport home? Maybe Steve and Gene talked about Gene's close call over southern Okinawa with Lieutenant Manley. How much time did they spend thinking about their plans to take advantage of the GI Bill when they got home?[11] What would it be like to see their families again? How would their hometowns seem different after what they had all been through? Steve had to be wondering, too, what would happen when he again met Necie face-to-face.

Marine Lieutenants Lynn, McDonald, and McCalpin all had destinations in mind and plans for the future, but they couldn't be sure how or whether their plans would pan out. As they sailed under the Golden Gate Bridge into San Francisco Bay on January 15, 1946, the three United States Marine Corps artillery officers did know one thing for sure. They had miraculously survived the war.

**Lt. Lynn sailing home on the USS *Adair*, January 1946**
(Photograph in family collection)

*January 4, 1946*
*Dear Necie,*

 *We're on the slow boat <u>from</u> China. It's like a milk run on a train trip. We seem to be stopping at every conceivable port in east Asia to pick up or drop off personnel of all different stripes. At least Bill and Gene are on board, too, so there's someone to shoot the bull with.*

 *Even after all we've been through, Gene is still smiling. He's planning on leaving the Marines as soon as he can and move back to Derry, PA. He and his high school sweetheart, Mary Jo, are already planning their wedding. Frank got word just before we left that he and Art Spiegel have been accepted at Harvard Law School. Once he's done with school, he's heading back home to St. Louis to begin a legal career. He's got big dreams of becoming a judge. Knowing him, I'd be willing to predict that he'll get it done. Art wants to be a judge, too, back in Ohio. They were just telling me that Bob McClean plans to stay in the Marines. He's accepted a regular commission. More power to him. I've had enough.*

 *Sure looking forward to sailing under that Golden Gate Bridge and stepping foot in the States again. Can't wait to see you, Necie...*
                 *Steve*

## 24
## Vernice
### Arlington, VA, and Washington, DC
### January–March 1946

*Life had a different shape; it had new branches and some of the old branches were dead.*[1]
—Beryl Markham, *West with the Night*

Vernice Milleville celebrated the New Year of 1946 drinking a cocktail (or two) and smoking with her friends in Washington, DC. She was enjoying the postwar city, and her administrative responsibilities in the Army Security Agency (ASA) were challenging and affirming. She worked hard at her job, and she liked it. Many of her wartime coworkers and friends had left town, but the ones who stayed were conscientious and intelligent. Together, they were getting a lot done in the postwar cryptographic units of the ASA.

Not all the women in the Lipstick Brigade who wanted to remain in government jobs were able to do so, but many did because the knowledge and skills they had acquired and demonstrated were valued by government agencies transitioning to new postwar roles. Other women were hired into the growing private sector in the Washington, DC, area. Businesses as well as research and development firms actually recruited former female government workers because the women had specialized knowledge of how certain government bureaucracies functioned.[1]

The fact of the matter is, though, that women working full-time in Washington (and elsewhere) in 1946 were under increasing social pressure to stop working, get married, and have babies. There was pressure even from strangers who would stop working women on the streets of Washington and express open disapproval of their working outside the home. On February 1, 1946, Jerry Klutz wrote in the article entitled "Men Again Taking Girls' Federal Jobs" printed in the *Washington Post*, "It's a historical fact that after every war a campaign is made openly to drive women out of the offices and back to the kitchens."[2]

Widely read magazines such as *Atlantic* and *Woman's Home Companion* ran articles like "Getting Rid of the Women" and "Give Back the Jobs." The *New York Times* and the *Washington Post* published articles warning working women they would become part of "a new generation of spinsters" if they remained in the workforce.³

In February 1946, six months after V-J Day, Vernice was notified she was being retained on staff even as the number of people in her unit was again being reduced "in line with new allocations." The evaluations of her work at the ASA convinced her superiors that she was one of the people the agency needed as it transitioned into a peacetime agency. Actually, by 1947, the country was entering what began to be called the Cold War between the Western Bloc (the United States and its allies) and the Eastern Bloc (the Soviet Union and its satellite states.)

By February, too, Steve was back in the United States receiving medical treatment at the Great Lakes Naval Hospital north of Chicago. On February 20, 1946, he received orders stating that he was relieved from active duty and granted a leave of absence for a period of sixty days plus travel time. How and where could they touch base again? How would their first meeting in over two years go? How would she feel about him when she actually spent time with him again? How would he feel about her? She knew a lot more about life than she had when they'd parted ways in Champaign in January 1944. She knew she had changed.

Somehow Steve figured out a way to travel to Washington to see Necie in late February. One blurry photo labeled "Feb. 1946" shows them together in front of a movie marquee in Washington, DC. It's clear from Vernice's personnel records that she didn't take time off from work, and it's a bit of a mystery how Steve could have arranged transportation across the country with the railroads so crowded, but in the photo, Vernice looks delighted to have him there. More than delighted really—overjoyed.

After their brief rendezvous, Vernice continued to work diligently at Arlington Hall Station through March. It wasn't clear what would happen next. In the meantime, Steve had his own affairs to tend to at home, and it wasn't practical for Vernice to pull the plug on a well-paying, interesting job in Washington, DC, now (or maybe ever). Besides, cross-country travel was difficult to arrange as troops coming home from Europe and the Pacific filled the railcars.

**Photo of Vernice in Washington, DC, taken by a friend, March 1946**
(Photograph in family collection)

Suddenly, at the end of March, the rug was pulled out from under Vernice. She received the shocking news on March 29 that her mother had been stricken with a massive cerebral hemorrhage. Vernice was needed back in Champaign immediately. Her superiors at the ASA granted her leave without requiring the normal two weeks' notice, and they helped her get travel papers. She dropped what she was doing and left Washington for "home."

# 25
# Steve
# Illinois
# January–March 1946

> To leave it all, and go back to normality: yes, that was undoubtedly the better option.
> —Maria Duenas, *The Time In Between*

*February 10, 1946*
*Dear Necie,*

*I finally made it to Great Lakes after waiting around in San Francisco for a train to bring me here. At least, I was able to spend the time with Gene and Bill. We'd probably seen enough of each other the last several months but it was better than being alone. They were as anxious as I was to head home.*

*I'm enclosing a photo Bill took of me on the USS Adair. He was able to get it developed in San Francisco while we were waiting for transport. Thought it might be good for you to see that I'm thin but otherwise okay. As soon as I can get medical clearance to get out of here, I'm going to snag a train heading for Washington. I'll wire the date.*

*Can't wait to see you...*

*Steve*

When he arrived in San Francisco on January 15, 1946, First Lieutenant Steve Lynn was ill. He'd picked up intestinal worms from some of the food he'd eaten in China. He was rapidly losing weight, unreasonably fatigued, and in considerable pain. On the same day the USS *Adair* arrived in port, he was told at the headquarters of the Department of the Pacific that he'd be given orders to travel to the Great Lakes Naval Hospital in northern Illinois for treatment.

Unfortunately, he wouldn't be able to get to Illinois very quickly. With so many troops arriving onshore from overseas, the railroads and the limited domestic airlines were unable to get the returning troops to their homes nearly as fast as they wanted to get there. The problem was especially acute on the Pacific coast during January 1946. Historian Samuel Morison reported, "Rickety old cars were pressed into service, but the situation was so bad that the railroads published advertisements apologizing for the shortage of transportation."[1]

Lieutenant Lynn had to check in with the Department of the Pacific headquarters four days in a row to get his transportation orders, and then he had to wait for the rail transport itself. Whether he felt well enough to enjoy any of the sights and sounds of postwar San Francisco during the time he was waiting to leave the city he never said.

To board the trains heading east, servicemen sailed first on one of the Southern Pacific rail ferries across the bay to Oakland. Some of the eastbound trains they boarded in Oakland had "mortuary cars" filled with flag-draped caskets attached to the end.[2] The trip across the country was uncomfortable, crowded, and long. He didn't arrive at the U.S. Marine Corps Separation Center and the Great Lakes Naval Hospital north of Chicago until February 7, more than three weeks after he had disembarked from the USS *Adair* in San Francisco. He was so sick by the time he finally arrived at Great Lakes that he had to spend ten days in the hospital.

While he was receiving medical treatment, Lieutenant Lynn was officially assigned to the Second Casual Company of the U.S. Marine Corps Separation Center. The food wasn't too bad. Fresh cold milk whenever he wanted it was a treat. Like so many in his generation, he'd grown up drinking fresh milk with every meal and sometimes in between, but all the Marines going overseas had been warned not to drink it there, and dehydrated milk (when it was available) just wasn't the same. The night before he left China on the USS *Adair*, fellow Marine artillery officer Lieutenant Dick Kennard wrote his mother, "Please fill that ice box with milk, cream, make some cake, too, for me."[3] Debarking from ships in San Francisco, San Diego, and Seattle, returning troops were offered fresh cold milk by Red Cross ladies as soon as they descended the gangplanks.

As he recuperated in the Great Lakes Naval Hospital, Lieutenant Lynn was restless and impatient with his treatment and recovery. He was chomping at the bit to see Vernice and his family. He was eager to get going with the rest of his life.

Finally, on February 21, he left Great Lakes on "terminal leave." Somehow, he found a way to catch a crowded train in Chicago heading east to Washington, DC, so he could visit Necie. He couldn't stay long, and she couldn't take off work, but at least they were able to see each other again after two long years. They hadn't been together since January 1944 when he'd been able to spend a few days with her in Champaign after he finished his training at Quantico and was on his way to Camp Pendleton, California, and the Pacific.

After their very brief rendezvous, he jumped on another train back to Chicago, where he caught an Illinois Central train headed south. Still wearing his uniform, in part because he didn't have any civilian clothes that fit him, Lieutenant Lynn received slaps on the back and "Welcome home!" greetings along the way. Some people recognized the First Marine Division insignia on his uniform. The division had a well-earned reputation among everyday folks who'd followed the war.

Like many of the returning veterans, Steve had a plan. After a brief stopover in Champaign, he was going back to the farm in southern Illinois to see his family. He'd missed his mother and sister Tillie very much, and, well, his father ... was his father. His father could use Steve's help getting the spring planting done, especially since Steve's brother, George "Joe" Washington, had been injured fighting in France. Steve also wanted to go see a recommended doctor across the Ohio River in Paducah, Kentucky, to see if he could finally get rid of the intestinal worms the naval doctors at Great Lakes hadn't completely eliminated with their treatment.

Steve stopped in Champaign for a couple of days to register for the summer term at the University of Illinois. Necie's parents, Millie and George Milleville, were delighted to see him and made room for him in their boardinghouse, the Illini Club. It was there that he ate the first home-cooked meals he'd had since he left the States two years earlier. Millie outdid herself, cooking all his favorite foods, and stood watching over him as he ate them.

Steve's academic plan was to finish the work for his mechanical engineering degree as soon as he could. With the financial assistance of the GI Bill, he could now do it without working fifty hours a week trying to scrape up enough money for room and board. He had some back pay saved, too, and he could take heavy course loads, focus on the coursework, and finish as quickly as humanly possible.

**Vernice's parents, Millie and George Milleville, March 1946**
(Photographs in family collection)

After enjoying more milk, cream, fresh meat, canned tomatoes, pickles, German cakes, and homemade cookies at Necie's parents' boardinghouse and getting their promise he could live there when he returned to campus, Steve jumped on the Illinois Central Railroad train headed for southern Illinois. With his rucksack in tow, he hopped down off the train in Metropolis and was greeted by his mother and father at the station. They were relieved and proud to see him. It had been three long years of waiting and worrying back on the farm near Brookport. His mother dressed up for the occasion, but her fancy dress didn't distract onlookers from her tears of happiness when Steve ran to give her a long embracing hug.

For the next few weeks, Steve followed the Paducah doctor's prescribed medical regimen which finally resolved his intestinal worm issue, and he patiently helped his father with the spring farm chores. Fortunately, his father's attitude and behavior toward Steve had changed, and they were able to work peaceably and productively together.

Steve's mother kept him fed, and he continued to gain back some of the weight he'd lost. It was pure pleasure to be able to walk down into the fruit cellar and grab a glass jar of preserved southern Illinois peaches. He spooned them into a bowl and poured fresh cream over the lot. He could polish off a whole jar in one sitting.

**Steve's mother, Elva Phillips Lynn, 1946**
(Photograph in family collection)

The early spring flowers were just starting to bloom in the woods up in the Shawnee Hills where his maternal grandparents' place was now being farmed by one of their sons, Truman. As February warmed into March, the southern Illinois trees started to gradually show new growth. The redbud trees turned pink, and the dogwood flower buds swelled with the increasing sunlight and warming temperatures. Migrating birds fluttered about in the shrubs along the fence lines and higher in the tree canopy. What a contrast to the images of Peleliu and Okinawa he still envisioned during his restless nights. And so many Marines he had known would never see such a beautiful springtime again.

Steve reconnected with his old teachers; favorite aunts, uncles, and cousins; and the friends (who had survived the war) from his high school days, and he shared stories with his brother Joe, who was recovering from the war injury to his right arm. Neither of them wanted to go hunting, though. Steve would never hunt any living creature again.

All in all, it was good to have the time at home to recover physically and prepare mentally for his next chapter back at school in Champaign. But when would he get to see Necie again?

They continued to write to each other, and now it was a bit easier to talk on the phone, too. The newly acquired phone service at the Lynn farm was on a party line (shared landline telephone circuit), and it wasn't always available (or very private), but it was better than nothing as they both bided their time and tried to figure out how the future might play out.

Sadly, the catalyst for their next meeting turned out to be Millie Milleville's sudden illness at the end of March. In tears, Vernice sent Steve an urgent telegram relaying the shocking news, and he dropped everything he was doing to figure out how he could get to Champaign to be there for her.

## 26
## Steve and Vernice
## Champaign, Illinois
## April–May 1946

**We are not the same persons this year as last; nor are those we love. It is a happy chance if we, changing, continue to love a changed person.**
## --W. Somerset Maugham, *The Summing Up*

Vernice Milleville was granted a paid leave from the Army Security Agency and arrived back in Champaign in time to see her mother before Millie Milleville died in Burnham City Hospital at the age of fifty-seven on April 14. It had been sixteen days since Millie's stroke had occurred. Vernice's paid leave had expired on April 4, but Vernice had requested an unpaid leave for another six weeks, which she was granted.

Steve Lynn traveled up to Champaign to be with Vernice, her father, George, and her sisters as soon as he could get a seat on an Illinois Central train. Thinking back over the years, Steve had known and come to care for Millie from his time spent with Vernice before the war. He had even lived in the family's boardinghouse on John Street before he joined the Marines. Millie had written to him regularly while he was overseas and sent him much-appreciated food packages, too. She had even provided his first home-cooked meals when he returned to the United States. She had treated him much like a son.

Steve helped the shocked family get back on its feet. He helped George with projects around the boardinghouse and kept the dejected and grieving man occupied with company and conversation. He spent time with Vernice and her three sisters as they arranged their mother's funeral service at St. John's Evangelical Lutheran Church in Champaign, where her mother had been a member. He stood nearby as they greeted the ninety-some friends and family who attended the service.

Necie's maternal grandparents had died around the age of sixty as well but were buried back in the St. Paul Lutheran Church cemetery near Altamont, Illinois. Instead of taking Millie's body back to Altamont, George and his daughters decided that Urbana's East Lawn Memorial Park would be Millie's final resting place. George bought enough burial plots to accommodate all the

Milleville girls and himself when their time came. Ludaemilia "Millie" Elizabeth Goers Milleville was laid to rest on April 16, 1946. She had lived to see all four of her daughters graduate from the University of Illinois. Two of her daughters were already married and had children. Millie had lived a good life, but it had been too short.

> **MILLEVILLE RITES TUESDAY AT ST. JOHN'S**
>
> Mrs. George Milleville, 57, 508 East John street, died at 9:35 p. m. Sunday at Burnham City hospital following an illness of two and a half weeks due to complications.
>
> The body was taken to the Owens funeral home. Funeral services will be conducted at 2:30 p. m. Tuesday from St. John's Lutheran church of which she was a member. Reverend J. G. Kaiser, pastor, will officiate and burial will be in East Lawn Memorial park.
>
> Mrs. Milleville was born Millie Goers, daughter of Mr. and Mrs. William J. Goers, Altamont, July 21, 1888. She was married to Mr. Milleville February 2, 1913. The family moved from Altamont in 1931.
>
> Mrs. Milleville leaves her husband, and four children: Anita Milleville, Oak Park; Mrs. Carl Wilfong, Flora; Mrs. Norman McQuown, New York city, and Bernice Milleville, Washington, D. C. She also leaves three grandchildren, Margaret Ann and Steven Paul Wilfong, and Kathryn McQuown; one sister, Mrs. John Schwerdtfeger, of Altamont; and four brothers, Arthur Goers, Champaign; Sam Goers, Altamont; Albert Goers, LaGrange, and Frank Goers, Sadorus.

Local Champaign-Urbana newspaper obituary for Millie Milleville, April 1946
(Clipping in family collection)

It was good for Steve and Vernice to spend the time together even though the occasion was saturated with sadness and shock. Sitting and talking quietly on the swing hanging from the ceiling of the Illini Club's front porch, they must have wondered if it was the right time to make any decisions about a future together. How well did they really know each other after the experiences they'd each had during the war? How had his horrific experiences at Peleliu and Okinawa changed him? How had her time of hard work and social independence in DC changed her? How had their views of the world and their views of their possible life together changed since they had known each other as young students meeting on John Street in 1941? Was the connection they felt before he'd gone into combat still there, or did they need some time to figure it out? What effect did the loss of Necie's mother have on her thinking? Maybe it was impossible for either of them to know for sure until they spent more time together. Should they wait a while before making any hard-and-fast decisions?

Vernice lingered in Champaign, spending time with her family and with Steve even after her unpaid leave expired on May 4. A notation in her personnel file indicates that the Army Security Agency personnel chief, D. Glen Starlin, reached out to her by teleprinter on May 13 wanting to know what her plans were. He even went so far as to say:

> If it is necessary for you to resign, and at a later date you are interested in reemployment, we will be glad to consider your application.

Vernice responded the same day, and she returned to work at Arlington Hall Station on May 14. Her services were still desired and needed in the Army Security Agency, and the pay was good. Was she still unsure about her own personal plans, or had she and Steve already laid out a plan for a future together?

## 27
## Steve
## Champaign, Illinois
## May–September 1946

**The combat veteran not only has to survive the experience, he has to learn to live with it the rest of his life.**
      —**Paul Fussell, as quoted by E. B. Sledge in** *China Marine*

*July 1, 1946*
*Dear Necie,*

*I found a cooler place to study down in the basement of the engineering building. The mid-summer heat and humidity reminds me a little bit of my farming days ... and my time spent in the south Pacific. I much prefer having my nose in my books here.*

*Your dad is doing okay but he's still missing your mom pretty badly. It's been quite a shock for him. I try to help him around the house as much as I can, and Norma and Anita visit when they can get away. He and I both really appreciate it when they bring food. Neither of us can cook like your mother could. I've been encouraging him to hire someone to come in to cook and clean, and I think he's almost convinced.*

*Norma's kids, Marge and Stevie, are a handful but really fun to have around. Dolores was here for a few days with little Kathy—what a cutie...*

                                                                                      *Steve*

**Vernice's sister Dolores and her daughter, Kathy, September 1946**
(Photograph in family collection)

Steve Lynn wasted no time using his GI Bill benefits to reenter school at the University of Illinois. During the 1946 twelve-week summer semester, which began shortly after Vernice returned to Washington, DC, he successfully completed three mechanical engineering courses as well as a course in theoretical and applied mechanics. The university also granted him an additional fifteen hours of credit toward graduation in basic and advanced military theory and physical education based on his "military service in World War II."

The university's granting Steve the additional credit based on his military service brings to mind an experience E. B. Sledge recounted in his memoir *China Marine*. Like Steve, Sledge served with the First Marine Division on Peleliu, on Okinawa, and in north China. As an infantryman, he endured the worst of the combat on both Peleliu and Okinawa, and he stood long, lonely, dark hours of guard duty in north China. He arrived back in the United States about six weeks later than Steve. He writes honestly and beautifully about his experiences, including his difficult adjustment returning to civilian life.

The event that might have resonated with Steve took place as Sledge was registering for class at Auburn University. Most universities questioned returning veterans about their training in the military upon their return to school. Could the training they received translate into course credit toward graduation? Three-quarters of the servicemen who served during World War II were not combat veterans, and many of them had received specialized training in the military to carry out their noncombatant responsibilities. The Auburn registrar interviewing Sledge couldn't find courses at Auburn that matched up with the weapons and tactics "schools" Sledge had trained in, and she grew frustrated:

> Finally, in desperation, she slammed her pencil on the table and said in a loud, exasperated voice, "Didn't the Marine Corps teach you anything?!" A gasp ran through the crowd, and you could have heard a pin drop. I didn't lose my temper, but I realized that, like most civilians, war to this lady meant John Wayne or the sweet musical *South Pacific*.
>
> Slowly placing my hands on the table, aware that all eyes were upon us, I said in a loud, calm voice: "Lady, there was a *killing* war. The Marine Corps taught me how

to kill Japs and try to survive. Now, if that don't fit into any academic course, I'm sorry. But some of us had to do the killing—and most of my buddies got killed or wounded."

She was speechless. There were many red faces among the obvious noncombatants present. I doubt if there were a half dozen infantrymen or tankers present.

She recovered her composure, looked me in the eye, and said, "I'm sorry; I apologize; I didn't understand." I told her she was very kind and I did not mean to upset her. "You didn't," she said, "You made me think." So I got credit for ROTC and PE, and the room returned to normal.[1]

Many of the combat veterans like Steve and E. B. returned home to find that their combat experiences had changed them in ways that made them feel just plain different from anyone else who had never experienced them. The horrifyingly vivid sights, sounds, and smells of combat and the feelings and thoughts veterans associated with them were not acceptable topics of polite conversation in postwar America. They made people uncomfortable. The veterans had to come to grips with the idea that most folks would never be able to understand what they had somehow survived. Sledge wrote, "We saw life through a different lens and always would," and conversation about the war "could be risky."[2] Civilians who had spent the war years at home and even noncombatant veterans really could not begin to imagine the price combat troops had paid to win the war.

The country was quickly moving on from the war. Combat veterans like Steve wanted to move on, too, but it wasn't always easy. At times, it was nearly impossible to keep the memories of the searing terror of combat and the haunting faces and voices of the dead contained within the rearview mirror.

In addition to quickly learning that honest disclosures about his combat experiences were unwelcome and brought up the memories he was trying to forget, Steve, like other veterans, struggled to understand why so many people seemed so concerned about so many insignificant things. Both his combat experiences and his observations of the malnourished, poverty-stricken people in postwar China forced him to question and be amazed at what American civilians complained about. Even later in life he would comment on the "luxuries" he never took for granted—luxuries like hot showers, clean cotton socks, home-cooked meals. He would marvel philosophically at people's lack of gratitude for these "simple" daily gifts so many Americans took for granted.

He also knew there was no way most people, even those he loved and who loved him, would ever really be able to understand what he and E. B. Sledge and so many other combat veterans were thinking. He didn't talk about it much, and he tried not to think about it too much, either.

The work and study required by his heavy course load at the university demanded a concentrated focus that often led to a peaceful night of sleep, but the vivid nightmares of combat continued with regularity. They were brought on especially by discussions about the war or reading about it, and Steve learned to avoid watching any films or TV programs about World War II. For years, he would read his favorite poetry or fiction writers late into the night to avoid going to sleep.

In *The University of Illinois Goes to War*, John Franch wrote about Steve and the other veterans who flooded onto the Urbana campus at the end of the war:

> The veterans were serious and in a hurry to graduate and begin a career. Many of them had families to provide for and did not have the time—or the inclination—to join campus groups, like fraternities. ... Perhaps not surprisingly, a certain amount of tension developed between the fresh-faced 17- and 18-year-old freshmen and the world-wise veterans.[3]

Turning twenty-four years old in June 1946, Steve was one of those veterans who was "serious and in a hurry." When the fall semester began on the Urbana-Champaign campus, he was one of the 11,200 veterans in the school enrollment of 18,378. It was the largest number of students in the school's history to that date. Steve, like many of the other veterans, was a man on a mission. He was there to earn his college degree and move on with his miraculously spared life. He wanted "normalcy" and a family ... with Necie.

*August 16, 1946*
*Dear Necie,*

*Anita left today to start her school year teaching business classes up in Oak Park. She was looking forward to it even though she's still worried about your dad and the Illini Club. I think he'll be okay. He's settling into his new life a bit better and starting to really get involved in the stock market. He records the price of every stock he owns in his ledger in the evening. He's becoming a serious student of how it all works. Nobody will be around to play his favorite hymns on the piano so he can sing along, but he's found a radio program on Sundays he can sing along to instead.*

*Final exams for the summer term are next week, and I think I'll do all right. I've already decided what classes to take in the fall term to keep me moving toward getting my degree as soon as possible.*

*Soon, I hope, you'll be here, too, and life will be happier...*

*Steve*

## 28
## Vernice
## Arlington, Virginia, and Washington, DC
## May–September 1946

And we'll reply when our children query what did you do in the war, I bought red tape for the Signal Corps.

> --Two of the last lines of the poem writton on
> The one-year anniversary of the cracking of
> Japanese code 2468 by code breakers Marjorie
> Miller and Ann August

After Vernice Milleville returned to Washington, DC, her job efficiency ratings continued to be very fine. She was good at her job, and she liked both it and her life in Washington enough to stay several months after many of her fellow workers had left town and Steve had returned to Illinois. As the hot, sticky summer months passed, however, the political and social times continued to change. The overt pressure on working women in Washington to "go home and start a family" continued to grow.

Additionally, some government employees were taking on a different attitude toward their employer after the war ended. In her personnel file is a copy of an affidavit she had to sign, swearing that:

> I am not engaged in any strike against the Government of the United States and that I will not so engage while an employee of the Government of the United States; that I am not a member of an organization of Government employees that asserts the right to strike against the Government of the United States and that I will not while a Government employee become a member of such an organization.

The penalty for being convicted of engaging in a strike against the "Government of the United States" was a fine of one thousand dollars or imprisonment for up to a year—or both. This legal notice reflected the concern about the massive "strike wave of 1945 and 1946."[1] Would crippling labor strikes by essential government workers also take place? The patriotic attitude of most Americans during the war years was transitioning into a new, more complicated attitude as "normalcy" returned.

Vernice continued to enjoy her friends and the city. A few photos she kept from that period catch her out and about seeing the sights in the Washington area. At least once, she and her friend Lili made it to the beach.

**Vernice (*left*) and her friend Lili at the beach, June 1946**
(Photographs in family collection)

Perhaps Vernice still had some hard thinking to do about the winds of change blowing in, her mother's death, and her personal and professional goals as she looked down the road ahead.

Or maybe not. Maybe she and Steve had already decided on a plan. She may have returned to Washington to work for another four months to earn money that could be added to Steve's accumulated back pay and GI benefits. Cumulatively it would help them get a more financially stable start in their marriage. She was now making a very respectable wage as a cryptographic clerk in Washington—at least twice what she could earn in Champaign, assuming she could even find a job there. Both Vernice and Steve knew from their Depression-era experiences all about the hardships that come with economic duress. Perhaps they both decided their being apart a few more months was worth the money she could make while Steve spent almost all of his waking hours trying to successfully complete a jam-packed academic load during the summer. Frugality and pragmatism were lessons they had both learned early and well.

Either way, by the end of the summer, they had both definitely made up their minds. They would get married. Vernice resigned from her position with the Army Security Agency on September 6, 1946. Her Notification of Personnel Action form from the War Department was signed by Jo Palumbo, the same person who had sworn her in to the Signal Service Agency that hot summer afternoon of July 1, 1944, when she arrived on "station" in Arlington, Virginia.

Official record of Vernice Milleville's end of service for the War Department, September 19, 1946
(Document in family collection)

A week later, on September 13, Stephen A. Lynn Jr. and Vernice Marilyn Milleville were married at Grace Lutheran Church in Champaign, Illinois. It was a small wedding attended by a few close friends and family members. Her sister Dolores signed the certificate as a witness, with Dolores's young daughter, Kathy, nearby. Steve and Vernice then traveled to the green, forested Pokagon State Park near Angola, Indiana, for a weekend honeymoon in the lodge by the lake.

When Vernice resigned from the Army Security Agency, she was admonished both verbally and in writing never to talk about the work she did for the agency—ever. The specific wording in the letter she received in late October 1946 (with a key passage underlined) was:

> We must always remember that information which affects the defense of the United States must be carefully preserved in periods of peace, as well as in war. Information which you were instructed not to reveal to unauthorized persons while you were employed at Arlington Hall should not now, <u>or at any time in the future</u>, be revealed.

She was also told in the same letter that if "any persons" should arouse her suspicions "by showing unusual interest" in her work, she should report the incident immediately. Her "patriotic cooperation" was desired in this matter. The fear of employees revealing secrets of America's "dark chamber" as Herbert Yardley did in 1931 lived on.

Vernice never did talk about the specifics of her work for as long as she lived. While she was alive, none of her four children nor any of her extended family would ever appreciate what important work she had done to help win the war. Potential future employers would never learn about all the skills she had acquired, the supervisory leadership she had demonstrated, the contribution she had made to the war effort, or the loyalty she had demonstrated to the oath she had taken. Looking back, one can clearly see that she dearly valued keeping those secrets long after the necessity of keeping them had passed. Her personnel file was not declassified until 2012, two years after she died at the age of eighty-eight.

*August 28, 1946*
*Dear Stevie,*

*I've been on the phone making all of the arrangements for our wedding at Grace. It won't be fancy, but it will be perfect.*

*The idea of going to Pokagon afterwards is really perfect, too. Thank you for setting it all up. I know how busy you've been studying for your final exams …*

*It's all so exciting, Stevie! Our new life together is about to begin …*

*Necie*

**Mr. and Mrs. Stephen A. Lynn Jr., September 13, 1946**
(Photograph in family collection)

## 29
## Steve and Vernice
## Illinois and Into the Future Together
## September 1946–March 1950

> It is something—it can be everything—to have found a fellow bird with whom you can sit among the rafters while the drinking and boasting and reciting and fighting go on below; a fellow bird whom you can look after and find bugs and seeds for; one who will patch your bruises and straighten your ruffled feathers and mourn over your hurts when you accidentally fly into something you can't handle.
> —Wallace Stegner, *The Spectator Bird*

The Pokagon State Park honeymoon was brief because Steve had to be back at the University of Illinois at Urbana-Champaign for class Monday morning. During the fall term of the 1946–1947 school year, he successfully completed five more mechanical engineering courses and another theoretical and applied mechanics course.

After they married in September, Steve and Vernice lived in a room in her father's boardinghouse on John Street in Champaign because any other housing in the area (and nationwide) was all but impossible to find after the war. University officials pulled out all the stops trying to find places for the flood of new students. Students were housed in the ice rink, the Men's Gym Annex, and the interior hall of the football stadium. The university even arranged with the U.S. government to house students at Chanute Air Field in Rantoul, twenty miles north of the campus. Every spare room, empty attic, or unused barn in the area became student housing. Steve and Necie felt fortunate to have a room, and they helped her father with the boardinghouse. Her sisters were no longer living in town, so George really appreciated having Steve and Vernice around as he struggled to find his way forward after Millie died.

In late September, the newly married couple carved out some time to visit Steve's family farm down in Massac County, Illinois, near Brookport. It was the first chance Vernice had to spend some time with her in-laws and really get an understanding of where Steve had grown up. His parents were friendly but maybe not too sure about their college-educated daughter-in-law. They may have wondered what she thought of them and their lives.

Steve showed her the Brookport High School building and talked about his teachers there. He drove her along the Pope and Massac County dirt roads to visit favorite aunts and uncles and his maternal grandparents' old farmstead. She spent some time with Steve's jolly sister, Tillie, her husband, Jay, and their new baby boy, Larry. Vernice met Steve's brother, Joe, too, and began to understand what Steve described as Joe's "easy-going" personality. Steve's oldest sister, Frances, was living out in California with her husband by that time.

**George Washington "Joe" Lynn and Steve with his mother, Elva, on the farm, September 1946**
(Photographs in family collection)

As they drove along the country roads under the clear blue autumn sky past the ripening farm fields, the creeks, the fence rows, and the thick southern Illinois woodlots, Steve told Vernice story after story about the people who lived in the farms they passed and incidents he'd experienced here and there as he'd grown up.

It's hard to know what she thought about it all. Visiting folks and seeing the sights in Massac County sure wasn't the same as being in the university town of Champaign or the urbane milieu of Washington, DC, but maybe it wasn't all that different from visiting her extended family down around Altamont, Illinois, as she was growing up.

**Steve and his father eating watermelon grown on the farm, September 1946**
(Photograph in family collection)

Back in Champaign, Steve and Vernice occasionally took some time out from studying and helping with the boardinghouse to attend some of the Illinois football games. In January 1947, the talented Illini team went on to beat UCLA, 45–14, in the Rose Bowl. The game itself, played in Pasadena, California, wasn't televised in those days, but movies of the big game were projected on a big screen in the Auditorium on the quad several times that month. Steve and Necie continued to be loyal Fighting Illini fans for the many years that followed.

In late autumn, Vernice and Steve learned they would soon be having their first child. Theirs would be one of the twenty-two million babies born in the United States between 1946 and 1951.[1] The news made them eligible to apply for one of the government surplus "homes" the university had moved to the military parade grounds west of Memorial Stadium on the south side of campus. Their application was one of nine hundred applications submitted for the 270 units available.[2] Reserved for married ex-servicemen university students with families, the clustered manufactured homes collectively formed a neighborhood, Stadium Terrace, swarming with babies and toddlers.

The Stadium Terrace homes were temporary remountable units moved to Champaign from Charleston, Indiana, only after the city of Champaign was promised the units would not be moved anywhere else within the city limits after the university was finished with them. The homes were meant to be used only for a short time as the World War II GIs finished their degrees, but the Korean War veterans followed them to campus, and affordable housing options remained a necessity for returning veterans. They weren't torn down and removed until 1967.[3]

The poorly winterized housing units were long and narrow—12 by 25.5 feet. They were nailed into foundation posts set into the ground. They had only one or two rooms with a small kitchenette, and they were heated by small coal stoves. Although certainly substandard by most measures, the units were highly sought after by the flood of married GIs returning to school.

When 1947 began, Steve and Necie were able to move into the new "neighborhood." They gladly paid the $30 a month (about $363 in 2021 dollars) for the one-bedroom unit located at 638 Stadium Terrace. The monthly fee paid both rent and "utilities," which included fuel for cooking and space heating, electricity for light, and water for drinking and bathing. For $4 more a month, residents could rent serviceable furniture.[4]

**Aerial View of Stadium Terrace, December 1946**
(Photograph reproduced by permission of the University of Illinois Archives)

Housekeeping and child-rearing were a challenge, with very few new appliances available as the war industries slowly transitioned to peacetime needs, and there were no disposable diapers in 1947. The Stadium Terrace neighborhood soon had playgrounds and dirt roads, and the camaraderie was unique as the veteran dads went off to class and the library. The new moms collectively cared for the innumerable babies and toddlers.

**Stadium Terrace unit (*top photo*) and playground supervised by moms, ca. 1946**
(Photograph reproduced by permission of University of Illinois Archives)

Within months after the remountables began to arrive, the Stadium Terrace Board was set up by the residents themselves to both interface with the University of Illinois Housing Division and self-govern the community. The neighborhood was divided into eight "wards," each of which elected its own representative to the board. The wives organized supervision for the playgrounds, lobbied for neighborhood improvements, and soon organized, wrote, published, and distributed a neighborhood newsletter, the *Prefabricator*.[5]

The mimeographed *Prefabricator* was published weekly during the school year and biweekly during the summer. It featured news about neighborhood quality-of-life issues (e.g., polio warnings, rat reduction tips, fire hazards, speeding drivers, loud radios, the easily broken vitreous china sinks) as well as listings of "free-time" suggestions such as on-campus plays, concerts, and lectures with titles including "Postwar France," "Nuclear Physics and Radio Activity," and "Pressure Groups in Congress." The "Trading Post" and "Swap Shop" sections of the newsletter carried a wide variety of notices, such as "Wanted: A good wash woman" and "For sale: Pre-war made bathinette and baby stroller." Babysitters offered their services for twenty-five cents per hour. The *Prefabricator* also shared ideas for coping with the living arrangements' shortcomings. For example, "A definite cooling aid (in the summer) may be utilized by keeping the door to your stove open. Honestly, it really helps circulation."[6]

A "Personals" column shared the news about who was sick, who died, who had a "lovely petunia bed," and whose relatives and friends were visiting from out-of-town. "Stork Visits," announcing new births in the neighborhood, was a regular feature.

Sometimes the *Prefabricator* carried important notices about upcoming rent increases and utility usage restrictions and how to obtain waivers. The Married Veterans Welfare Office in the university's Division of Special Services for Veterans started using the newsletter to share information on services for the veterans and their wives—how to obtain refrigerators, how to get spousal identification cards, times and locations for meetings for expectant wives on preparing for "baby's arrival," early infancy, and emotional issues of veterans and new parents.

After Steve and Necie moved into the neighborhood early in 1947, the *Prefabricator* included a "call to action" by the neighborhood's residents to contact their U.S. representative to support the Rogers/Langer Bill. If passed, the bill would raise the GI subsistence pay for veterans taking educational courses under the GI Bill from $64 a month (about $903 in 2021 dollars) to $125 a month plus $10 for every child. The article claimed that the cost of living had risen 30 percent during the previous nine months, and it was nearly impossible for the student veterans and their families to keep their heads above water unless they had some financial reservoir of savings to draw on.[7] Steve and Necie had a bit of a financial cushion thanks to the money Vernice had saved from her work in Washington, DC, and the back pay Steve had saved when he was in the Marine Corps.

While awaiting the birth of their first child during the second semester of the 1946–1947 school year, Steve polished off two more mechanical engineering classes as well as two electrical engineering classes and an engineering law course. He was more driven than ever to complete his degree and begin a family-supporting career. He and Vernice hoped to have several children, and in those times, he was the assumed breadwinner. The self-discipline he had learned in the Marine Corps helped him keep his focus while spending long days and nights in the engineering labs and library. Necie spent the time helping her father, getting to know the neighbors, preparing for the new baby, and attending the Thursday evening Bridge Club for wives and Illini Theater Guild performances on campus.

Necie and Steve welcomed their first child, Julia, in June 1947, just nine months after their honeymoon and before Steve graduated. Their baby daughter had plenty of playmates, and Vernice had neighbors with whom to share mothering and homemaking responsibilities while Steve studied. No one asked Vernice what she had done during the war, but she couldn't and wouldn't have told them the complete story anyway. In her quiet moments of solitude, Vernice undoubtedly pondered the essentially treeless, muddy "yards" and "roads" of Stadium Terrace and compared them with the green, tree-filled neighborhoods where she had lived and worked in Arlington, Virginia. Her new married life in central Illinois was sure different from living in the wartime Washington, DC, area.

One can imagine Vernice sitting on the front porch step of her one-bedroom remountable home in Stadium Terrace on a hot, humid summer afternoon sipping a glass of percolated iced coffee while her baby daughter napped inside. Setting aside the latest edition of the *Prefabricator*, she may have paused to wonder if the life she had known in Washington, DC, not even a year earlier had been real or just a dream. One hopes she was happy with her decision to leave the Army Security Agency (ASA), get married, and start a family with Steve. One hopes, too, that she felt like one Women's Air Corps member who had worked for the SSA during the war years who said, "I feel that what I did was worthwhile in helping to win the war, even realizing at that time I was merely a tiny, tiny cog in the wheel."[8]

As Vernice adjusted to her new roles as mother and wife, Steve earned his degree during the 1947 summer session by successfully completing two more mechanical engineering classes and two more electrical engineering classes. He was awarded his Bachelor of Science degree in mechanical engineering from the University of Illinois at Urbana-Champaign on October 5, 1947. He had returned to school determined to complete his degree, and he had done it in short order.

> **Stephen Lynn to Get U. of I. Degree**
>
> Stephen A. Lynn, Jr., son of Mr. and Mrs. Steve Lynn, route 1, is one of more than 1000 students at the University of Illinois, Urbana-Champaign who are candidates for degrees at the close of the summer semester in October. He is a candidate for the degree of Bachelor of Science in Mechanical Engineering.
>
> Commencement exercises will be October 5, with the procession at 3 p.m. (daylight saving time) and ceremonies in the University auditorium at 3:30 p.m. President Lydon O. Brown of Knox College will be the speaker, and President George D. Stoddard of the University of Illinois will confer the degrees. The ceremonies will be broadcast by the University's non-commercial radio station, WILL (580 kc.).
>
> With the University operating on a three-semester schedule since the beginning of the war emergency, many students are completing their work at other than the traditional June commencement time, and three commencements now are held at Illinois each year--in June, February and October.

Steve's graduation announcement in one of the local Massac County papers
(Clipping in family collection)

In mid-1947, there were seven hundred married veteran applicants awaiting placement in Stadium Terrace and the other married student housing neighborhoods on campus.[9] Consequently, the Lynn "home" was quickly reoccupied by another veteran's family when Steve and Necie left town and headed to Dayton, Ohio. Steve had been hired immediately upon graduation by Delco Products, a division of General Motors. Having switched back to the production of automobiles and pickup trucks after producing tanks and other military vehicles during the war years, General Motors was expanding exponentially to meet the postwar demand. Steve first designed production parts and then became part of a team of engineers designing and opening new manufacturing facilities in various locations in the United States and around the world. First stop was Dayton, Ohio, then Richmond, Indiana, then Caracas, Venezuela, and back to Queens,

New York. Vernice was the glue that held the growing family together as it moved from one location to another.

On April 27, 1948, Steve accepted appointment as "First Lieutenant (Permanent)" in the Marine Corps Reserve. The oath of office was executed a week later. His rank of first lieutenant had been "temporary" since it was assigned "in the field" after the Peleliu campaign back in January 1945. A few months later, however, Steve resigned from the Marine Corps Reserve, effective October 20, 1948. Perhaps he made the decision as he watched events in Korea continue to unravel. By October 1950, the First Marine Division—including Steve's former unit, the Eleventh Marines—was fighting there. His higher priorities by that time were his family and his civilian career, and he may have felt he'd already done his duty with the U.S. Marine Corps in the Pacific.

**Vernice, Julie, and Steve, May 1948**
(Photograph in family collection)

Steve's honorable discharge from the U.S. Marine Corps Reserve was mailed to him at the home he shared with Vernice and their young daughter at 4708 Greenwich Village Avenue, Dayton 6, Ohio, on December 14, 1948. On April 8, 1949, five of the six awards he had earned for his service in the Pacific were officially delivered.

They included two Presidential Unit Citations awarded to the First Marine Division, Reinforced, for service on (1) Peleliu and Ngesebus and (2) Okinawa; the American Campaign Medal; the Victory Medal World War II; and the China Service Medal No. 2306 for service in China 1945–1946.

**American Campaign Medal, Victory Medal World War II, and China Service Medal**
(Wikipedia images in the public domain)

On March 20, 1950, Stephen A. Lynn Jr. received the actual Distinguished Flying Cross medal he had earned back in 1945 "**For extraordinary achievement while participating in aerial flights while serving as an air observer for a Marine artillery regiment on OKINAWA SHIMA, RYUKU ISLANDS, from 1 April to 2 1 June, 1945.**" With the delivery of the DFC medal to his home with Necie, Steve could feel that his service with the United States Marine Corps in the Pacific theater of World War II was complete. He had done his part to "win the war," and it was officially over.

Unofficially, the war never entirely ended for Steve Lynn. Steve's "combat fatigue," or what today we would call posttraumatic stress disorder, did not incapacitate him as it did many other combat veterans. He worked hard at his career, first as a mechanical engineer and then as a business manager and leader. He often transplanted his family (which grew to four children), accepting new job offers in two cities in Indiana, the Chicago suburbs, and South Carolina before eventually taking root in south Florida, where he became the president and CEO of a small manufacturing company. Additionally, he and Necie profitably managed real estate investments in south Florida, and they both invested wisely in the stock market.

Nevertheless, Steve never completely shed the psychological scars inflicted by his war service. He taught his children to turn on the light if they woke up at night so no one was wandering around the house in the dark. They learned, too, never to sneak up on him or to watch war-themed movies or TV shows when he was home. Looking back, one can see that his lifelong restlessness, insomnia, nightmares, flashbacks, and occasional rage emanated at least in part from the mind-searing experiences he endured on the Pacific islands of Peleliu and Okinawa in 1944 and 1945. Sadly, he relived those experiences periodically and sometimes dramatically until he died at the age of ninety in 2013, three years after Vernice's death. A United States Marine Corps Honor Guard attended his memorial service and formally presented a commemorative American flag to our family to recognize his service to the country.

Rest in peace, Mom and Dad … and thank you.

## Acknowledgments

I had a lot of help researching and writing this book.

To garner personal details about the prewar lives of my parents, I relied in part on family stories, letters, and photos provided by Margaret Wilfong Metcalfe, Kathy McQuown Connell, Julie Lynn, Sally Lynn Chase, Stephen Wilfong, Paula Weaver, Jeff Vieregg, Craig Vieregg, and Joseph Chase. Genealogical records accessed through Ancestry.com were invaluable in providing facts about their lives.

Debbie Hammack Christiansen at the Brookport Library helped me acquire photos of my dad and his teachers during his high school years. Coincidentally, Debbie's father attended Brookport High School during the same years my dad did. Pat Lockard organizes and maintains the genealogy resources available in the Metropolis Library. She kindly assisted me both at the library and from afar when I was grasping for an understanding of the Lynn/Phillips family land holdings and lifestyle in southern Illinois. Pat also diligently searched vintage local newspapers for photos and wartime articles about my dad. Debbie and Pat are among those unsung heroes in our country who with limited resources maintain local records and artifacts that are invaluable in a project like this one.

The multidecade collection of the Champaign High School yearbook the *Maroon*, housed at the Champaign Public Library, provided a new look into my mother's teenage years. How could any one person have been involved in so many activities at one time? The yearbooks also paint a picture of prewar life and times in that central Illinois community. Staff members at the Champaign County Recorder Office in Urbana helped me decipher the property records telling the story of my mom's parents' real estate transactions during the 1930s and 1940s.

The University of Illinois at Urbana-Champaign obviously played a huge role in my parents' stories, as it has in mine. Without the assistance of the incredible staff at the University of Illinois Archives, this story would have been much thinner and less revealing. Linda Stepp provided tips for navigating the archives and ferreted out the information on Club Topper. Cara Setsu Bertram, Anna Trammel, Heidi Charles, Jameatris Rinkus, and Katie Nichols all played roles in helping me access old student directories, scholarship confirmations, the wartime climate on campus, and information about and photos of Stadium Terrace and Illinois Theatre Guild plays. Tracking down and accessing original copies of the *Prefabricator*, the newsletter published by the residents of Stadium Terrace in the postwar years, was thrilling, and it could have been accomplished only with their assistance. The University of Illinois Archives staff also guided me through the process of obtaining my parents' archived student transcripts.

Thank you, too, to the University of Illinois Alumni Association. My page-turning wanderings through the wartime and postwar editions of the *Illio*, the University of Illinois yearbook housed at the Alice Campbell Alumni Center in Urbana, afforded my mind the opportunity to imagine life on campus during that unique period.

Comprehending Lieutenant Lynn's U.S. Marine Corps records and experiences was probably the most challenging part of the research I completed for this narrative. Opening the tattered manila envelope filled with the orders my father received as an officer in the Corps was analogous to opening a huge box stuffed with thousands of questions written on tiny bits of paper. All the acronyms, coded locations, abbreviations, time stamps, names... What did they mean? Who were the mentioned people? With what historical events did the orders correlate? Where were these places? What happened there? What was my father doing there? How did he get there? Whom did he know there? Every single question that I answered through painstaking research raised more questions I felt compelled to investigate. It all triggered a deep dive into the history, records, and operational details of the U.S. Marine Corps both before and during World War II.

Paul Grasmehr, the reference coordinator at the Pritzker Military Museum and Library in Chicago, gave me ideas and direction early in the research process. He provided useful suggestions about whom to contact in the U.S. Marine Corps History Division and what kinds of questions to ask.

Annette Amerman, the branch head of the Historical Inquiries and Research Branch of the Marine Corps History Division, provided valuable information on the Fifty-Second Replacement Battalion, aerial observation during the war, histories of both the Eleventh Marines and VMO-3, and direction and ideas for further research. Jim Ginther, a guest senior archivist in the Archives Branch of the Marine Corps History Division at the time, spent time looking for relevant pilot log books, after-mission debrief sheets, and morning reports. I yearn for the daily detail some of these records might have provided if they still existed, but I was unable to find them in spite of the ideas he gave me. I greatly appreciate the efforts of the overworked staff of the Marine Corps History Division at Quantico.

A very special thank you goes to Steve "Smitty" Smith, curator, and Leon Simon, mechanic and restorationist, at the Flying Leathernecks Aviation Museum in San Diego. Mr. Simon gave up part of a weekend in October 2017 to patiently answer my questions and to give me, my husband, and my son all the time in the world to explore the partially dismantled Stinson L-5 Sentinel (OY-1 "Grasshopper") and the SBD-1 aircraft in a restricted hangar out of public view. My dad "spotted" from an SBD-5 before landing on Peleliu, and he spent way too many hours flying under fire in the unarmored, fabric-covered OY-1 in the skies over both Peleliu and Okinawa. We took pictures of the planes, sat in the OY-1, examined the controls, and imagined being in my dad's "seat" during those flights. It was a very powerful experience, and it was very kind of both Mr. Simon and Mr. Smith to make it possible.

One of my sons, Craig Vieregg, flew us to San Diego in a small plane to visit the Flying Leathernecks Aviation Museum. It added to the experience. Additionally, he shared web photos and videos of the still remaining Stinson L-5 "Grasshoppers" and helped me understand the plane's operational controls. Thank you, Craig.

Barbara Rossow, my "sister" and friend, realized as she patiently listened to what I was learning about the Eleventh Marines that we had even more in common than we thought. Her father, Lieutenant Seeley G. Lodwick, also served in the Eleventh Marines and fought in the First Marine Division battles of New Gloucester, Peleliu, and Okinawa. She shared the photos and the artillery manuals he saved from his service. Undoubtedly our fathers knew each other in the Pacific. How amazing that their two daughters know and care for each other now.

The Wheaton Public Library in Wheaton, Illinois, has an impressive collection of books and other resources on World War II military and code-breaking operations as well as access to off-site books, newspapers, and journals that are difficult to find. I feel so fortunate to have had this library close at hand, and I thank the staff for helping me when I ran into difficulties finding the sources I sought.

Many thanks to the staff at the U.S. National Archives in St. Louis for providing the assistance I needed to acquire both my father's archived military personnel record and my mother's official civilian personnel record. I had been warned that the process would be aggravating and time-consuming, but it was not. I appreciate the work the archives staff does on a daily basis.

I also need to recognize and thank the staff members who study, conserve, and provide access to the Still Photo Collection of the U.S. National Archives in College Park, Maryland. By providing me the opportunity to slowly sift through the thousands of photos taken of the Marines on Pavuvu, Peleliu, and Okinawa and in North China, they gave me poignant insight I could have acquired in no other way.

One of the most exciting and unexpected moments in the research process was seeing my father's name in a book's description of Marine observers' flights off the USS *Petrof Bay* near the coast of Okinawa on April 2, 1945. A special thank-you to Rick Cline for keeping such detailed notes of the ship's operations and personnel when he served during World War II and then sharing them in his book *Escort Carrier WWII: War in the Pacific on the Aircraft Carrier USS Petrof Bay*.

In addition to providing family information, Ancestry.com and Fold3.com provided essential records such as military muster rolls, war diaries, action reports, etc. These records were invaluable in parsing out fine details of people and operations. They gave me the pieces of the puzzle

I needed to figure out who was where when and with whom as well as on-the-ground, in-the-moment detail.

Tina Louise Mead, then associate chief librarian, and her intern Crispien Van Aelst at the Pritzker Military Museum and Library in Chicago provided introductory background information on women in cryptography and their recruiting, and they guided me to further research options related to cryptanalysis, Arlington Hall Station, and the women who worked there.

The research staff of the Center for Cryptologic History at the National Security Agency located in Ft. Meade, Maryland was an incredible partner in my search to understand what my mother actually did at Arlington Hall and even exactly where she worked. They also provided access to fascinating and comprehensive declassified documents recounting the history of American cryptography before and during the war. I can't imagine having learned what I did without that partnership.

I am much indebted to Liza Mundy, who wrote *Code Girls: The Untold Story of the American Women Code Breakers of World War II*, for the amazing work she did in telling the stories of the American women working at Arlington Hall and elsewhere. In the same vein, Cindy Gueli provided innumerable stories about what life was like for women working in the Washington, DC, area in her book *Lipstick Brigade: The Untold True Story of Washington's World War II Government Girls*. Both of these books were crucial in helping me understand the tenor of my mother's experiences.

I am obviously indebted as well to the historians who labored so rigorously to record the details of the events recounted in this narrative. Their work is represented in the bibliography. Each of them provided a slightly different slant on the events they recorded. Reading their work both educated me and challenged me to read between the lines, ask more questions, and investigate more deeply. As I read and reread different accounts of the same historical events, I was struck by how both the "fact" and the interpretation of those events sometimes varied with the storyteller and when the story was told. I have tried to get it "right" to the best of my ability. Any errors I have made are mine alone.

All the many contributors to Wikipedia, too, deserve recognition for not only providing information and photos of events, people, places, ships, and equipment but also for providing their sources for the contributed entries. On more than one occasion, the listings of cited references and bibliographic sources for Wikipedia entries gave me direction for more in-depth research on my own. Wikimedia Foundation, Inc., the 501-3C nonprofit organization that organizes it all, deserves more support for its work.

Lori Meek Schuldt deserves a special thank-you. Her attention to detail and her probing questions and suggestions as she copy edited my manuscript gently compelled me to carefully reevaluate what I had written. This book is immeasurably better than it would have been without her assistance.

Finally, and most important, I want to express my heartfelt thanks to those people who encouraged and sustained me during the painfully long writing process. Mary Carroll Moore expressed genuine interest in the project when I attended her weeklong writing class at the Madeline Island School of the Arts. Her storyboarding technique and writing style suggestions were very helpful. Jeff and Cindy Crosby, wonderful writers and friends, read an early draft and prodded me to continue my efforts. John Heneghan, Tom Mitchell, Julie Lynn, and Barbara Rossow followed suit and cheered me on when I wondered whether I should continue. My sons, Jeff and Craig Vieregg, both contributed thoughtful ideas and supported the writing process. They also seemed to really appreciate the effort I was making to record this family history.

Most of all, I want to express immeasurable gratitude to my husband and best friend, Jim Vieregg. He listened patiently when I shared the "discoveries" I made doing the research for this book, and he was always amazed by them, too. What more could one ask for?

# NOTES

*Don't Just Look—See! My Parents' War* relies heavily on the official government personnel records of Stephen A. Lynn and Vernice Marilyn Milleville obtained from the United States National Archives. Information from these records is not annotated because the records are not readily available to most readers. The same is true for the dates and locations extracted from Lieutenant Lynn's U.S. Marine Corps orders, which he kept in a manila envelope until he died in 2013. Finally, the information on academic course loads and titles for both Steve and Vernice was extracted from their student transcripts obtained from the Archives of the University of Illinois at Urbana-Champaign. Full source citations for other works in these notes are listed in the bibliography at the end of the book.

### Chapter 1: Steve, Massac County, Illinois, 1934–1940
Epigraph: Gibran, *Prophet*, p. 80.

### Chapter 2: Vernice, Champaign, IL, 1931–1940
1. "Factory Is Donated to Keep Firm in Altamont," *Decatur Daily Review*, April 5, 1935, p. 10.
2. "Buys Half Interest," *Decatur Daily Herald*, August 14, 1937, p. 5.

### Chapter 3: Steve and Vernice, University of Illinois at Urbana-Champaign, September 1940–March 1943
Epigraph: Vance, *Hillbilly Elegy*, p. 25.
1. McNeill et al., *American Home Front*, p. 54.
2. McNeill et al., p. 59.
3. Ebert quoted in Franch, *University of Illinois Goes to War*, p. 1.
4. Franch, p. 1.
5. Editorial quoted in Ebert, *Illini Century*, p. 159.
6. Franch, *University of Illinois Goes to War*, p. 23.
7. Willard letter quoted in Ebert, *Illini Century*, p. 160.
8. Harno quoted in Ebert, *Illini Century*, p. 148.
9. University of Illinois SLC Archival Program, "Student Life at Illinois."
10. Timmins, "I Times," p. 33.
11. McNeill et al., *American Home Front*, p. 61.

### Chapter 4: Steve, San Diego, CA, and Quantico, VA, March 1943–January 1944
Epigraph: Sledge, *With the Old Breed at Peleliu and Okinawa*, p. 315.
1. Sledge, p. 8.
2. Sledge, p. 8.
3. Craf, "Stanford GSB during World War II," p. 3.
4. Sledge, *With the Old Breed at Peleliu and Okinawa*, p. 11.
5. Condit, Diamond, and Turnbladh, *Marine Corps Ground Training in World War II*, p. 164.
6. Condit, Diamond, and Turnbladh, p. 160.

7. Condit, Diamond, and Turnbladh, p. 163.
8. Sledge, *With the Old Breed at Peleliu and Okinawa*, p. 12.
9. Sledge, p. 13.
10. Condit, Diamond, and Turnbladh, *Marine Corps Ground Training in World War II*, p. 195.
11. Sledge, *With the Old Breed at Peleliu and Okinawa*, p. 15.
12. Condit, Diamond, and Turnbladh, *Marine Corps Ground Training in World War II*, p. 57.
13. Condit, Diamond, and Turnbladh, p. 247.
14. McCall, introduction to *Pacific Time on Target*, p. 12.
15. Donner, *Pacific Time on Target*, p. 17.
16. Condit, Diamond, and Turnbladh, *Marine Corps Ground Training in World War II*, p. 76.
17. Condit, Diamond, and Turnbladh, p. 80.
18. Condit, Diamond, and Turnbladh, p. 248.
19. Fleming, Austin, and Brelay, *Quantico*, p. 78.
20. Condit, Diamond, and Turnbladh, *Marine Corps Ground Training in World War II*, p. 267.
21. Condit, Diamond, and Turnbladh, p. 270.

### Chapter 5: Vernice, Champaign, IL, March 1943–January 1944

Epigraph: Powers, *Echo Maker*, p. 450.
1. Franch, *University of Illinois Goes to War*, p. 9.
2. Franch, p. 12.
3. *Illinois Alumni News* quoted in Franch, pp.15–16.
4. Franch, p. 19.
5. Franch, pp. 9–10.

### Chapter 7: Steve, California, January–March 1944

Epigraph: Maugham, *Of Human Bondage*, p. 615.

### Chapter 8: Vernice, Champaign, IL, February–March 1944

Epigraph: Coehlo, *Alchemist*, p. 23.
1. Duffin, "Percentage of the U.S. Population Who Have Completed Four Years of College."
2. Gueli, *Lipstick Brigade*, p. 11.
3. Cavna, "Wonder Woman's Power Ride."
4. Horten, *Radio Goes to War*, p. 2.
5. Gueli, *Lipstick Brigade*, p. 2.
6. Gueli, p. 72.
7. Mundy, *Code Girls*, p. 9.

### Chapter 9: Steve, California, At Sea, New Caledonia, and Pavuvu, April–June 1944

Epigraph: Sledge, *With the Old Breed at Peleliu and Okinawa*, p. 33.
1. Rottman, *U.S. Marine Corps World War II Order of Battle*, p. 255.
2. Frank and Shaw, *Victory and Occupation*, p. 682.
3. Frank and Shaw, p. 682.

4. Sledge, *With the Old Breed at Peleliu and Okinawa*, p. 24.
5. Sledge, p. 24.
6. Sledge, p. 28.
7. Sledge, p. 28.
8. McMillan, *Old Breed: A History*, p. 3.
9. Shaw, *Opening Moves*, p. 1.
10. McMillan, *Old Breed: A History*, p. 4.
11. McMillan, p. 4.
12. McMillan, pp. 6, 14.
13. McMillan, p. 134.
14. McMillan, p. 134.
15. Frank and Shaw, *Victory and Occupation*, p. 522.
16. McMillan, *Old Breed: A History*, p. 137.
17. McMillan, p. 145.
18. Clark, *Battle History of the United States Marine Corps, 1775–1945*, p. 177.
19. Garand and Strobridge, *Western Pacific Operations*, p. 90.
20. Sledge, *With the Old Breed at Peleliu and Okinawa*, p. 32.
21. Hough, *Assault on Peleliu*, p. 26.
22. Snead, "*Obscure but Important*, p. 18.
23. Sledge, *With the Old Breed at Peleliu and Okinawa*, p. 32.
24. Snead, "Obscure but Important," p. 18.
25. Hough, *Assault on Peleliu*, p. 26.
26. Rottman, *Marine Corps World War II Order of Battle*, p. 129.
27. Snead, "Obscure but Important," p. 17.
28. Hough, *Assault on Peleliu*, p. 27.
29. McMillan, *Old Breed: A History*, p. 3.

### Chapter 10: Vernice, Champaign, IL, and Washington, DC, April–June 1944

Epigraph: Gueli, *Lipstick Brigade*, p. 96.
1. "Capitol Limited (B&O Train)."
2. Mundy, *Code Girls*, p. 30.

### Chapter 11: Steve, Pavuvu in the Russell Islands, July–August 1944

1. Rottman, *U.S. Marine Corps World War II Order of Battle*, p. 124.
2. Emmet, *Brief History of the 11th Marines*, p. 17.
3. Watson and McCalpin, "Aerial Spotters," p. 46.
4. Watson and McCalpin, p. 46.
5. Slappey, *Marine Observation Squadron Three, 1 May 1944 to 31 May 1944*, p. 5.
6. Slappey, *Marine Observation Squadron Three, 1 June 1944 to 30 June 1944*, p. 4.
7. McMillan, *Old Breed: A History*, pp. 257–258.
8. McMillan, p. 258.
9. McMillan, p. 256.
10. Watson and McCalpin, "Aerial Spotters," p. 48.

11. Hough, *Assault on Peleliu*, p. 27.
12. Sledge, *With the Old Breed at Peleliu and Okinawa*, pp. 34–35.
13. "Bob Hope—Pavuvu."
14. McMillan, *Old Breed: A History*, p. 267.

## Chapter 12: Vernice, Arlington, VA, July–August 1944

Epigraph: Mundy, *Code Girls*, p. 11.
1. Mundy, p. 208.
2. Official Civilian Personnel file for Vernice M. Milleville, "Oath of Office, Affidavit, and Declaration of Appointee," page not numbered.
3. Official Civilian Personnel file for Milleville.
4. Official Civilian Personnel file for Milleville.
5. Gueli, *Lipstick Brigade*, p. 4.
6. Gueli, p. 30.
7. Gueli, p. 103.
8. Lake, "28 Acres of Girls," p. 103.
9. Parrish, *Ultra Americans*, p. 90.
10. Wilcox, *Sharing the Burden*, p. 8.
11. Gilbert and Finnegan, *U.S. Army Signals Intelligence*, p. 18.
12. Gilbert and Finnegan, p. 18.
13. Gilbert and Finnegan, p. 234.
14. Gilbert and Finnegan, pp. 19–20.
15. Fagone, *Woman Who Smashed Codes*, p. 120.
16. Gilbert and Finnegan, *U.S. Army Signals Intelligence*, p. 23.
17. Gilbert and Finnegan, p. 4.
18. Gilbert and Finnegan, p. 24.
19. Mundy, *Code Girls*, p. 99.
20. Mundy, p. 101.
21. Parrish, *Ultra Americans* p. 82.
22. Parrish, p. 80.
23. Gilbert and Finnegan, *U.S. Army Signals Intelligence*, p. 54.
24. Gilbert and Finnegan, p. 55.
25. Gilbert and Finnegan, p. 56.
26. Gilbert and Finnegan, p.63.
27. Gilbert and Finnegan, p. 89.
28. Gilbert and Finnegan, p. 50.
29. Gilbert and Finnegan, p. 10.
30. Budiansky, *Battle of Wits*, p. 226.

## Chapter 13: Steve, Peleliu in the Palau Island Group, September–October 1944

Epigraphs: Sledge, *With the Old Breed at Peleliu and Okinawa*, p. 156; Sloan, *Brotherhood of Heroes*, p. 311.
1. Rottman, *U.S. Marine Corps World War II Order of Battle*, p. 344.
2. Garand and Strobridge, *Western Pacific Operations*, p. 97.
3. Garand and Strobridge, p. 67.
4. Garand and Strobridge, p. 73.

5. Lewin, *American Magic*, p. 257.
6. Rottman, *U.S. Marine Corps World War II Order of Battle*, p. 347.
7. Garand and Strobridge, *Western Pacific Operations*, p. 65.
8. Morison, *History of United States Naval Operations in World War II*, vol. 12, p. 39.
9. Garand and Strobridge, *Western Pacific Operations*, p. 110.
10. McMillan, *Old Breed: A History*, p. 307.
11. Hough, *Assault on Peleliu*, p. 40.
12. Sledge, *With the Old Breed at Peleliu and Okinawa*, p. 71.
13. Pyne quoted in Berry, *Semper Fi, Mac*, p. 71.
14. Morison, *History of United States Naval Operations in World War II*, vol. 12, p. 40.
15. Garand and Strobridge, *Western Pacific Operations*, p. 130.
16. Garand and Strobridge, p. 127.
17. Sledge, *With the Old Breed at Peleliu and Okinawa*, p. 80.
18. Garand and Strobridge, *Western Pacific Operations*, p. 150.
19. Garand and Strobridge, p. 151.
20. Slappey, *Marine Observation Squadron Three, 1 September, 1944 to 30 September, 1944*. (All daily events for VMO-3 in September 1944 are recorded in this war diary.)
21. Ross, *Peleliu: Tragic Triumph*, pp. 267–68.
22. Alexander, *Storm Landings*, p. 121.
23. Shoemaker quoted in Ross, *Peleliu: Tragic Triumph*, p. 235.
24. Ross, p. 296.
25. Garand and Strobridge, *Western Pacific Operations*, p. 161.
26. Garand and Strobridge, p. 189.
27. McMillan, *Old Breed: A History*, p. 320.
28. Emmet, *Brief History of the 11th Marines*, p. 20.
29. Garand and Strobridge, *Western Pacific Operations*, p. 218.
30. Sledge, *With the Old Breed at Peleliu and Okinawa*, p. 147.
31. Moran and Rottman, *Peleliu 1944*, p. 83.
32. Slappey, *Marine Observation Squadron Three, 1 October, 1944 to 31 October, 1944*. (All daily events for VMO-3 in October 1944 are recorded in this war diary.)
33. McMillan, *Old Breed: A History*, p. 335.
34. Sloan, *Brotherhood of Heroes*, p. 315.
35. History.com Editors, "Battle of Peleliu."
36. Hallas, *Devil's Anvil*, p. 279.
37. Ross, *Peleliu: Tragic Triumph*, p. 338.
38. Rottman, *U.S. Marine Corps World War II Order of Battle*, p. 347.
39. Moran and Rottman, *Peleliu 1944*, p. 91.
40. Garand and Strobridge, *Western Pacific Operations*, p. 281. Italics mine.
41. Hough, *Assault on Peleliu*, p. 198.
42. Hough, p. 199.

Chapter 14: Vernice, Arlington, VA, September–October 1944

Epigraph: Mundy, *Code Girls*, p. 241.
1. Marshall quoted in Lewin, *American Magic*, p. 232.
2. Mundy, *Code Girls*, p. 220.
3. Gilbert and Finnegan, *U.S. Army Signals Intelligence in World War II*, p. 10.
4. Marshall quoted in Gilbert and Finnegan, *U.S. Army Signals Intelligence in World War II*, p. 105.
5. National Security Agency, "The Japanese Army Problem Memorandum," p. 60.
6. National Security Agency, "The Japanese Army Problem Memorandum," p. 57-58.
7. National Security Agency, "The Japanese Army Problem Memorandum," p. 62.
8. Mundy, *Code Girls*, p. 118.
9. For an entire series of World War II–era posters, see National Archives Catalog, "World War II Posters, 1942–1945."
10. Budiansky, *Battle of Wits*, pp. 261–62.
11. Mundy, *Code Girls*, p. 252.
12. Carlyle quoted in Lewin, *American Magic*, p. 153.

Chapter 15: Steve, Pavuvu Revisited and En Route to Okinawa, October 1944–March 1945

Epigraph: Sledge, *With the Old Breed at Peleliu and Okinawa*, p. 180.
1. Sledge, p. 166.
2. Sledge, p. 169.
3. Brown quoted in Frank and Shaw, *Victory and Occupation*, p. 88.
4. Alexander, *Storm Landings*, p. 155.
5. Sledge, *With the Old Breed at Peleliu and Okinawa*, p. 174.
6. United States Marine Corps, *III Corps Artillery, III Phib Corps Action Report, 1 April-30 June 1945*, p. 12.
7. Alexander, *Final Campaign*.
8. United States Marine Corps. *11th Marines, First Marine Division Special Action Report*, p. 12.
9. Henderson quoted in Frank and Shaw, *Victory and Occupation*, p. 89.
10. Frank and Shaw, *Victory and Occupation*, p. 90.
11. Donner, *Pacific Time on Target*, p. 48.
12. Sloan, *Brotherhood of Heroes*, p. 328.
13. Sloan, p. 329.
14. Leckie, *Okinawa*, p. 62.
15. Donner, *Pacific Time on Target*, p. 52.
16. U.S. Marine Corps Order No. 2445-40/5 (7/49-gwl) issued March 4, 1945, from the Commanding Officer of the Headquarters, III Amphibious Corps c/o Fleet Post Office, San Francisco (copy in Lieutenant Stephen "A" Lynn personal file).

17. Morison, *History of United States Naval Operations in World War II*, vol. 12, p. 50.
18. Toll, *Twilight of the Gods*, p. 161.
19. Morison, *History of United States Naval Operations in World War II*, vol. 12, p. 50. Ulithi Anchorage vintage footage online provides a bird's-eye view of some of the anchorage as Lieutenant Lynn would have seen it flying over it in 1945. See CriticalPast, "U.S. Fleet of Warships at Anchor Off Ulithi Atoll"; MyFootage.com, "1940s World War II: Ulithi, Anchorage."
20. Toll, *Twilight of the Gods*, p. 161.
21. Morison, *History of United States Naval Operations in World War II*, vol. 14, p. 110.
22. Beckett, "Top Secret: U.S. Naval Base at Ulithi." The website containing this source, War History Online, also contains numerous photographs and a map providing a closer look at Ulithi, including the recreation area on Mog Mog.
23. Cline, *Escort Carrier WWII*, pp. 148–60. All the daily events recorded on the USS *Petrof Bay* are described in these pages.
24. Morison, *History of United States Naval Operations in World War II*, vol. 14, p. 100.
25. Sloan, *Ultimate Battle: Okinawa*, p. 43.
26. Donner, *Pacific Time on Target*, p. 56.
27. Emmet, *Brief History of the 11th Marines*, p. 22.

## Chapter 16: Vernice, Arlington, VA, and Washington, DC, November 1944–March 1945

Epigraph: Gueli, *Lipstick Brigade*, p. 5.

1. Gueli, p. 95.
2. Gueli, p. 4.
3. Evans quoted in Gueli, p. 19.
4. She recounted the story to me and others. A high-level KGB defector publicly revealed in a book written in 1990 that the Russians had infiltrated Arlington Hall by 1945 with the placement of a man named Bill Weisband, who worked there for several years. See "Arlington Hall."
5. Gueli, *Lipstick Brigade*, p. 134.
6. Lichty quoted in Gueli, p. 150.
7. Moyers quoted in Gueli, p. 150.
8. Mundy, *Code Girls*, p. 125.

## Chapter 17: Steve, Okinawa, April–June 1945

Epigraphs: 117 Cong. Rec. S46371 (daily ed. December 11, 1971) (quotation of Admiral Halsey); Frank and Shaw, *Victory and Occupation*, p. 377.

1. Sherrod, *History of Marine Corps Aviation World War II*, p. 370.
2. Appleman et al., *Okinawa: The Last Battle*, p. 75.

3. Slappey, *Marine Observation Squadron Three, 1 April, 1945 to 30 April, 1945*. (All daily events for VMO-3 in April are recorded in this war diary.)
4. Garrett, *Marine Observation Squadron Six, 1 April, 1945 to 30 April, 1945*. (All daily events for VMO-6 in April are recorded in this war diary.)
5. Ambler, *Marine Observation Squadron Two, 1 April, 1945 to 30 April, 1945*. (All daily events for VMO-2 in April are recorded in this war diary.)
6. Parker and Bartha, *A History of Marine Observation Squadron Six*, p. 7.
7. Cline, *Escort Carrier WWII*, p. 159.
8. Isely and Crowl, *U.S. Marines and Amphibious Warfare*, p. 564.
9. Isely and Crowl, p. 563.
10. Isely and Crowl, p. 561.
11. Yahara, *Battle for Okinawa*, p. 33.
12. McMillan, *Old Breed: A History*, p. 368.
13. Toll, *Twilight of the Gods*, p. 615.
14. Frank and Shaw, *Victory and Occupation*, p. 185.
15. United States Marine Corps, *11th Marines, First Marine Division Special Action Report*. One action item in this report conflicts with the VMO-3 war diary's accounting of the air observers' location. It states that the observers were based at Yontan Airfield until just a few days before the end of the battle when they moved to Itoman. The VMO-3 war diary refers to the transfer of the observers to Kadena Airfield in May, which required the VMO pilots to pick them up before each mission as described in the narrative. See Slappey, *Marine Observation Squadron Three, 1 April, 1945 to 30 April, 1945*.
16. Foster, *Okinawa 1945*, p. 100.
17. Sherrod, *History of Marine Corps Aviation World War II*, p. 386.
18. Frank and Shaw, *Victory and Occupation*, p. 193.
19. Frank and Shaw, pp. 192–93.
20. Brown quoted in Alexander, *Final Campaign*.
21. Yahara, *Battle for Okinawa*, p. 25.
22. Hodge quoted in Frank and Shaw, *Victory and Occupation*, p. 204.
23. Frank and Shaw, p. 206.
24. Sherrod, *History of Marine Corps Aviation World War II*, p. 395.
25. Sloan, *Ultimate Battle: Okinawa*, p. 154.
26. Frank and Shaw, *Victory and Occupation*, p. 218.
27. Slappey, *Marine Observation Squadron Three, 1 May, 1945 to 31 May, 1945*. (All daily events for VMO-3 in May are recorded in this war diary.)
28. Sherrod, *History of Marine Corps Aviation World War II*, p. 406.
29. Frank and Shaw, *Victory and Occupation*, p. 219.
30. Appleman et al., *Okinawa: The Last Battle*, p. 255.
31. Garrett, *Marine Observation Squadron Six, 1 May, 1945 to 31 May, 1945*. (All daily events for VMO-6 in May are recorded in this war diary.)

32. Toll, *Twilight of the Gods*, p. 615.
33. Sherrod, *History of Marine Corps Aviation World War II*, p. 405.
34. Astor, *Semper Fi in the Sky*, pp. 341–42.
35. Foster, *Okinawa 1945*, p. 169.
36. Alexander, *Final Campaign*. Italics mine.
37. Slappey, *Marine Observation Squadron Three, 1 June, 1945 to 30 June 1945*. (All daily events for VMO-3 in June are recorded in this war diary.)
38. Frank and Shaw, *Victory and Occupation*, p. 340.
39. Seward, *Marine Observation Squadron Seven, 1 June, 1945 to 30 June, 1945* (all daily events for VMO-7 in June are recorded in this war diary); Garrett, *Marine Observation Squadron Six, 1 June, 1945 to 30 June 1945* (all daily events for VMO-6 in June are recorded in this war diary).
40. Yahara, *Battle for Okinawa*, p. 219.
41. Rottman, *U.S. Marine Corps World War II Order of Battle*, p. 376.
42. Yahara, *Battle for Okinawa*, p. 43.
43. Giangreco, *Hell to Pay*, p. 20.
44. Hammel, *War in the Western Pacific*, p. 274.
45. Hammel, p. 274.
46. Schultz, "Breaking Point," p. 2.
47. Frank and Shaw, *Victory and Occupation*, p. 369.
48. Frank and Shaw, p. 369.
49. Sloan, *Ultimate Battle: Okinawa*, pp. 310–11.
50. Toll, *Twilight of the Gods*, p. 633.
51. Frank and Shaw, *Victory and Occupation*, p. 377.
52. Henderson quoted in Frank and Shaw, p. 377.
53. Donner, *Pacific Time on Target*, p. 112.
54. Parker and Bartha, *History of Marine Observation Squadron Six*, p. 9.
55. Seward, *Marine Observation Squadron Seven, 1 July, 1945 to 31 July, 1945*.

## Chapter 18: Vernice, Arlington, VA, and Washington, DC, April–June 1945

Epigraphs: Baime, *Accidental President*, pp. ix, 35.
1. Skates, *Invasion of Japan*, p. 135.
2. Baime, *Accidental President*, p. 254.
3. Churchill quoted in Baime, p. 255.

## Chapter 19: Steve, Oahu, Hawaii, July 1945

Epigraph: Schultz, "Breaking Point," p. 2.
1. Del Valle, *First Marine Division Action Report, NANSEI SHOTO*, p. 16.
2. Reese, "New Views on Aerial Spotters," p. 58.
3. Watson and McCalpin, "Aerial Spotters," p. 48.
4. Baime, *Accidental President*, p. 324.

## Chapter 20: Vernice, Arlington, VA, and Washington, DC, July–August 1945

Epigraphs: Giangreco, *Hell to Pay*, pp. 92, 103.

1. Skates, *Invasion of Japan*, p. 136.
2. Skates, p. 137.
3. Giangreco, *Hell to Pay*, p. 214.
4. Lewin, *American Magic*, p. 287.
5. Skates, *Invasion of Japan*, p. 138.
6. Giangreco, *Hell to Pay*, pp. 218–19.
7. Rikiei quoted in Giangreco, *Hell to Pay*, p. 76.
8. Skates, *Invasion of Japan*, p. 140.
9. Giangreco, *Hell to Pay*, p. 80.
10. Giangreco, p. 240.
11. Giangreco, p. 221.
12. Toll, *Twilight of the Gods*, p. 652.
13. Skates, *Invasion of Japan*, p. 142.
14. Baime, *Accidental President*, p. 300.
15. Truman quoted in Baime, p. 340.
16. Giangreco, *Hell to Pay*, p. 110.
17. Giangreco, p. 112.
18. Mundy, *Code Girls*, p. 329.
19. Baime, *Accidental President*, p. 353.
20. Skates, *Invasion of Japan*, p. 249.
21. Giangreco, *Hell to Pay*, p. 204.
22. Nicholson quoted in Gueli, *Lipstick Brigade*, p. 212.
23. Smith, *Emperor's Codes*, p. 275.
24. Mundy, *Code Girls*, p. 331.

### Chapter 21: Steve, Oahu, Hawaii, August 1945

Epigraphs: Michener quoted in Giangreco, *Hell to Pay*, p. 279. Van Kirk quoted in Baime, *Accidental President*, p. 337.
1. Baime, *Accidental President*, pp. 344–45.
2. Baime, p. 345.
3. Toll, *Twilight of the Gods*, p. 747.
4. Sledge, *With the Old Breed at Peleliu and Okinawa*, p. 313.
5. Sledge, *China Marine*, p. 9.

### Chapter 22: Vernice, Arlington, VA, and Washington, DC, Sept–Dec 1945

Epigraph: Markham, *West with the Wind*, p. 238.
1. National Security Agency, "Post War Transition Period", p. 32.
2. National Security Agency, "Post War Transition Period, ASA", p. 42.
3. National Security Agency, "General Cryptanalytic Problem Recommendations," p. 91.
4. National Security Agency, "Post War Transition Period, ASA", p. 31.
5. National Security Agency, "General Cryptanalytic Problem Recommendations," p. 39.
6. Gueli, *Lipstick Brigade*, p. 214.
7. Gueli, p. 214.

### Chapter 23: Steve, Tientsin, North China, and Home, Sept–Dec 1945
Epigraph: Sledge, *China Marine*, p. 101.
1. North China Marines (http://www.northchinamarines.com/id1.htm) is a website with the names of those Marines taken prisoner, what prison camps they were taken to, and whether or not they survived the war to be rescued or released.
2. Sledge, *China Marine*, p. 36.
3. Sledge, p. 40.
4. Nagano quoted in Frank and Shaw, *Victory and Occupation*, p. 581.
5. Sledge, *China Marine*, p. 27.
6. Marshall quoted in Morison, *History of United States Naval Operations in World War II*, vol. 15, p. 17.
7. Morison, vol. 15, p. 17.
8. Morison, vol. 15, p. 20.
9. Rottman, *U.S. Marine Corps World War II Order of Battle*, p. 546.
10. Kennard, *Combat Letters Home*, p. 163.
11. President Franklin D. Roosevelt signed the Servicemen's Readjustment Act of 1944 (the GI Bill) into law on June 22, 1944, as the first group of veterans returned home. Under the GI Bill, the government covered tuition, books, and fees up to $500 per school year (about $7,648 in 2021 dollars) and paid a monthly allowance for each veteran who served at least ninety days and received an honorable discharge. In 1947, veterans composed nearly half of all college admissions. By 1956, about 49 percent of the sixteen million World War II veterans had participated in some type of education or training program under the GI Bill. Gueli, *Lipstick Brigade*, p. 217.

### Chapter 24: Vernice, Arlington, VA, and Washington, DC, January–March 1946
Epigraph: Markham, *West with the Wind*, p. 197.
1. Gueli, *Lipstick Brigade*, p. 219.
2. Klutz quoted in Gueli, p. 222.
3. Gueli, p. 224.

### Chapter 25: Steve, Illinois, January–March 1946
Epigraph: Duenas, *Time In Between*, p. 638.
1. Morison, *History of United States Naval Operations in World War II*, vol. 15, p. 21.
2. Toll, *Twilight of the Gods*, p. 781.
3. Kennard, *Combat Letters Home*, p. 161.

### Chapter 26: Steve and Vernice, Champaign, IL, April–May 1946
Epigraph: Maugham, *Summing Up*, p. 36.

### Chapter 27: Steve, Champaign, IL, May–September 1946
Epigraph: Sledge, *China Marine*, p. 149.
1. Sledge, pp. 134–35.
2. Sledge, p. 131.
3. Franch, *University of Illinois Goes to War*, p. 28.

## Chapter 28: Vernice, Arlington, VA, and Washington, DC, May–September 1946

Epigraph: Mundy, *Code Girls*, p. 241.

1. In response to the massive labor strikes of 1945 and 1946, Congress overrode President Truman's veto in 1947 to pass the Taft-Hartley Act, which restricted the powers and activities of labor unions.

## Chapter 29: Steve and Vernice, Illinois and Into the Future Together, September 1946–March 1950

Epigraph: Stegner, *Spectator Bird*, p. 213.

1. Gueli, *Lipstick Brigade*, p. 225.
2. University of Illinois at Urbana-Champaign Archives, "Stadium Terrace, Champaign, Illinois, 1946: Interpretation," Resource Identifier arh4001, p. 1.
3. Urbana Free Library, "Living in Stadium Terrace," p. 2.
4. University of Illinois at Urbana-Champaign Archives, "Stadium Terrace," p. 1.
5. Stadium Terrace Board, *Prefabricator*, June 10, 1946. This collection of newsletters is contained in four cardboard boxes in the University of Illinois Archives. It was first printed in March 1946 and ceased publication in 1971.
6. Stadium Terrace Board, *Prefabricator*, June 10, 1946.
7. Stadium Terrace Board, *Prefabricator*, February 5, 1947.
8. Wilcox, *Sharing the Burden*, p. 15.
9. Stadium Terrace Board, *Prefabricator*, June 30, 1947. The actual inflation rate was 8.33 percent during 1946 and 14.36 percent during 1947, according to Webster, "U.S. Inflation Rate." A bill increasing the monthly subsistence pay was passed in the U.S. Senate in July 1947 but wasn't passed in the U.S. House of Representatives and signed by the president until February 1948.

# BIBLIOGRAPHY

*Don't Just Look—See! My Parents' War* relies heavily on the official government personnel records of Stephen A. Lynn and Vernice Marilyn Milleville obtained from the United States Archives, their academic transcripts obtained from the Archives of the University of Illinois at Urbana-Champaign, and the retained U.S. Marine Corps orders kept by Steve Lynn in a manila envelope until he died in 2013.

-----------------------------------------

Alexander, Col. Joseph H., USMC (Ret.). *The Final Campaign: Marines in the Victory on Okinawa*. World War II Commemorative Series. Washington, DC: Marine Corps Historical Center, 1996. https://www.ibiblio.org/hyperwar/USMC/USMC-C-Okinawa/index.html.

Alexander, Col. Joseph H., USMC (Ret.). *Storm Landings: Epic Amphibious Battles in the Central Pacific*. Annapolis, MD: Naval Institute Press, 1997.

Ambler, John A. *Marine Observation Squadron Two, 1 April, 1945 to 30 April, 1945*. World War II War Diaries, 1941–1945. Washington, DC: National Archives, 1945.

Anderson, Willis B. *Marine Observation Squadron Two, 1 May, 1945 to 31 May, 1945*. World War II War Diaries, 1941–1945. Washington, DC: National Archives, 1945.

Appleman, Roy E., James M. Bruns, Russell A. Gugeler, and John Stevens. *Okinawa: The Last Battle*. Washington, DC: Center of Military History, United States Army, 1993.

"Arlington Hall." Wikipedia. Updated December 14, 2020. https://en.wikipedia.org/wiki/Arlington_Hall.

Astor, Gerald. *Semper Fi in the Sky: The Marine Air Battles of World War II*. New York: Presidio Press, 2005.

Baime, A. J. *The Accidental President: Harry S. Truman and the Four Months That Changed the World*. Boston: Houghton Mifflin Harcourt, 2017.

Beckett, Jack. "Top Secret: U.S. Naval Base at Ulithi Was for a Time the World's Largest Naval Facility." War History Online. Published October 14, 2017. https://www.warhistoryonline.com/world-war-ii/hidden-ulithi-naval-base.html.

Berry, Henry. *Semper Fi, Mac: Living Memories of the U.S. Marines in World War II*. New York: Arbor House, 1982.

"Bob Hope—Pavuvu." Posted March 22, 2011. Video, 0:43. https://www.youtube.com/watch?v=XOmhqqCfJE0.

Budiansky, Stephen. *Battle of Wits: The Complete Story of Codebreaking in World War II*. New York: Free Press, 2000.

Campbell, Douglas E. *U.S. Navy, U.S. Marine Corps, and U.S. Coast Guard Aircraft Lost during World War II Listed by Aircraft Type*. Vol. 3. Morrisville, NC: Lulu Press, 2011.

"Capitol Limited (B&O Train)." Wikipedia. Updated April 17, 2021. https://en.wikipedia.org/wiki/Capitol_Limited_(B%26O_train).

Cavna, Michael. "Wonder Woman's Power Ride." *Chicago Tribune*, May 31, 2017.

Clark, George B. *Battle History of the United States Marine Corps, 1775-1945*. Jefferson, NC: McFarland, 2010.

Clark, George B. *Treading Softly: U.S. Marines in China, 1819-1949*. Westport, CT: Praeger, 2001.

Cline, Rick. *Escort Carrier WWII: War in the Pacific on the Aircraft Carrier USS Petrof Bay*. Placentia, CA: R. A. Cline. 1998.

Coelho, Paulo. *The Alchemist*. New York: HarperCollins, 1998.

Condit, Kenneth W., Gerald Diamond, and Edwin T. Turnbladh. *Marine Corps Ground Training in World War II*. Washington, DC: Historical Branch, G-3 Division, Headquarters, U.S. Marine Corps, 1956. ttps://archive.org/stream/marinecorpsgroun00unit/marinecorpsgroun00unit_djvu.txt.

Craf, John R. "Stanford GSB during World War II." *Stanford Business School Bulletin*, March 1943. https://www.gsb.stanford.edu/stanford-gsb-experience/news-history/history/stanford-gsb-during-world-war-ii.

CriticalPast. "The U.S. Fleet of Warships at Anchor Off Ulithi Atoll in World War II HD Stock Footage, 6 December 1944." Posted April 7, 2014. Video, 2:10. https://www.youtube.com/watch?v=Ip8hhbQ7oho.

DeChant, John. "Devil Birds (Peleliu)." *Marine Corps Gazette* 31, no. 7 (July 1947), ProQuest Military Collection.

DeChant, John. "Devil Birds: The Battle for Okinawa." *Marine Corps Gazette* 31, no. 10 (October 1947), ProQuest Military Collection.

Del Valle, Gen. Pedro. *First Marine Division Action Report, NANSEI SHOTO (Okinawa) Operation, 1 April-June, 1945*. World War II War Diaries, 1941–1945. Washington, DC: National Archives, 1945. (Declassified December 31, 2012.)

Donner, Christopher S. *Pacific Time on Target: Memoirs of a Marine Artillery Officer, 1943–1945*, Kent, OH: Kent State University Press, 2012.

Drea, Edward J. *MacArthur's Ultra: Codebreaking and the War Against Japan, 1942–1945*, Lawrence: University Press of Kansas, 1992.

Drea, Edward J., and Joseph E. Richard. "New Evidence on Breaking the Japanese Army Codes." *Intelligence and National Security* 14, no. 1 (1999): 62–83. https://www.doi.org/10.1080/02684529908432524.

Duenas, Maria. *The Time In Between*. Detroit: Gale Cengage Learning, 2011.

Duffin, Erin. "Percentage of the U.S. Population Who Have Completed Four Years of College or More from 1940–2019, by Gender." Statista. Accessed October 18, 2020. https://www.statista.com/statistics/184272/educational-attainment-of-college-diploma-or-higher-by-gender/

Ebert, Roger. *Illini Century: One Hundred Years of Campus Life*. Urbana: University of Illinois Press, 1967.

Emmet, Robert. *A Brief History of the 11th Marines*. Washington, DC: Historical Branch, G-3 Division, Headquarters, U.S. Marine Corps, 1968.

Fagone, Jason. *The Woman Who Smashed Codes: A True Story of Love, Spies, and the Unlikely Heroine Who Outwitted America's Enemies.* New York: HarperCollins, 1917.

Fisher-Alaniz, Karen. *Breaking the Code: A Father's Secret, A Daughter's Journey, and the Question That Changed Everything.* Naperville, IL: Sourcebooks, 2011.

Fleming, Charles A., Robin L. Austin, and Charles L. Braley. *Quantico: Crossroads of the Marine Corps.* Washington, DC: History and Museums Division, Headquarters, U.S. Marine Corps, 1978.

Foster, Simon. *Okinawa 1945: Final Assault on the Empire.* London: Arms & Armor Press, 1994.

Franch, John. *The University of Illinois Goes to War.* Urbana: University of Illinois Archives' Student Life and Culture Archival Program, 2007.

Frank, Benis M., and Henry I. Shaw Jr. *Victory and Occupation.* Vol. 5 of *History of U.S Marine Corps Operations in World War II.*, Washington, DC: Historical Branch, G-3 Division, Headquarters, U.S. Marine Corps, 1968.

Garand, George W., and Truman R. Strobridge. *Western Pacific Operations.* Vol. 4 of *History of U.S. Marine Corps Operations in World War II.*, Washington, DC: Historical Division, Headquarters, U.S. Marine Corps, 1971.

Garrett, Donald R. *Marine Observation Squadron Six, 1 March, 1945 to 31 March, 1945.* World War II War Diaries, 1941–1945. Washington, DC: National Archives, 1945.

Garrett, Donald R. *Marine Observation Squadron Six, 1 April, 1945 to 30 April, 1945.* World War II War Diaries, 1941–1945. Washington, DC: National Archives, 1945.

Garrett, Donald R. *Marine Observation Squadron Six, 1 May, 1945 to 31 May, 1945.* World War II War Diaries, 1941–1945. Washington, DC: National Archives, 1945.

Garrett, Donald R. *Marine Observation Squadron Six, 1 June, 1945 to 30 June, 1945.* World War II War Diaries, 1941–1945. Washington, DC: National Archives, 1945.

Gayle, Gordon D. *Bloody Beaches: The Marines at Peleliu.* Washington, DC: Marine Corps Historical Center, 1996.

Giangreco, D. M. *Hell to Pay: Operation DOWNFALL and the Invasion of Japan, 1945–1947.* Annapolis, MD: Naval Institute Press, 2009.

Gibran, Kahlil. *The Prophet.* New York: Alfred A. Knopf, 1981.

Gilbert, James L., and John P. Finnegan, eds. *U.S. Army Signals Intelligence in World War II: A Documentary History*. Washington, DC: Center of Military History, United States Army, 1993.

Gueli, Cindy. *Lipstick Brigade: The Untold True Story of Washington's World War II Government Girls*. Washington, DC: Tahoga History Press, 2015.

Hallas, James H. *The Devil's Anvil: The Assault on Peleliu*. Westport, CT: Praeger, 1994.

Hammel, Eric. *Marines on Peleliu: A Pictorial Record*. Pacifica, CA: Pacifica Military History, 2013.

Hammel, Eric. *War in the Western Pacific: The U.S. Marines in the Marianas, Peleliu, Iwo Jima, and Okinawa, 1944–1945*. Minneapolis: Zenith Press, 2010.

History.com Editors. "Battle of Peleliu." Updated August 21, 2018. http://www.history.com/topics/world-war-ii/battle-of-peleliu.

Horten, Gerd. *Radio Goes to War: The Cultural Politics of Propaganda during World War II*. Berkeley: University of California Press, 2002.

Hough, Frank Olney. *The Assault on Peleliu*. USMC Historical Monograph. Washington, DC: Historical Branch, G-3 Division, Headquarters, U.S. Marine Corps, 1950.

Isely, Jeter A., and Philip A. Crowl. *U.S. Marines and Amphibious Warfare*. 1951. Reprint, Princeton, NJ: Princeton University Press, 2015.

Keegan, John. *Intelligence in War: Knowledge of the Enemy from Napoleon to Al-Qaeda*. New York: Alfred A. Knopf, 2003.

Kennard, Richard C. *Combat Letters Home: A U.S. Marine Corps Officer's World War II Letters from Peleliu, Okinawa and North China September 1944 to December 1945*. Bryn Mawr, PA: Dorrance, 1985.

Lake, Elinor. "28 Acres of Girls: Arlington Farms." *Reader's Digest*, July 1944, 36-38.

Leckie, Robert. *Okinawa: The Last Battle of World War II*. New York: Penguin Books, 1995.

Lewin, Ronald. *The American Magic: Codes, Ciphers and the Defeat of Japan*. New York: Farrar, Straus and Giroux, 1982.

Madigan, Tim. "Their War Ended 70 Years Ago; Their Trauma Didn't." *Washington Post*, September 11, 2015.

Maier, Milton H. *Military Aptitude Testing: The Last Fifty Years*. Monterey, CA: Defense Manpower Data Center, 1993.

Manning, Molly Guptill. *When Books Went to War: The Stories That Helped Us Win World War II*. New York: Houghton Mifflin Harcourt, 2014.

Markham, Beryl. *West with the Wind*. New York: North Point Press, 1997.

Maugham, W. Somerset. *Of Human Bondage*. New York: Bantam Books, 2006.

Maugham, W. Somerset. *The Summing Up*. Garden City, NY: Doubleday, Doran, 1938.

McCall, Jack H. Introduction to *Pacific Time on Target*, by Christopher S. Donner, 1–16. Kent, OH: Kent State University Press, 2012.

McMillan, George. *The Old Breed: A History of the First Marine Division in World War II*. Washington, DC: Infantry Journal Press, 1949. (Good photos and anecdotes.)

McNeill, Allison, Richard C. Hanes, Sharon M. Hanes, and Kelly Rudd, eds. *American Home Front in World War II*. Vol. 1, *Agricultural Mobilization*. Detroit: UXL, 2005.

Moran, Jim, and Gordon Rottman. *Peleliu 1944: The Forgotten Corner of Hell*. Praeger Illustrated Military History. Westport, CT: Osprey Publishing, 2004. (Fascinating photographs and well-drawn maps.)

Morison, Samuel Eliot. *History of United States Naval Operations in World War II*. Vol.12, *Leyte, June 1944–January 1945*. Boston: Little, Brown, 1962.

Morison, Samuel Eliot. *History of United States Naval Operations in World War II*. Vol.14, *Victory in the Pacific, 1945*. Boston: Little, Brown, 1962.

Morison, Samuel Eliot. *History of United States Naval Operations in World War II*. Vol.15, *Supplement and General Index*. Boston: Little, Brown, 1962.

Mundy, Liza. *Code Girls: The Untold Story of the American Women Code Breakers of World War II*. New York: Hachette Books, 2017.

MyFootage.com. "1940s World War II: Ulithi, Anchorage." Posted May 22, 2012. Video, 2:11. https://www.youtube.com/watch?v=BEgsA07E9Ok.

National Archives Catalog. "World War II Posters, 1942–1945." Accessed November 24, 2020. https://catalog.archives.gov/search?q=*:*&f.ancestorNaIds=513498&sort=naIdSort%20asc.

National Security Agency Central Security Service (NSA CSS). "Cryptologic Hall of Honor: Elizebeth S. Friedman." Accessed May 31, 2021. https://www.nsa.gov/about/cryptologic-heritage/historical-figures-publications/hall-of-honor/Article/1623028/elizebeth-s-friedman/.

National Security Agency Central Security Service (NSA CSS). "Cryptologic Hall of Honor: William F. Friedman." Accessed May 31, 2021. https://www.nsa.gov/about/cryptologic-heritage/historical-figures-publications/hall-of-honor/Article/1623026/william-f-friedman/.

National Security Agency Central Security Service (NSA CSS). Center for Cryptologic History. "General Cryptanalytic Problem Recommendations Resulting from a Control Office Survey, 31 August, 1945." Accessed September 8, 2021. https://www.nsa.gov/Portals/70/documents/news-features/declassified-documents/friedman-documents/reports-research/FOLDER_488/41718889075819.pdf.

National Security Agency Central Security Service (NSA CSS). Center for Cryptologic History. "Historic Photographs of NSA and its Predecessor Organizations." Accessed August 25, 2021. https://www.nsa.gov/news-features/declassified-documents/arlington-hall/.

National Security Agency Central Security Service (NSA CSS). Center for Cryptologic History. "The Japanese Army Problem Memorandum, 26 June 1945." Accessed August 26, 2021. https://www.nsa.gov/Portals/70/documents/news-features/declassified-documents/friedman-documents/reports-research/FOLDER_488/41719029075835.pdf.

National Security Agency Central Security Service (NSA CSS). Center for Cryptologic History. "Post War Transition Period, The Army Security Agency, 1945-1948." Accessed September 8, 2021. https://www.nsa.gov/Portals/70/documents/news-features/declassified-documents/army-security-agency/asa-history-1945-1948-post-war-transition.pdf.

Nichols, Charles S., Jr., and Henry Shaw Jr. *Okinawa: Victory in the Pacific*. Washington, DC: Historical Branch, G-3 Division, Headquarters, U.S. Marine Corps, 1955.

Parker, Gary Wallace, and Frank M. Bartha. *A History of Marine Observation Squadron Six*. Washington, DC: History and Museums Division, Headquarters, United States Marine Corps, 1982.

Parkyn, Michael. "Operation Beleaguer: The Marine III Amphibious Corps in North China, 1945-49." *Marine Corps Gazette* 85, no. 7 (July 2001): 32–37.

Parrish, Thomas. *The Ultra Americans: The U.S. Role in Breaking the Nazi Codes*. New York: Stein and Day, 1986.

Polesie, Herbert, dir. *Marines in the Making*. Metro-Goldwyn-Mayer, 1942. Posted May 20, 2020. Video, 9:04. https://www.youtube.com/watch?v=toPyVzqX7ys.

Powers, Richard. *The Echo Maker*. New York: Picador, 2007.

Reese, Paul. "New Views on Aerial Spotters." *Marine Corps Gazette* 29, no. 2 (February 1945): 58, ProQuest Military Collection.

Ross, Bill D. *Peleliu: Tragic Triumph—The Untold Story of the Pacific War's Forgotten Battle*. New York: Random House, 1991.

Rottman, Gordon L. *U.S. Marine Corps World War II Order of Battle: Ground and Air Units in the Pacific War, 1939–1945*. Westport, CT: Greenwood Press, 2002.

Rutecki, Gregory W. "Peleliu as a Paradigm for PTSD: The Two Thousand Yard Stare." *Hektoen International Journal* 9, no. 4 (Fall 2017). http://hekint.org/volume-9-issue-4-fall-2017/.

Schultz, Duane. "The Breaking Point: Combat Stress in WW II." *Warfare History*, September 30, 2016.

Seward, William A. *Marine Observation Squadron Seven, 1 June, 1945 to 30 June, 1945*. World War II War Diaries, 1941–1945. Washington, DC: National Archives, 1945.

Seward, William A. *Marine Observation Squadron Seven, 1 July, 1945 to 31 July, 1945*. World War II War Diaries, 1941–1945, Washington, DC: National Archives, 1945.

Shaw, Henry I., Jr. *Opening Moves: Marines Gear Up for War*. Marines in World War II Commemorative Series, PCN 190 003115 00. Washington, DC: Marine Corps Historical Center, 1991.
http://www.ibiblio.org/hyperwar/USMC/USMC-C-Opening/.

Shaw, Henry I., Jr. *The United States Marines in North China, 1945–1949*. Washington, DC: Historical Branch, G-3 Division Headquarters, U.S. Marine Corps, 1968.

Sherrod, Robert. *History of Marine Corps Aviation World War II*. Washington, DC: Combat Forces Press, 1952.

Skates, John Ray. *The Invasion of Japan: Alternative to the Bomb*. Columbia: University of South Carolina Press, 1994.

Slappey, Wallace J., Jr. *Marine Observation Squadron Three, 1 February, 1944 to 29 February, 1944*. World War II War Diaries, 1941–1945. Washington, DC: National Archives, 1945.

Slappey, Wallace J., Jr. *Marine Observation Squadron Three, 1 March, 1944 to 31 March, 1944*. World War II War Diaries, 1941–1945. Washington, DC: National Archives, 1945.

Slappey, Wallace J., Jr. *Marine Observation Squadron Three, 1 April, 1944 to 30 April 1944*. World War II War Diaries, 1941–1945. Washington, DC: National Archives, 1945.

Slappey, Wallace J., Jr. *Marine Observation Squadron Three, 1 May, 1944 to 31 May, 1944*. World War II War Diaries, 1941–1945. Washington, DC: National Archives, 1945.

Slappey, Wallace J., Jr. *Marine Observation Squadron Three, 1 June, 1944 to 30 June, 1944*. World War II War Diaries, 1941–1945. Washington, DC: National Archives, 1945.

Slappey, Wallace J., Jr. *Marine Observation Squadron Three, 1 July, 1944 to 31 July, 1944*, World War II War Diaries, 1941–1945. Washington, DC: National Archives, 1945.

Slappey, Wallace J., Jr. *Marine Observation Squadron Three, 1 August, 1944 to 31 August, 1944*. World War II War Diaries, 1941–1945. Washington, DC: National Archives, 1945.

Slappey, Wallace J., Jr. *Marine Observation Squadron Three, 1 September, 1944 to 30 September, 1944*. World War II War Diaries, 1941–1945. Washington, DC: National Archives, 1945.

Slappey, Wallace J., Jr. *Marine Observation Squadron Three, 1 October, 1944 to 31 October, 1944*. World War II War Diaries, 1941–1945. Washington, DC: National Archives, 1945.

Slappey, Wallace J., Jr. *Marine Observation Squadron Three, 1 February, 1945 to 29 February, 1945*. World War II War Diaries, 1941–1945. Washington, DC: National Archives, 1945.

Slappey, Wallace J., Jr. *Marine Observation Squadron Three, 1 March, 1945 to 31 March, 1945*. World War II War Diaries, 1941–1945. Washington, DC: National Archives, 1945.

Slappey, Wallace J., Jr. *Marine Observation Squadron Three, 1 April, 1945 to 30 April, 1945*. World War II War Diaries, 1941–1945. Washington, DC: National Archives, 1945.

Slappey, Wallace J., Jr. *Marine Observation Squadron Three, 1 May, 1945 to 31 May, 1945*. World War II War Diaries, 1941–1945. Washington, DC: National Archives, 1945.

Slappey, Wallace J., Jr. *Marine Observation Squadron Three, 1 June, 1945 to 30 June, 1945*. World War II War Diaries, 1941–1945. Washington, DC: National Archives, 1945.

Sledge, E. B. *China Marine: An Infantryman's Life after World War II*. New York: Oxford University Press, 2002.

Sledge, E. B. *With the Old Breed at Peleliu and Okinawa*. New York: Presidio Press, 2010.

Sloan, Bill. *Brotherhood of Heroes: The Marines at Peleliu, 1944 — The Bloodiest Battle of the Pacific War*. New York: Simon & Schuster, 2005.

Sloan, Bill. *The Ultimate Battle: Okinawa 1945 — The Last Epic Struggle of World War II*. New York: Simon & Schuster Paperbacks, 2007.

Smith, Michael. *The Emperor's Codes: The Breaking of Japan's Secret Ciphers*. New York: Arcade Publishing, 2000.

Snead, David Lindsey. "Obscure but Important: The United States and the Russell Islands in World War II." *Journal of America's Military Past* 96, no. 3 (Spring/Summer 2003): 5–30. Reprinted in *Faculty Publications and Presentations* 22 (Summer 2003), Liberty University, https://digitalcommons.liberty.edu/hist_fac_pubs/22/.

Stadium Terrace Board. *The Prefabricator,* March 1946–1971. University of Illinois Archives, Urbana.

Stegner, Wallace. *The Spectator Bird.* New York: Penguin Books, 1990.

Timmins, Mary. "I Times: A Capsule History of the People and Events That Shaped the University of Illinois." *Illinois Alumni* 30, no. 3 (2017): 33.

Toll, Ian W. *The Conquering Tide: War in the Pacific, 1942–1944.* New York: W. W. Norton, 2015.

Toll, Ian W. *Pacific Crucible: War at Sea in the Pacific, 1941–1942.* New York: W. W. Norton, 2012.

Toll, Ian W. *The Twilight of the Gods: War in the Western Pacific, 1944–1945.* New York: W. W. Norton, 2020.

United States Marine Corps. *III Corps Artillery, III Phib Corps Action Report, 1 April–30 June 1945.* Washington, DC: National Archives, 1945. (Declassified December 31, 2012.)

United States Marine Corps. *11th Marines, First Marine Division Special Action Report on Artillery, Nansei-Shoto (Okinawa), 1 April–30 June 1945.* Washington, DC: National Archives, 1945. (Declassified December 31, 2012.)

University of Illinois at Urbana-Champaign Archives, "Stadium Terrace, Champaign, Illinois, 1946," December 1946. Resource Identifier arh4001. Includes photograph image Negative Number 8703, RS 39/2/22, Box BUI–Stadium Terrace, Folder BUI–Stadium Terrace Nov–Dec 1946, ID 0003719, CONTENTdm file 73431171572002_stadiumterrace.jpg, and two-page "Interpretation" descriptive text. For photograph image, see https://archon.library.illinois.edu/index.php?p=digitallibrary/digitalcontent&id=3817.

University of Illinois Student Life and Cultural (SLC) Archival Program. "Student Life at Illinois: 1940–1949; 1941." Accessed July 7, 2021. https://archives.library.illinois.edu/slcold/researchguides/timeline/decades/1940.php.

Urbana Free Library. "Living in Stadium Terrace: Housing the University of Illinois' G.I. Students." *Local History and Genealogy* (blog), November 8, 2015. https://urbanafreelibrary.org/blogs/2015/11/10/living-stadium-terrace-housing-university-illinois%E2%80%99-gi-students.

Vance, J. D. *Hillbilly Elegy: A Memoir of a Family and Culture in Crisis*. New York: Harper Publishing, 2016.

Vandegrift, A. A. *Once A Marine: The Memoirs of General A. A. Vandegrift*. As told to Robert B. Asprey. New York: W. W. Norton, 1964.

Vento, Carol Schultz. *The Hidden Legacy of World War II: A Daughter's Journey of Discovery*. Camp Hill, PA: Sunbury Press, 2011.

Walton, Rodney Earl. *Big Guns and Brave Men: Mobile Artillery Observers and the Battle for Okinawa*. Annapolis, MD: Naval Institute Press, 2013.

Watson, Thomas A., and F. W. McCalpin. "Aerial Spotters." *Marine Corps Gazette* 28, no. 10 (October 1944), ProQuest Military Collection.

Webster, Ian. "U.S. Inflation Rate in 1947: 14.36%." CPI Inflation Calculator. Accessed June 11, 2021.
http://www.in2013dollars.com/inflation-rate-in-1947.

Wilcox, Jennifer. *Sharing the Burden: Women in Cryptology during World War II*. Ft. Meade, MD: Center for Cryptologic History, National Security Agency, 1998.

World War II War Diaries, 1941–1945, *III Corps Artillery, III Phib Corps Action Report on Operations on the Invasion and Occupation of Okinawa Gunto, Ryukyu Islands, 4/1–8/30/1945*. Washington, DC: National Archives, 1945.

World War II War Diaries, 1941–1945, 25 March–25 May 1945, *USS Petrof Bay*. Washington, DC: National Archives, 1945.

World War II War Diaries, 1941–1945, 1 March–25 May 1945, *USS Tulagi*. Washington, DC: National Archives, 1945.

Yahara, Col. Hiromichi. *The Battle for Okinawa: A Japanese Officer's Eyewitness Account of the Last Great Campaign of World War II*. Hoboken, NJ: John Wiley & Sons, 1995.

www.ingramcontent.com/pod-product-compliance
Lightning Source LLC
LaVergne TN
LVHW021946060526
838200LV00043B/1939